IMP

THE COMPLETE STORY

George Mowat-Brown

CROWOOD

First published in 2003 by
The Crowood Press Ltd
Ramsbury, Marlborough
Wiltshire SN8 2HR

www.crowood.com

British Library Cataloguing-in-Publication Data
A catalogue record for this book is available from the British Library.

ISBN 1 86126 619 7

Typeset by Servis Filmsetting Ltd, Manchester

Printed and bound in Great Britain by CPI Bath

Contents

Acknowledgements

The completion of this book would not have been possible without the tremendous assistance of those involved with the original Imp and Linwood projects, today's enthusiasts, and Scottish and English archivists alike.

Special thanks must go to Bob Saward and Ron Wisdom for their illuminating exposition on the styling of the Imp, Jim Pollard for his enthusiastic recollections of Linwood and Coventry, and Richard Sozanski and Roger Swift for their specialist knowledge and patience in dealing with my detailed questions. The reader will also realize the specialist information provided by Allan Lloyd Davies, Tim Fry, Clare Bunkham (Prudential Archive), Lord Rootes, Alan Fraser, and the librarians at Kirkwall and Ealing Public Libraries – not to mention the large number of helpful Imp enthusiasts scattered over the globe, including Dion Fluttert and Gary Henderson – to whom the author would like to extend his appreciation of their efforts. Special gratitude is expressed to Helena Mowat-Brown for her enormous contribution acting as research assistant to this volume.

The author would like to thank Jim Pollard, Bob Saward, Ron Wisdom, Richard and Antoni Sozanski, Roger Swift, Lord Rootes, Dale Drinnon, Anna Whelan, Simon Benoy, John Bullock, Mark Davison (Ron Poore Collection), the Scottish Screen Archive (production stills from *Young at Heart*), Ted Walker (Ferret Fotographics), and the Imp Club for permission to reproduce photographs from their collections.

Extracts from the Prudential Archive, L. J. K. Setright's *Drive On!*, Geoffrey Rootes' *Carpe Diem*, Tony Benn's *Diaries*, *Motoring Which?*, and the Marc Boxer cartoon (courtesy of Anna Ford) are reproduced with permission of the author, family or publisher.

Introduction

The sixties might have started with the British Prime Minister talking of the 'Wind of Change' in the statesmanlike manner we had come to expect from our leaders, but few British manufacturers could have realized what the end of colonial domination would mean. For that matter, and closer to home, there was the question of how much society was changing and whether this would have commercial ramifications – even if Rootes Motors was putting the finishing touches to its exciting new factory in Scotland and commenced manufacturing its all-new car. Harold Macmillan was still the Prime Minister in 1962, but his sobriquet was changing from SuperMac to Mac the Knife, and the scandal of his cabinet minister's sexual exploits with Christine Keeler remained merely rumour. Britain was, however, on the verge of irreversible social change: our elders and betters were openly parodied on television in the satirical *That Was the Week That Was*, and the Beatles had released *Love Me Do*.

While it was clear for all to see the danger of President Kennedy playing a global version of nuclear Russian roulette with Khrushchev's missiles in Cuba, the emergence of the new social order from the safe conformity of the 1950s did not seem to be a great threat to our flourishing industries – not even the likes of Honda making its first car seemed worthy of notice. New cars might not necessarily be bigger, but they were most certainly better, and in a time when motoring was such fun everyone would buy whatever was produced. The Imp was launched at a time when *From Me to You* and *Please Please Me* were challenging our cultural perception; our motoring tastes would take a little longer to change. This volume is about the Imp, but I consider that the context of the latter-day history of the company is so integral to the story of the Imp, that this is also dealt with in some detail.

With an eye on this book's subtitle, *The Complete Story*, I realize the impossibility of achieving this for the Hillman Imp. Not only has a lot of the politically and commercially sensitive material yet to be released into the public domain, but I remain convinced that most of the major decisions were made during shoots at Glenalmond or Ramsbury – Harold Macmillan being a regular guest at both these estates of Lord Rootes – the complete story having gone to the grave with its principal perpetrators. Another statement of Macmillan, 'Abroad, you may be a statesman; at home, you're a politician', kept running through the mind when considering the trials and tribulations of the complete tale.

George Mowat-Brown
Westray

Is this where some of the most speculative plans were aired? The Prime Minister, the Rt Hon. Harold Macmillan, shoots with Sir William Rootes on the latter's Glenalmond estate, Perthshire.

1 The Journey Begins

In the beginning

Earlier in the century, Britain had been rather slow off the mark when it came to producing these new-fangled horseless carriages, but after the First World War it became the major European producer. With its protected markets at home and in the Empire, Britain's motor industry was in a favoured position that would cause complacency among its producers. This led to British designs being rather outdated from both the technical and production-engineering standpoints, and a rudimentary marketing strategy seemed unnecessary. Only when considering the latter half of the twentieth century do we now feel that a handful of the British designers were at least as innovative as their foreign counterparts, albeit not always with the support of the patrician owners for whom they worked. Fortunately, Sir William Rootes let two very young designers in the family firm follow through their ideas for a different type of car: a small car at that, for the respectable, some might say staid, family firm to show that it could address the socially changing marketplace that was now embracing the British working classes. These two designers, Mike Parkes, aged 24, and Tim Fry, aged 20, commenced with the youthful conviction that would eventually lead to the production of the Hillman Imp — an outstanding design and execution of their initial concept. What we instantly recognize as the Imp would require the enormous contribution of Ron Wisdom and Bob Saward to allow the Apex project to metamorphose into the Imp.

The Rootes Band, photographed c.1872, comprised family members. The brass instruments have modern valves.

Family Rootes

William Edward Rootes, later Lord Rootes of Ramsbury, the first baron, was born in 1894 at Goudhurst into a family of substance, or, as his son put it, 'There is evidence that the family was of some local importance in the Weald of Kent.' William was educated at Cranbrook School, a local minor public school. William's first encounter with automobiles was nearly his last: aged ten, he crashed the family's car, but fortunately he and his brother Reginald escaped unscathed. He later experienced some success as a long-distance endurance motorcyclist and racer.

William's entrepreneurial mettle was displayed as a schoolboy through a chicken-rearing business which financed the interregnum between his unfinished apprenticeship at Singer Motors and his naval air service. Ever the countryman, in 1931 William purchased the 650-acre Stype Estate near Hungerford, Wiltshire, for its shooting rights – an essential appurtenance for someone in his position. This estate would quintuple in size during William's twenty-year stewardship. In 1946, William added to his portfolio the 16,000-acre Glenalmond estate near Perth, Scotland. In agrarian circles, he was known for his knowledge of pedigree Aberdeen Angus cattle and Hampshire Down sheep, and he was president of the society for the former. He regularly occupied three homes – Wiltshire, Perth, and the town house in Shepherds Close, Mayfair, London, which was two minutes' walk from the office.

William played a prominent establishment role as part of his Second World War effort, acting as the chairman of the Shadow Aero-Engine Committee and the Supply Council, and visiting France to assess Allied transport needs for the Government. He was accompanied by B. B. Winter, Rootes' director of engineering, the later supporter of the Apex/Imp development. At a localized level, William chaired Coventry's Reconstruction and Coordinating Committee, which was responsible for repairing the city's war damage, and used his contacts with the English Establishment assiduously. Sir William, as he became in 1942, remained a regular visitor to North America, and his understanding of the American market, combined with the expertise he acquired while serving on the Overseas Trade Development Council, meant that Rootes was always the leading British exporter, and this led to his appointment as chairman of the Dollar Exports Council. Lord Rootes also served education through the Committee on Education and Training of Students and the British Council. His final prominent public role was as the principal fund-raiser for the establishment of the University of Warwick – one of the highly successful universities established as part of Harold Wilson's enlightened higher-education expansion programme.

Lord Rootes died on 12 December 1964, following the rapid onset and progress of liver cancer.

Reginald Rootes (in 1945, Sir Reginald), the brother of William, was born in 1896 at Goudhurst and educated at Cranbrook School. After abandoning a rosy future as an Admiralty civil servant, as someone who understood the implications of things financial, Reginald joined his brother in business. He visited Chrysler and Chevrolet in 1926 and brought back new ideas on assessing markets and production, later returning to America to study Ford's production methods after reviewing Rootes' new acquisitions. He also established a subsidiary in Argentina in time for the British Exhibition of 1931.

Sir Reginald was the first post-war president of the Society of Motor Manufacturers and Traders (SMMT). He was based at Humber in Coventry and Devonshire House, London. It was he who nearly amalgamated Rootes and Morris Motors in the 1950s. In 1965 he succeeded William as chairman of Rootes, with his planned retirement in 1967 to be coincident with Chrysler's take-over, but this was the year of his death.

Sir Reginald was a lifelong Kentish farmer, with a preference for Jersey cattle.

Geoffrey Rootes, son of William (and later the second baron), was born at Loose, near Maidstone, in 1917 of 'Anglo-Saxon English stock with a rural background', and died in 1992. He was educated at Harrow School and at Christ Church, Oxford, where he read modern languages, but came down before graduating to gain experience in Rootes.

Geoffrey was taken on an eventful round-the-world tour between school and university with the intention of meeting significant Rootes' customers and business people. He appeared to display a certain level of social skill with the daughters of the international establishment and was at ease with American automobile people such as Cord, Ford, Bendix and the senior management of Chrysler and General Motors – a useful preparation for his prescribed destiny.

Geoffrey saw active service in the Supplementary Reserve of the Royal Army Service Corps, in which he rose to the rank of major, with the British Expeditionary Force at Dunkirk, in East Africa, the Middle East and North Africa, and finally in Italy. Additionally to Devonshire House, he was based at Humber, having previously spent time in the machine shops and foundry in Coventry and with Sunbeam-Talbot-Darracq in Barlby Road and in Acton. He became the chairman of Rootes (Scotland) Limited, and remained head and managing director of the Manufacturing Division. He was deputy-chairman of Rootes Motors Ltd in 1965, and chairman in 1967, remaining with the new company until 1973, allegedly to safeguard the interests of the British shareholders.

Geoffrey was a great committee man, his many positions extending from those of the motor trade, through industry in general, to those concerned with education and the arts, with many at a local level. His motor industry committee service included successive posts with the SMMT, the National Advisory Council, the National Economic Development Committee (including presenting its report, 'Economic Prospects for the Motor Industry'), the Motor Industry Research Association and the Institute of the Motor Industry. On a wider platform, his memberships included the Confederation of British Industry, the British National Export Council and the Institute of Directors. Following his retirement, he accepted non-executive positions on the boards of Lucas Industries and Rank Hovis McDougal, and was chairman of the First National City Trust Company (Bahamas).

Geoffrey's rural interests were represented by the Game Conservancy, the Kennet Valley Fishing Association, the Royal Society for the Protection of Birds, the Wildfowl and Wetlands Trust, and the World Wildlife Fund. His other work reflects his passions: Councils of Cranfield Institute of Technology and Warwick University, Coventry Cathedral Festival, the Royal Society of Arts, the Royal Academy, the Tate Gallery and the Courtauld Institute and Gallery. At a more local level, he was president of the St John Ambulance for Berkshire and a trustee of the Duchy of Somerset Hospital. After retirement, the second Lord Rootes lived at Glenalmond until its sale in 1981.

In an unsupportive statement, Tony Benn opined that, 'Rootes is not an exciting person. He has just got to the top by having the right father, as so often happens.' The author feels that Lord Rootes fulfilled his commercial destiny, but that his real fulfilment lay in his rural and wildlife interests, languages, education and training, and the arts.

Brian Rootes, William's younger son, was born in 1919 and died at Glenalmond in 1971, aged 52, having never enjoyed robust health. For much of his career, he was based in New York, where he was responsible for the North American market and was knowledgeable about the Latin-American markets, where Rootes supplied CKD kits for local assembly. Brian headed the Export Division of Rootes.

Timothy Rootes, son of Reginald, held various posts, including Director of Sales and Service for the manufacturing division, and directorships of Rootes Motors, Humber Limited and Rootes Limited. It is suggested that 'his true heart lay with events on the turf propelled by four legs, rather than wheels'.

Nicholas Rootes, son of Geoffrey, succeeded to the barony as the third Lord Rootes in 1992 and is unconnected with manufacturing.

The Rootes brothers made a formidable partnership of complementary gifts – administrative and marketing. They also possessed the gift of being able to anticipate the trends that both the industry and their own customers would follow. Whilst true of the earlier stages in their careers, for the same understandable reasons as blighted the prosperity of British mass-producers of vehicles later in the century, the Rootes brothers seem to have misread the ramifications of the enormous social changes that were to take place after the Second World War, and were to fail to capitalize on addressing these changes through preparing their company to profit from them. It is often said that the Imp would be their glo-rious swansong, the right car at almost the right time, but possibly made in the wrong place and abysmally marketed. For the reasons that will become evident through this book, the author, for a number of complex reasons, would not be wholly in agreement about the Imp being manufactured in the wrong place: the swansong for Rootes Limited, however, is undeniable, but what a glorious attempt to reinvigorate the fortunes of the company.

The first ambitious project of Rootes, the Hillman Wizard of 1931, might not have realized the envisaged car-for-all-countries, but the Minx – named by brother Reginald in preference to the intended Merlin or Witch – of the following year did, and it would endure on successive models for nigh on forty years. The Minx established the idea of Rootes as a significant producer, as well as a distributor, and William had gone to immense trouble over its release. The Wizard had been launched at London's Albert Hall with much razzmatazz (an advertising idea to be copied by Ford for its Y model the following year), but the publicity was far more impressive than the reality of the metal. Because of this, William personally took a prototype Minx on a European tour and subsequently delayed its extravagant launch until its shortcomings, as he perceived them to be, had been eradicated. It seems remarkable that having learnt from this cautionary tale, the company would not adopt a similar strategy for the Imp, when it was clear to all that the prognosis was not likely to be that of an uncomplicated birth.

Following their natural inclinations as salesmen, the Rootes brothers aimed their marketing at the different strata of the British middle-class customers through promoting the marque identities of their separate manufacturers so that each retained its distinctive identity within a general perception of being 'built to last': Humbers were analogous to affordable luxury (envy-making objects of the desire of others, but not too ostentatious), Sunbeam and Sunbeam-Talbot with a sporting image (but again, the marketing message was tempered, so that these fine cars were not exclusively the provenance of the rakish cad), and the public were encouraged to think of Hillman as a more modest product, but still a good-quality, well-made one, that was a notch above its competitors.

By 1936, the six main volume producers of private cars in the United Kingdom were Morris, Ford, Austin, the Rootes Group, Standard and Vauxhall. The most comprehensive, the Nuffield organization in the form of Morris, were producing five times the output of Vauxhall and over double that of the Rootes Group. It is often said that the British motor industry was based in the West Midlands, and while this was true of most of the component

suppliers, these largest six manufacturers, often referred to as 'the Big Six', were distributed over the southern half of the country, being based in or near Oxford (Cowley), Dagenham in Essex, Birmingham (Longbridge), Coventry (Rootes Motors and Standard) and Luton in Bedfordshire respectively. Annual production of British automobiles pre-Second-World-War would peak near 400,000 in the later 1930s, but by 1939 there would still be only two million registered cars on British roads. It is worth recalling that even after the industrial recovery, one in eight of the British population remained unemployed – better than nearer the start of the decade, which reached a social state when almost 20 per cent of the male population were seeking employment. During this decade, British automobile production overtook the French to become the largest in Europe – a situation that would persist until 1956.

Even by the late 1930s, all-steel bodywork and all-synchromesh gearboxes (despite the number of Alvis patents for the latter) were a feature of an American vehicle, and unitary-construction or monocoque bodies, 'over-square' short-stroke engines and independent suspension were more the contribution of mainland European manufacturers. There were some exceptions, as Rootes' Hillman Minx, announced in 1939, was of monocoque construction and the Rootes brothers' cognizance of Chrysler's use of compliant engine mountings and the appeal of synchromesh gearboxes had not gone unnoticed.

Politicians have always enjoyed pontificating on motoring, especially the fiscal aspects, but they have rarely had an understanding of the technical implications or the social impact of the results of letting their speech-writers loose on the subject. For many decades in Britain, the annual taxation of motor cars, the Road Fund Licence, was based upon a curious and unpopular classification – the Royal Automobile Club horsepower-rating. This was one factor that caused British engine designers to retain the long-stroke, small-bore engine.

Establishment of the Rootes Group of Companies

Many British automobile producers progressed from production of the bicycle to motorized transport. With the Rootes family, the progression was analogous, but that of commerce rather than manufacture. The father, William Rootes, in addition to being a minor Victorian composer and director of the Rootes Band, was the proprietor of a successful Kent bicycle shop, to which he added an automobile agency. William Rootes' business was up to date in possessing electricity and rejoicing in the telephone number of Hawkhurst 1. Rootes senior's elder son, William, went to Coventry, joining Singer Motors as an apprentice. Like most young men, William Edward was eventually 'called up' for active service, and in 1914 became a sub-lieutenant in the Royal Naval Volunteer Reserve, to be demobilized before the end of the war to help a pioneering concept – an aero-engine refurbishment and repair facility, Lea Engineering, in Pudding Lane, Maidstone, Kent. William Edward's brother, Reginald, an Admiralty civil servant, joined the Maidstone enterprise in 1919. Was this a case of Reginald making and controlling the money and William spending it? William turned his peace-time attentions to establishing an automobile sales and distribution business: Rootes Ltd was the result. Of the dynamics of the company's sibling partnership, William's son, Geoffrey, wrote in his autobiography, *Carpe Diem*:

> My uncle (later Sir Reginald Rootes) was a person for whom I had an enormous admiration. We had much in common and later he was very much my guide and mentor in my life in industry . . . It has often been said that my father and my uncle were complementary to one another and that their respective qualities, which were so well balanced, were one of the main reasons for their success. I believe this to have been true. My father was the extrovert, enthusiastic and energetic salesman, whereas my uncle was the sound administrator and organizer, who nevertheless had considerable financial and commercial flair.

With a gesture that typifies his future business acumen, William placed a large order for Singer cars, utilizing financial guarantees. The business flourished and his father joined him as the new car dealership moved to Maidstone (the first official record of the incorporation of a Rootes company is 26 September 1917). The expanding business moved to Long Acre, London, via New Bond Street, prospering to the stage

that in 1926 it acquired showrooms and offices in the palatial, redeveloped Devonshire House, Piccadilly, in the prosperous West End of central London. Devonshire House was constructed upon the site of the Duke of Devonshire's London house (demolished in 1924).

Acquiring large but under-capitalized distributors, the brothers established themselves as a large distributor – probably the largest in Europe and the foremost in the United Kingdom. From Rootes' depot in Chiswick, West London, the Rootes Group was supplying everything from the Austin Seven to the products of Alvis, Bentley, Chevrolet and Rolls-Royce to the entire British Empire. But not all of Rootes' expansionist plans came to fruition: William's wish to take over Austin, and his later cloak-and-dagger intention of buying out William Morris's stake in the Cowley-based Pressed Steel Company, were stymied. Through William's friendship with Edward G. Budd of Philadelphia, who devised the process of pressing motor-body panels, Rootes realized the potential of pressed panels and monocoque construction of cars, but it had been Morris who had persuaded Budd to co-found the Pressed Steel Company.

During the economic recession of the 1920s, most manufacturers had little money to undertake necessary modernization or restructuring. Three financially ailing interdependent companies – the Hillman Car Co., Humber Ltd and Commer Cars – caught the eye of the Rootes brothers. With the backing of the Prudential Assurance Company, the brothers acquired a financial interest in the manufacturing of what they were distributing, the entire deal being completed in 1929. (Commer Cars in Luton had been bought by Humber, literally Hillman's next-door neighbour, with which it had effectively merged.) The Rootes brothers had gone from being a sales and distribution business to that of a manufacturer. The structural model seems to be that Rootes Securities owned Rootes Limited, which was the holding company for the separate manufacturers: therefore there would never be a 'Rootes Imp'.

Rootes' initial restructuring was by way of long-overdue modernization and rationalization of production. By 1935, the company started acquiring, or taking a controlling interest in, new opportunities through adding other failing and/or under-funded concerns to the group: Karrier Motors and Thrupp & Maberly (coachbuilders), followed by Clement Talbot, British Light Steel Pressings, and the Sunbeam

Establishment of the Rootes Group of Companies *continued*

Motor Company (having previously bought Sunbeam's commercial vehicles). However, even if it seemed painful, the rationalization was not sufficiently extreme to ensure a healthy future for the company: at the commencement of the group, it offered fifty-four vehicle types, twenty-two different engines and forty-two car-body styles, whereas afterwards there were still thirty-two vehicle types on offer.

Although the Rootes board would add dozens of smaller companies to the Rootes Group, it started the post-war period by disposing of some. For example, the electric trolley-buses and commercial vehicles made by the likes of Sunbeam were sold to Guy as the sale of part of Sunbeam-Karrier. The Karrier municipal commercial vehicles (the post-war dustcart with a crescent-shaped refuse enclosure comes immediately to mind) and Commer lorries continued, and while not as fêted as the domestic automobiles, they made a considerable contribution to the profits of Rootes Securities – the Dunstable facility was greatly increased in size to cope with the demand for commercial vehicles. In some ways, the commercial side of Rootes was more integrated: it acquired Tilling Stevens, whose associated Vulcan Motors produced such magnificent commercial engines as the extraordinary TS3, which saw service in Commer trucks all round the world (with cabs by British Light Steel Pressings), as well as coaches made by the Dartford subsidiary, John C. Beadle. Post war, Rootes was renowned for possessing one of the most successful public relations departments.

The Government's Royal Automobile Club Taxation Formula

The RAC formula was a simple one: the square of the cylinder's diameter in inches, multiplied by the number of cylinders, divided by 2.5. Expressed arithmetically, this was $(D^2 \times n)/2.5$. Models were sometimes named thus, the smaller ones being 8hp, while the more expensive to tax were 30hp.

The formula was initially based on sound thinking that assumed three constants – that the mechanical efficiency would be 75 per cent, the mean effective pressure was $90lb/in^2$ and the piston speed remained 1,000ft/min. Engine designers increasingly exceeded these, and the model name would reflect both the RAC hp and the often-exaggerated estimated bhp output. By the time Wolseley discontinued this practice, one of the last to do so, and well after this fiscal system was used, its 18/85 model was 18hp and the output was a claimed 85bhp.

Along with the other members of 'the Big Six', Rootes entered the war in secure financial shape and with a clear public perception of the different niches occupied by its various marques. Rapidly, the car producers and engineering concerns abandoned frivolities like automobiles to focus on the war effort. This meant that most manufacturers dismantled their production lines and went over to manufacturing munitions, aero components – both engines and airframes – lorries, tanks, and various types of armaments and military equipment. Rootes did produce a few cars, but not for civilian motoring – Humber was designated as one of the principal suppliers of vehicles to be used as senior military staff cars, and some Hillman Minxes were modified for usage by lesser mortals. The lack of private car production and the devastation wrought on car factories once hostilities commenced resulted in an overwhelming transformation of the motoring industry. An equally significant effect for post-war manufacturing facilities was inaugurated three years before the outbreak of the war, however.

Austerity with Ingenuity?

If the decade leading up to the war could be seen as having a profound effect upon the composition of the British motor industry, the emergence of the post-war economy would certainly prove a testing time for the producers of such unessential items as private motor cars. The Board of Trade had granted a limited agreement in 1944 to develop post-war

Shadow Factories

In 1936, the recently ennobled Lord Austin of Long-bridge, a peerage given as much for his support of the atomic work of Lord Rutherford at the Cavendish laboratory in Cambridge as his automobile manufacturing, was given the task of establishing a series of 'shadow factories'. Rootes would also occupy a similar position. The scheme, technically the Government Aircraft Schemes, was, through volume manufacture of airframes and aero-engines, to prepare for the impending conflict by increasing both capacity and trained personnel to ensure the country's necessary rearmament. The Government financed the infrastructure – bearing the cost of both the factories and the machinery – whilst the automobile manufacturers were invited to set up and run these rented facilities. Unsurprisingly, given the chairmanships of this scheme, the first factory with its own runway, which produced Fairey aircraft, was operated by Austin and shadowed the Longbridge facility. Once war was declared, a second Shadow Factory Scheme, this time far more comprehensive, resulted in a huge expansion of available manufacturing centres, and, it is said, a burgeoning of peerages and knighthoods for the complicit motor industry.

The term 'shadow' was chosen to denote the proximity of these new facilities to an existing plant, but a few of them were also extremely well camouflaged. The most amazing of the hidden factories was a subterranean one run by the Rover Company at Drakelow in Worcestershire. Whereas most of these factories had post-war lives either through becoming the basis of the parent company's new car production or remaining as aircraft factories, Drakelow would enjoy the dubious distinction of being turned into an underground nuclear bunker for the Regional Seat of Government of Defence Region No. 9!

Rootes' pre-war shadow factory was at Speke, near Liverpool, where it produced Bristol Blenheim bombers. As a premonition of what would follow later in Scotland, Rootes had the experience of coordinating a factory that took just over a year to be transformed from a field of cabbage to full industrial production. The most significant post-war car factory for Rootes was constructed in 1940 at Ryton-on-Dunsmore, near Coventry, as 'Number 2 Aero Engine Shadow Factory'. The Hercules aero-engines made at Ryton were not that far removed from those understood by automobile manufacturers – nearby Rover was working with jet engines. When Rootes returned to car production, the Ryton facility would build the various generations of Hillmans, Humbers, Sunbeams, Talbots and Peugeots. Through Government influence, the Hillman Imp would never be assembled there, but Ryton would host many stages in its development and testing. The Ryton-on-Dunsmore shadow factory, along with that of Rolls-Royce, was equipped with a special unit devoted to engine testing; these buildings would be of tremendous benefit for automobile experiment and sophisticated testing of engines and components, and in Ryton's case, this was where the Apex would develop and evolve into the Imp.

models, and some manufacturers had been deploying a few staff on unofficial development. Most new vehicles, however, were similar to those that had been in production beforehand – this is markedly true of those from 'the Big Six'. Despite industry being awash with innovative designers and engineers, most of whom had either amassed their experience, or cut their teeth, through displays of ingenuity during the war, it has to be said that captains of the British automobile industry were slow to notice that the social order had changed irrevocably. The conservatism and complacency of the owners and senior management of the British industry would cause it and them to bumble along waiting for the status quo to return. Their failure to address, or second-guess, what British society would be demanding sowed the seeds for the financial, industrial and social problems that would follow – virtually realizing the demise of the British motor car industry. The post-war development of Britain's rekindled aspirations in world trade provided a challenge for the Rootes brothers, who played a leading role in attempting to organize the exports of the industry, initially with some successes: Rootes would be the first British company to establish an Australian assembly plant, and wearing his hat as the chairman of the Society of Motor

Manufacturers and Traders, William was prominent in organizing the first British motor show to be held in New York in 1950. Three years later, there were 800 Rootes dealers in North America, and Rootes (Canada) Limited had also been established – William's expertise gained as chairman of the Dollar Exports Council was of tremendous benefit to his company.

In the longer perspective, however, Rootes would follow a similar course to most of the other major players, so even its more speculative and innovative ideas like the Hillman Imp would never achieve the level of success, or provide sufficient financial reward, for the design and innovative thinking to seem worthwhile.

Although there was the obvious pent-up home demand from the victorious British public for new cars, the prevalent mood of austerity and the Government's continued imposition of rationing of consumables (including petrol), combined with the punitive taxation of what it considered inessential, dampened down the public demand and enthusiasm. If the aspirant owner of a new car did not mind paying the supplemental purchase tax of a third of its list value, which had been so for some years, then he was likely to be stymied through not being able to obtain the necessary Government permit to spend his money on such a frivolity. The new Government was coming to terms with repaying the large sums the country had borrowed to fund its rearmament during the previous years – no agreement was more on the Chancellor of the Exchequer's mind than the 'Lend-Lease' programme with the United States. For the manufacturers, who also experienced huge shortages of steel and coal for some years, it was startling to have to comply with the populist Government slogan, 'Export or die'. This was more of a Government edict than an encouragement, and it meant that the products of such manufacturing as there was were destined for export. This accounts for the gargantuan efforts made by the manufacturers at

events such as the motor show in New York City. Not only did the Ministry of Supply operate a quota system for the number of new vehicles that would be allowed on to the British market, but by way of 'Covenant Regulations' there was a restriction on the resale of cars to a second owner. Neither of these schemes would experience a significant relaxation until 1952. The concentrated effort to export British vehicles to the United States would continue to have a beneficial effect until the early 1960s, and would account for many marques and models of all shapes and sizes, including the Sunbeam Imp, briefly appearing on the American market.

As part of the reparations after the war, the German motor industry was inspected by the victors, but it was thought that there was little of interest to the British industry. A few specialist producers acquired, by way of the spoils of war, German automobile designs, but little commercial interest was shown by the official Rootes Commission, appointed to assess the viability of transferring production of German models to England. The newly formed Car Division of the Bristol Aeroplane Company was one of the few English firms to benefit. With the cooperation of the War Reparations Board and BMW, who preferred to see its designs travel westwards rather than in an easterly direction, Bristol gained the knowledge and design of the pre-war BMW 326, 327 and 328 models. Aspects of the chassis and suspension of these would form the basis of the new Bristol 400, whilst the hemispherical 6-cylinder engine of the 328 would power its future cars for over a decade, and would also be supplied to other sporting manufacturers like AC and Frazer Nash.

The attentive reader is probably wondering why the Volkswagen Beetle, as it became known, was not part of this appraisal. It was: but the Rootes Commission (a Government committee comprising car manufacturers chaired by Sir William Rootes) deemed it to be unsuitable and uncompetitive, concluding that it was unlikely to survive for longer than

Hitler and his entourage visit the Rootes Motors' stand at the 1939 Berlin Motor Show.

a couple of years! William Rootes had discussed the *Kraft durch Freude Wagen* with Hitler, Goering and Goebbels when they visited the Rootes stand at the 1939 Berlin Motor Show – at that time, more on William's mind was the significant impact on increased British unemployment caused by the German Government's subsidizing of its native industry, especially the automotive sector.

So where did the cessation of hostilities leave the Rootes Group, other than with the addition of new former-shadow facilities at Ryton and Speke, but without the Volkswagen? Rootes emerged from the war in more robust financial shape than many, but with pretty restricted fare to offer to the public. Not that there were sufficient raw materials to engage in true mass production in this time of rationing – even if it had had a shiny new car to put it in, most of the British population would not have been able to acquire very

much petrol by any legal means! Several thousand examples of the pre-war monocoque Minx had been produced in a military form, but now it could be produced for civilian use, albeit mainly to be exported, as were models bearing Sunbeam-Talbot and the more prestigious Humber badges. There was little here that would not have been familiar to the pre-war buyer, with the top-of-the-line being represented by the large 4.1-litre Humbers, also with side-valve engines. As Rootes was moving its former Talbot assembly lines from Ladbroke Hall, Barlby Road (between Scrubs Lane and Ladbroke Grove), North Kensington, London, to its new Ryton-on-Dunsmore factory, so as to free the London site to become its new service depot, Renault was surprising everyone with an all-new car – the 4CV of 1946. The 4CV was arguably more suitable as a Gallic 'people's car' than the Teutonic Beetle; a tiny car perhaps, but a full

15

Kraft durch Freude Wagen – the Beetle

How did this failed dream of the Third Reich become an iconic metaphor of German industry? The answer reveals many shortcomings of custom and practice that was British industry. With typically Fascist nomenclature, the *Kraft durch Freude Wagen* (Power-through-Joy Car), referred to as the *KdF Wagen*, was announced by the Third Reich in 1937, with the *Gesellschaft Zur Vorbereitung des Deutsche Volkswagens (GeZuVor) mbH* (Company for planning the German People's Car Ltd) being created the following year to attend to its production and marketing; later it was understandably known as *Volkswagenwerk GmbH*. A huge new factory was built at a new town called KdF-Stadt. It is the *New York Times* that is frequently attributed with the invention of the nickname of Beetle (in German, *Käfer*).

After the invasion of Poland, the 'people's car' enjoyed little civilian production, with the KdF factory turning to producing military versions of the *KdF Wagen* – the Nazi Jeep-equivalent *Kübelwagen* that so excelled in the North African campaigns, the *Kommandeurwagen* and an amphibious *Schwimmwagen*. Kdf-Stadt was captured by American troops, but allocated to the British Sector. The bombed-out factory was considered as primarily of military significance – it had also been a parts supplier for the V-1 rocket-like 'flying bombs' – so it befell the British administration to dismantle it. The town council changed its name to that of a nearby fourteenth-century castle, Wolfsburg, and a Maj Ivan Hirst of the Royal Electrical and Mechanical Engineers took charge of the situation. Through his initiative, Hirst became the third cog in the chain that started with Hitler's socio-political-motoring fantasy, solved by the Austrian Ferdinand Porsche's plagiaristic engineering ingenuity, and now to be brought to a civilian motoring reality. (It should be pointed out, as it has some relevance to the rear suspension of the Imp, that Hans Ledwinka, the Czech engineer and designer of the Tatra that was much admired by Hitler, received several million Deutschmarks in out-of-court settlements for Ferdinand Porsche's patent infringements.)

Dismissing the conscripted workforce, Hirst organized the factory utilizing the few original workers and former Nazi officials that remained, these being joined daily by German refugees fleeing from the adjacent Russian sector. The workforce dealt with repairing and rebuilding the British and American military vehicles, but using mothballed spares for the civilian *KdF*, Hirst completed an example that caused the British military to order a large number, some of which went to the German Post Office. Within a year, the Wolfsburg Motor Works was able to produce a thousand vehicles a month and was employing a workforce of 8,000. An example was sent to England for appraisal and found wanting by Sir William Rootes; it proved to be slower than his own Raymond Loewy-influenced new four-door, four-seater Hillman Minx Phase III – the car Rootes was aiming directly at the same sociological group, the lower-middle class. The Rootes Commission's report, annexed with an unfavourable Humber evaluation of a captured *Kübelwagen*, concluded that the Beetle could not 'be regarded as an example of a first-class modern design to be copied by the British industry'. It was offered to other manufacturers: the Morris board's consideration was reduced to a footnote, and Ford seems to have been reserved about embarking upon running an ex-Nazi facility, possibly because of a sensitivity that many producers had about the composition, nature and conditions of their own German workforces during the years of conflict. The French Government seemed more interested, but its industry was busily producing its indigenous answer to the same problem.

The British Army did not wish to run a car factory, and it could not give it away. So Hirst, the visionary major described by Sir William Rootes as 'a bloody fool', managed to attract Heinrich Nordhoff from the still-moribund General Motors' subsidiary, Opel, to run the plant while the British military government transferred the trusteeship to the State of Lower Saxony. Nordhoff, who remained with the operational responsibility for nearly twenty years, capitalized on this phoenix-like recovery through a most remarkable transparent managerial style that accrued enormous loyalty. Nordhoff's challenge seems to have been all the more impossible when one remembers that Volkswagen lacked a single dealer, distributor of either cars or parts, or any support. But thanks to Hirst, it did have an advantage – it was the first back into production. By any commercial measure, the Volkswagen became the world's most successful passenger vehicle, with production running into the twenty-millions, spread over several continents.

It is said that Lord Rootes regretted his handling of this situation for the remainder of his life.

four-seater, of monocoque construction and with fully independent suspension. Like the Beetle and the Imp, Fiat 600, NSU Prinz, and Simca 1000 to come, the 4CV was rear-engine powered. The car had a production-span of fifteen years, while the water-cooled engine lived on for a life of well over thirty years. The Sunbeam-Talbot name would survive its relocation to the Midlands and live on until the new Sunbeam of 1953, Rootes having coined the composite marque in 1938, would finally put it to rest in 1954. The Sunbeam name would enjoy a Linwood incarnation, being used on Imps destined for some overseas markets and the quite separate marketing ploy of branding some of the upmarket and sporting variants of the Imp thus for home consumption. It would adorn the bonnets of Chrysler and Talbot's products in a life post-Imp.

The British Motoring Bazaar

The complacency of the British manufacturers in the post-war bazaar is understandable: at home they were selling in a protected marketplace that did not allow the importation of foreign vehicles until 1953, and if the manufacturers were conservative, then their customers were even more so – a situation that nearly all the mass-producers were keen to reinforce, supported by the majority of motoring journalists, who purveyed the subliminal message that the emerging strange foreign cars were not real cars at all. As in many other aspects of life, Britain knew best: a convenient mantra for the industrial oligarchy to promulgate. After the war, the automobile industry's importance to the country's economy was as a gigantic contributor to the national balance of payments, the overdue decline of which, coincidentally, would be synchronous with the production fortunes of the Imp. The automobile industry had always produced a healthy surplus to the United Kingdom's balance of payments when the value of exports was compared with imports, and this was a status quo

that Rootes, like every other British producer, assumed would continue, *ad infinitum*. Alas, following some fluctuation between 1972 and 1974, which was virtually a point of equilibrium for the country's motor industry, the position would continue to deteriorate, and the industry would remain a significant drain on the country's balance sheet for most of the remaining century.

British society of the 1950s was still firmly rooted in the 1930s, and would remain so for another decade. This ethos might have been fertile ground for the later explosion in Britain of satirical entertainment like *Beyond the Fringe*, but it was also nurturing the seeds of its own downfall. Motoring was still the provenance of the well-heeled or those who aspired to appear so – owning and driving a car might have become an aspirant middle-class preoccupation during the 1930s, with people wanting to demonstrate their freedom beyond the fast-expanding suburbs, but accepted ownership by the masses was still to happen. It is instructive to see film footage of the workforce of the factories of the time: huge flocks of bicyclists emerging from car works – those who assembled automobiles could afford neither to buy nor to run the product of their daily toils; this was left to the finger-pointing and bean-counting classes.

It is worth recalling an obvious assumption of social economists, that the principal influence on a customer's decision to make a large capital expenditure – and for many people a car will only be surpassed by their home – is the perceived relationship between their wealth and the cost of the item, within their perception of the general context of prices within the economy. Governments like to stimulate or suppress retail spending, both directly and indirectly, and manufacturers have learnt that subversion of the economists' principles elevates their sales figures. In Britain, cars were traditionally expensive – they could only seem otherwise if they were less costly, especially at the 'entry level' of the family saloon. The Imp would become part of the sociological change that involved the popularization of private motoring.

To avoid the Government's import restrictions prior to 1953 and to alleviate the punitive import taxes imposed on foreign vehicles after this, a number of continental manufacturers set up small assembly plants within Britain. Other than minor trim items, little of these cars would include items sourced from British manufacturers. The Renault 4CV, for example, from 1949 was assembled for the British market at the Renault factory in Western Avenue, Acton, West London, while from 1953 its interesting Gallic compatriot, the Citroën 2CV, which had been launched in France in 1948, was assembled at Citroën's British assembly plant in Slough, west of London and connected to it by the Great West Road. Simca would follow its fellow countrymen to Kew, West London. Even if it was going to play a minor role in the later development of the Apex, one can see why the original 2CV Citroën was thought quite so peculiar by the British public: its 2-cylinder, air-cooled engine of 375cc produced only 9bhp (enlarged to 425cc and 12bhp in 1955), and was more akin to what the English would expect to find in a piece of agricultural machinery, rather than a full four-seater motorcar in which they might be tempted to carry the family!

A year after the lifting of the importation ban on foreign vehicles, which allowed the Beetle to be sold in Britain, the chauvinistic public were hardly beating a path to the doors of these exotic emporia. The sales of foreign vehicles registered by 1954 were still less than one per cent of registrations, and it took until 1958 for this figure to nudge over one per cent of the market, a finding that caused great consternation at the time. It was the calm before the commercial bloodbath that was to come. The dropping of all import restrictions in 1959, other than an import tax of an extra 30 per cent added to foreign vehicles, was to set the scene for the forthcoming shift in the motoring public's steadfast loyalty for the home-made product.

These apparently weird and wonderful foreign vehicles might not sell in large numbers, but it is worth remembering when looking at even the earliest fantasies of what would become the Hillman Imp that the designers were as well acquainted with these cars as they were with the offerings of their British competitors, such as the British Motor Corporation's Morris Minor and Austin A30, Ford's Popular, and Standard's Eight. Apart from an experimental early pre-war flight of fancy that was known as Little Jim, and a Volkswagen-inspired, twin-cylinder, rear-engined car, Rootes had never addressed the small-car segment of the market, and would not do so until the Hillman Imp.

In 1954, things were, in some ways, starting to look up for the British motorist wanting a new post-war car nigh on a decade after the end of hostilities. This would be the last year that would seem to be a 'seller's market' for the manufacturers, and the native purchaser would be able again to hone his skills at negotiating a discount, or haggling over the deal, that would have caused him to feel at home in an Eastern bazaar. As early as 1948, the arcane RAC vehicle taxation system had given way to a flat-rate licensing system that no longer took account of the size of the engine, but in many other ways the automobile was the traditional Government 'cash cow' for raising revenue, which also meant direct or indirect social control. Accompanying this vehicle taxation reform was the imposition of an additional purchase tax of two-thirds the list price on any vehicle costing over £1,000. This luxury-band of tax would fluctuate greatly and apply to all new cars at differing rates until it was reduced in 1962 to what would seem at the time to be a reasonable 25 per cent. The less direct fiscal manipulation came through restrictions on credit, especially the popular 'hire purchase' schemes. To make sure the people understood, prime ministers would deliver such appropriated American sentiments as Sir Harold Macmillan's 'Let's be frank about it: most of our people have never had it so good!' As things

British were still clearly best in the public's mind, the stimulation of retail sales would benefit indigenous manufacturers and would not jeopardize the country's balance of payments through adding to imported goods. Hire purchase schemes were not new; they stemmed from the 1920s, but when Morris Motors established this with the United Dominions' Trust, that was a time when British salaries were the highest in Europe and the price of cars marginally lower than the European equivalent.

Just when things were starting to look as if the British motor industry might have an easier time than for many a decade, the next couple of years would change this optimism to what would later in the century be termed crisis management. A series of crises, some large, others, considered in isolation, small, would eventually sound the death knell for the large, independent, mass-producers of the British motor industry. The commercial events of the next couple of decades would leave the Government without the social control it had been able to exercise in the past by manipulating this industry – one that will be viewed by historians as a child of the twentieth century. The Government itself, through the nationalization of key players, would become at arm's length a car producer, but the global view of the multinational company would prevail and huge swaths of the manufacturing base would come and (mainly) go, unaffected by the political sentiment of the Government of the time.

Sir William Rootes exchanged his Wiltshire home, the Stype Estate, for Ramsbury Manor, a large estate with this imposing Charles II house on the far side of the lake. Because of its colossal running costs, it was sold after Sir William's death.

The Times, They Are a-Changing

The immediate period that lead up to Hillman's official announcement in 1960 of the Imp started in 1955 with the minor irritations of the Government again fiddling with the rate of purchase tax through increasing it, and imposing new restrictions. Meanwhile the signs of industrial unrest were articulated through strikes by the workforce of newspapers and the docks: but this did not prevent the Conservative Government being returned for another term. This next administration would encounter huge international political problems, with Colonel General Abdel Nasser, the Egyptian President, nationalizing the Suez Canal. This would cause the face of European motoring to be changed for ever in a succession of ever-more-significant 'oil crises'.

Sir William Rootes was to add to the Rootes Group by his traditional method of finding a struggling small firm, taking it over, then rationalizing it − ironically, a fate that would befall the Rootes Group itself when a larger fish, in the form of Chrysler, entered the European pond in the 1960s. Sir William's final target of late 1955 was Singer, a badge that would find favour on the better-equipped Imps, as the Singer Chamois. The year following the acquisition of Singer would see the emergence of a new generation of the Rootes bread-and-butter car, the Hillman Minx, while the ongoing rationalization of the entire Rootes Group, which had already rationalized the big-engined Humbers out of existence, would see many of the other Humbers disappear by 1957. Sir William's talks of the same year, which might have led to a Rootes Group merger with Standard and Triumph, came to nought because of a complication about the Massey Harris/Ferguson tractor interests. Likewise, separate exploratory discussions with Morris and Austin concerning possible mergers with Rootes Securities withered on the vine.

Whether the Rootes brothers were perceived by their workers as beneficent autocrats or not, there is no doubting that until it received the attentions of Chrysler, Rootes was a glorified family enterprise. The board would have an enormous hands-on influence on the Imp, as during its gestation period the largest twenty shareholders in Rootes owned 55 per cent of the voting capital of the company, with 34.4 per cent being in the hands of the chairman and managing director, Sir William. (Brother Reginald, of course, was the other significant shareholder.) Son Geoffrey would become the chairman of Rootes Motors (Scotland) Ltd, and he would have overall responsibility for the production stages of the Imp.

Although the level of reorganization seemed disruptive at the time to the individual firms that found themselves melded into the Rootes Group of companies, it could be said to have been an example of too little, too late. The constituent parts of the group might survive, even at times flourish, under its more dynamic corporate management, but with the benefit of hindsight, it is difficult to see how the company might have been a long-term success story. Industrial and economic historians disagree about which of the industry's many separate contemporaneous shortcomings was chiefly to blame for its eventual demise, but most agree that the British mass-producers' choice to ignore what is frequently referred to as the 'Fordist' approach, especially after Ford UK's move from Old Trafford, Manchester, to the new factory in Dagenham, Essex, was a fatal error. For all the American production values that it espoused, not even Ford managed to implement fully its American-inspired production methods in the United Kingdom, nor, for that matter, were many of these methods well suited to the volume of cars produced by the European manufacturers or the workplace culture of the British workforce. The 'Fordist' approach, however, had a more fundamental effect on these age-old customs and practices that were left virtually untouched by the rationalization taking part in plants like those of Rootes.

Despite the reorganization and its awareness of the American way of doing things, Rootes was still producing lots of models with not enough commonality between their components for great enough savings to be achievable. The norm of the buying public was for small styling changes to make the fare on offer to them many and various. Another characteristic that had grown up with the industry in Britain, and remained unchanged at Rootes, was the outsourcing of a large number of the component-parts of their vehicles; this meant that many of a car's constituent parts were outwith the control of the company, and in times of industrial unrest Rootes had not only its own employees to worry about, but also the effects of industrial action from the multitude of suppliers of essential components over which the company had little or no control. Being a very much more modern and innovative design than the rest of the Rootes range, the Imp would add considerably to this problem, even if it was produced in relatively large numbers for a Rootes car. Ironically, at the time of its launch, Rootes was happy to be complicit in the advertising of the many separate companies that were contracted to supply components for this exciting new model.

2   Engine in the Boot

Pick Up My Guitar and Play?

Well, a pencil, anyway: Parkes and Fry were not part of The Who's anti-revolutionary ethos, even if they thought that 'The change, it had to come/We knew it all along'. The junior co-designer of the Imp, Tim Fry, in his Foreword to David and Peter Henshaw's wonderfully detailed account of the history of the Imp project, *Apex: the Inside Story of the Hillman Imp*, states, 'I picked up my pencil and with a clean sheet of paper started designing what was ultimately to become the Hillman Imp.' Whilst this might in essence be true – Mike Parkes and Tim Fry were not attempting to fulfil some specification resulting from consumers' wish-list surgeries or focus groups – like all radical departures their flights of fancy took off from the more predictable context of what was the available in engineering terms, and Bob Saward, with his team of stylists, would present these ideas to an unsuspecting public in a form that would seem both practical and acceptable. Saward was astonished when he first joined Rootes to discover there was no coordinated 'product planning'.

The best way for Parkes and Fry to establish the engineering norm was to see what others were up to and to offer up to their own detailed scrutiny the more interesting small cars that were available. Rootes Securities purchased an example of each new model from its competitors. Correctly reading the sociological change in Britain, both engineering designers were convinced that their new car would need to be what would be recognized as small. Tim Fry says of their other preoccupations: 'Youthful enthusiasm above all made the car fun to drive, with good handling and controls. Since we lacked the wisdom to know what could not be done, the result was that whatever features we thought it needed, it should have.' So as Mike Parkes, who had a parallel career as a racing driver, demanded, the car's fun quotient embraced such aspects as the predictability of its overall performance. To a driver like Parkes, high levels of handling,

Who's Who – the Apex/Imp Project	
Bernard B. Winter/ Peter Ware	Director of Engineering, Rootes Motors; technical director
A. Craig Miller	Chief Engineer, Rootes Motors; concept team leader
Harry Whyte	Chief (Chassis) Designer, Rootes Motors
Mike Parkes	Project Engineer
Tim Fry	Coordinating Engineer
Leo Kuzmicki	Engine Design; Deputy Chief Engineer
Adrian 'Bill' West	Transmission Engineer
Bob Saward	Body and Interior Styling; Assistant Chief Stylist (to Ted White, Rootes)
Ron Wisdom	Styling Department
Ken Sharpe	Chief Development Engineer
Ken Davies/ Bob Croft	Body Engineering
C. Drury	Project Engineer, Pressed Steel Company

roadholding and speed were important, but predictability would dominate the car's development hierarchy. These preoccupations resulted in the Imp being a 'driver's car' that was capable of impressive point-to-point journey times as well as being much appreciated by those who preferred the competitive track to the trunk road.

As a 'Happy Birthday to the Hillman', following a year's production, *Autocar* pondered on the complete story of a car:

> Where does the story of a car start? When the first seeds of thought begin to germinate in a designer's mind or when the first production cars roll off the line? To the army of project engineers, not to mention the many smaller outside firms called in for specialist component and sub-contract work, the latter part is more the end of the story. The task of tooling a factory for a new design of car is formidable, expensive and, in many facets, uncertain. The task of setting up a new industry, in a new development zone, for a new car would frighten many manufacturers off, but Rootes have successfully achieved just this with their new assembly plant for Hillman Imps at Linwood.

As with many young men who were 'keen on cars', Parkes and Fry found all their personal cars fun, and were constantly attending to them and attempting to liberate their cars' untapped potential. In the 1950s, of course, motoring was much more fun than the daily chore it became for many some decades later. Tim Fry speaks with enjoyment of these earlier times, whether it was being whizzed round in Mike Parkes' Sunbeam Alpine S-T 90, trying a Lotus Type 11, or trips in his own 175cc Fichtel & Sachs, single-cylinder Messerschmitt KR175 that he acquired from his father. Fry tells an amusing tale of Parkes driving him and a luckless friend in the two-seater Messerschmitt which was chosen as the most likely candidate after they pooled their combined petrol allowances in the post-Suez

petrol rationing of ten gallons a month: 'Parkes drove the Messerschmitt with three of us from Oxford to London – the third person's feet were sticking out of the window most of the time!' Parkes' Alpine was left-hand drive, but he decided to convert it to right-hand operation, which meant that for a period it was equipped with a surfeit of steering wheels – something an observant policeman on point duty decided to run for his life from! As far as the description 'youthful enthusiasm' is concerned, this is an attribute Fry has continued to display throughout life, with the firm belief that the 'target of enthusiasm is the product'. Fry even got enthusiastic about a sewage gas filter when he was designing it!

Parkes and Fry realized that Rootes had a range of Hillman cars that were available in several sizes and levels of trim, but none was particularly compact or cheap, and times were a-changing – the working man would no longer feel content to cycle to work on his bicycle. For motoring to become more egalitarian, cars in the United Kingdom were going to have to get smaller and cheaper. The accepted version of the start of the tale is Bernard B. Winter from the Technical Division of Rootes approaching these young designers based at Humber – in 1955, Mike Parkes and Tim Fry were only 24 and 20 years old respectively – when Rootes' pre-war evaluation of a small car, the Little Jim experimental project, was unknown to the youthful pair. According to Tim Fry's recollection, having ideas above their station, it was they who initially approached B. B. Winter. Fry recounts, 'We knew it all! [Rootes comprised] fossils making boring cars.' On emerging from Winter's office with what they took to be his support, Parkes followed an expletive with 'What have we done? We said we would do it, so we'd better go off to do it!' They started with little more than their belief that their youthful enthusiasm and idealism would result in an interesting small car. Parkes would later admit that when he and Fry turned their attention to designing their car, they assumed

---

Mike Parkes (1931–77)

Michael Johnson Parkes was born in 1931 at Richmond, Surrey, the son of John Joseph Parkes. Mike chose his family well: J. J. Parkes is remembered as the former managing director and chairman of Alvis (which had a broader manufacturing base than Rootes – aero-engines, military vehicles, cars, and the largest British manufacturer of printing machines), but during Mike's childhood, Parkes senior was known for his aero expertise, which led to him being a fellow of the Royal Aeronautical Society. One of the founders of Airwork Limited, Mike's father progressed to de Havilland Aircraft via a time spent working for what would become part of Rootes. The Parkes household was a stimulating place to grow up as J. J. had a wide range of interests, which included sailing, flying, electronics and amateur radio.

After public school, Mike entered the three-year training/apprenticeship course at Rootes Motors. On graduating from there he became one of the principals of this narrative. Mike stayed at Rootes through the transformation of Apex into the Imp, leaving in 1962 to join Ferrari as a test and development engineer. Concomitant with his Imp development, Mike was taking part in different types of racing at a club level, and his successes in Lotus cars led to him being a reserve driver for them in the 1958 *Grand Prix d'Endurance les 24 Heures du Mans* race in a Type 11, and actually racing a Type 14 in 1960. Although he was not to qualify, David Fry (coincidentally, Tim Fry married his step-daughter) offered Mike his Formula 2 Fry-Climax car in the 1959 British Grand Prix.

It was as a long-distance sports-car racer that Mike shone, representing Ferrari at Le Mans from 1961 to 1967 and 1970 to 1972, scoring two second places, a third and a seventh. Interestingly, he was the official Rootes' team reserve-driver for its Sunbeam Tiger attempt in 1964. Between 1963 and 1966 he also had considerable success for Ferrari at Monza, Spa, Reims, Nürburgring and Sebring. Mike made his Formula One debut, again with Ferrari, coming second in the 1966 French Grand Prix, the position he was to repeat at Monza. Silverstone would be his first GP win in 1967, followed by a dead heat in the Syracuse GP. It is reputed that Enzo Ferrari did not like Mike risking his life and limb as a mere racing driver, thinking of him as an excellent test engineer. When Mike crashed heavily on the opening lap of the Belgian GP, this was the end of his Formula One career. Although recovery ensued, Mike restricted his racing to sports-cars and managing racing teams for Ferrari and the Fiat 128 touring-car team.

Mike's final development work was on the mid-engined Lancia Stratos, as fitted with the 2.4-litre V6 Ferrari engine, which had been based upon a Bertone design. Mike helped the final stages of rally development of this 200bhp car, as he had taken over as chief development engineer for Lancia, and transformed it into the Group 5 Silhouette racing version of 560bhp. Parkes distrusted front-wheel-drive cars, and it was while driving a Lancia Beta Coupé near Turin on a wet August night in 1977 that he was killed in a road accident.

Rootes had little intention of adding such a vehicle to its range. It was not uncommon for the board to want to know what could be done – what we would call a feasibility study. It is said that the British motor industry was at its best from the concept to prototype stages; from there on, there was a multitude of skills and knowledge that still had to be acquired for industry to survive in the freer marketplace of the century's end. Rootes' inability to benefit from the brilliance of the Imp could serve as an example of this. When industrial historians bandy such phrases as it 'never achieved its full potential', or 'never received the public acclaim/recognition it deserved', what is meant is that the brilliance of its design was clear to all, but it was poorly manufactured and/or not marketed correctly – in other words the production company did not know how to make and sell an excellent product that might have had a Phoenix-like effect on the company. Not that the industry is short of contrary examples – bad designs that were terrible cars, even with a brief sales success if allocated a large enough marketing budget. Up to the production-engineering stage, the Imp looked like taking the European industry by storm.

To the Drawing Board

Following the vaguest suggestions to the design team, one point of departure was to look at what continental manufacturers had already produced. What was available in addition to the curious micro- or bubble-cars of the period, such as those made by Goggomobil, Heinkel, Messerschmitt and the BMW Isetta series, which must have been approaching a test of how basic a car could be and pose the question of what a miniature car might comprise? Along with the Renault 4CV and the Citroën 2CV, Fiat had, in 1955, replaced its Topolino 500 series with the innovatory 600 – a basic design that would be made available with many sizes of engine. Parkes and Fry assessed what motoring and engineering compromises had been struck by their designers,

and realized that these vehicles provided some of what they desired, but no single model offered roominess and comfort, along with what could be described as 'fun to drive' and economy. It was envisaged that the new car would be about the size of small cars from Rootes' British competitors, but larger than the bubble-cars. The designers knew that their car would have to be acceptable within the image that Rootes had created for its products. L. J. K. Setright's comment on small cars comes to mind: 'It is important to distinguish between the truly small and the merely insubstantial.'

Tim Fry remembers the appraisal process of the new models of competitors: he and Parkes would 'thrash the living daylight out of everything'. The foreign vehicle that sticks in his mind was the Citroën 2CV. Although it was

Tim Fry

Tim Fry was born in 1935 into the same branch of the family as the prison reformer Elizabeth Fry (it is his wife who hails from the Bristol branch of eponymous chocolate-manufacturing fame). Tim was educated at Marlborough College, where he seems to have excelled at Latin to the point that the school was preparing him to read classics at the University of Cambridge, but he wanted to study automobile design, and so got himself accepted for the most reputable scheme – the Rootes one at Humber – which he started a week late (to attend Le Mans) in 1953.

Tim's first job for Rootes was to assist with the facelift of the Sunbeam Rapier: 'We reintroduced the S-T radiator grille, made it look more upmarket and longer through the tricks of the trade with chrome.' Less glamorously, he was also designing parts for Commer trucks. After the Imp and Asp, Tim spent eight months at Chrysler in Detroit – sent as an engineer, but working in the styling department. Tim always tried to resist (unsuccessfully, until he founded his own company) the artificial division between engineering and styling of a product. His life-long belief is that 'The customer sees the single entity – if you do not think of it as such, something suffers.'

On his return, Tim turned his attentions to shaping

the exterior of the new Avenger. He altered the boot and added the characteristic L-shaped tail-lights, which was subsequently updated from Detroit. Tim's later positions were as 'Chief Stylist of Advanced Styling' and 'Chief Engineer of Advanced Styling', but he spent most of his time on cooling and electrical systems. He left Rootes in 1970 because he felt he was being 'promoted to positions I did not like', and receiving a 'fantastic redundancy deal' he founded Smallfry of Wolston, near Coventry. Smallfry's early consultancy work, with Peter Knott, Tim's brother-in-law and former colleague, was working on actuators for operating valves for Rotork, where his brother was the managing director. He has since designed patrol boats, a catamaran ferry, Hydrovane road compressors, tractor chassis, a telephone, a one-piece clothes peg, and plastic garden furniture for B&Q. It is perhaps the Sea Truck that brought Tim the largest recognition after the Imp, as it obtained a Design Council Award and the 1975 Prince Philip Designer's Prize.

Whether talking about the Imp, which he still holds in some esteem, or even his clothes peg, Tim absolutely exudes enthusiasm for his work and the idea of design in general, and he is still fully engaged with his Smallfry projects.

not a fast car *per se*, they were astonished by its performance over virtually any terrain, how much fun it was to drive (it sounded as if the word 'recklessly' should have formed part of this description), and of course it accommodated four passengers in some degree of comfort. On completion of their appraisal, such had been the vigour of testing its 'fun' quotient that the 2CV had to make a detour via Parkes' family garage to have the wheels straightened and made circular again!

The carefully contrived Rootes Group's image was that of rather upmarket, albeit conservative, cars compared to those of its competitors. Even in those days before men in smart suits with their fresh business studies degrees would hold tremendous sway, the Rootes brothers realized that if their manufacturing concern was to flourish, any purchaser of one of their marques could make his purchase with the confidence that he was paying a little more for those extra little touches.

The board of Rootes was eager to sanction each step in the progress of new vehicles. This was especially true at the styling stages. Bob Saward recalls, 'We used to drag the full-size model out onto the playing fields in Humber Road, under wraps – then the Rootes family would come and view it.' After the family's final viewing of the Imp, Geoffrey Rootes commented to the stylists: 'We didn't change it, did we?' Things were not always this unanimous. Timothy Rootes – the mention of whose name seems to exhort comments from former employees about his sartorial elegance and his knowledge and love of the turf, rather than his attempts at styling, where he was nominally placed – was responsible for some small detail that the board was viewing. William commented, 'You have this all wrong!', to which came the instant reply, 'Yes sir . . .'. On another occasion, the family was viewing the Super Minx, which was to gain four headlamps, while the base model would be left with a single pair and two empty orifices requiring attention. This time it was son Geoffrey, who had suggested a cruciform ornamental grille to disguise these, and William, on seeing them, exclaimed, 'Eyes in your arse!' This solution was not proceeded with.

The engineering-design pair also took as a starting point a few fundamental concepts of what such a small car should be able to achieve: carrying two adults with two children

This is where the bubble-car look takes its first step towards a squared-off 'proper' car. There is still a long way to go, but Ron Wisdom's sketches have become three-dimensional and the 'Slug' is setting out on its journey to become the Imp.

WWK 752

was one principal input to their thinking, and they felt this should be achievable in a vehicle that could progress at 60mph and under favourable conditions and speeds achieve 60mpg. It is worth remembering quite how uneconomical the average British family saloon was at this time, and it is interesting to compare this conceptualization with the one, reputedly imposed by the *Reichsverband der Automobilindustrie*, on Ferdinand Porsche when he was designing the Beetle. Porsche was supposed to meet the criteria of carrying two adults and three children, being able to cruise on the new autobahns at 60mph (100km/h), achieving 33mpg (8.6ltr/100km) with an air-cooled reliable engine, costing under 1,000 RM (c. £200), and capable of carrying three soldiers and a machine-gun!

Being practical designers, and not having to be concerned about their car's militaristic possibilities, Parkes and Fry's reputed starting point for this small car was to begin with the four seats, then design a minimal shell around the putative new buyer's family. Whilst this is partially true, Fry's comment 'that we were trying to replace the popular motorcycle and sidecar combination' was foremost in the collective mind – minds that were delighted with their inaugural run: the car returned 83mpg (3.4ltr/100km) and a top speed of 56mph (90km/h).

This car, like many vehicles they inspected, was significantly smaller than the norm of the day; so where to site the running gear? This is a good example of them working from first principles. Rather than follow, with embellishments, the *Système Panhard* that had dominated the layout of cars since the 1890s, the designers realized the benefit in a small vehicle of locating the engine and gearbox at the same end as the driven wheels – but which end? Since the pre-war days of Alvis, Cord and Citroën, front-wheel drive had been a possibility, but there was a problem that was costly to solve: if the driven wheels were also going to be the steered wheels, then special joints were required to cope with the angularities involved when providing power to the wheels, whatever angle they were; the simple much-utilized universal joint of the seventeenth-century scientist Robert Hooke was much more suitable for prevalent orthodoxy than driving the steered wheels. Decades later, front-wheel drive would become the low-cost solution to the layout of every small car, but this would only be after the BMC Mini solved the problem through the use of a low-cost, constant-velocity joint, significantly cheaper than those available to their rivals like SAAB or Citroën. Fortuitously for Alec Issigonis and his Mini, Hardy-Spicer of the UK produced such a constant-velocity joint, the Birfield, that was after the thirty-year-old Czech ball-bearing design by Hans Rzeppa. Citroën knew of Rzeppa's design, but this British version was at a price that could be used in a cheaper car – it having being developed by the British patent-holders, Unipower of Shipley, Yorkshire, for submarine conning-tower control gear.

Like the designers of the highly influential Fiat 600, Parkes and Fry realized the simplicity of rear-wheel drive with a rear-mounted engine. Not that this was without its problems requiring their attention – the most obvious was the bad reputation that many rear-engined vehicles had acquired as far as their road-holding was concerned. Predictable and fun it might be in skilled hands, but this was to be a mass-production vehicle that could and would be driven by drivers who would possess a wide range of competence. The accepted wisdom was that even with untutored hands at the steering wheel, however many vices most of the front-wheel-drive cars exhibited, and in some cases these were considerable, when the limit of adhesion of the tyres was being approached somehow the car would scrabble round a bend with the driver reacting in a 'natural' and unthinking way to the resultant shortcomings of his folly. In stark contrast, however, the rear-engined car would be facing the direction whence one had come! It was clear, however it was to be achieved, that acceptable road-holding for the Imp would not be good enough – it had to be exemplary and surpass that of its more conventional competitors. Under 'Six main headings for SALES SUCCESS', sent to its dealers, Rootes would claim for the Imp's engine location 'all technical advantages of both rear and front engine layout'; further justification for this assertion was not forthcoming. It is ironic to realize that one of the shortcomings of front-wheel drive would contribute to Mike Parkes's untimely death when driving an ordinary road-going Lancia Beta Coupé many years later.

Back to the Drawing Board, but Getting There . . .

When the rapidly evolving small-car project was presented to Rootes, the board was sufficiently interested to authorize the preparation of working prototypes, which were to acquire the sobriquet 'the Slug'. Parkes and Fry were allocated to the company's research department at Ryton-on-Dunsmore, near Coventry – the former test facility for aero-engine refurbishment. This billet remained the home of the engineering development of what became the Apex project. Ryton was an exceptionally convenient location, as it was close, not only to the Rootes styling studio at Humber, but

also to the other necessary skilled specialists who would be required during the various stages of turning this speculative theoretical venture into a reality. It is difficult today to adjudge just when the Slug became the Apex, as those working on the former frequently attributed the latter's name to it.

The Apex was developed into the pre-production Imp by a closely knit team of fewer than one hundred contributors. Bernard B. Winter's successor, Peter Ware, was a huge supporter of the project, and all who worked for him claim that he pushed for the Imp at the highest managerial levels. The part of the former aero-engine testing facility devoted to the Apex engineering development was a self-contained unit of workshops and the like – the idea of testing components in this way, whether destructively or not, was a new idea. The omens were right for this small Rootes vehicle, and time would become increasingly of the essence of putting the car into production. In these pre-computer-design days, the initial stage was to take the design drawings, make clay models, then engage panel-beaters and fabricators to realize these designs in metal for the working prototypes. Here the proximity of specialists was of enormous assistance to the Apex.

To speed up the building of a running

While not as basic as the original Parkes/Fry ideas for the Apex, this is minimal if not minimalist. The thickness of the seat backs does not invite one to try them, and the front parcel shelf is just what the name implies, albeit an extremely deep one. The indentations revealed by the surface of this photograph suggest that tracings have been taken off it to design a different binnacle and instruments with shorter stalks protruding from the side.

prototype, the front suspension from a Goggomobil was utilized complete. This accorded with the Parkes and Fry decision to use swing-axle suspension at both ends of the car for cost as well as simplicity reasons, despite the problems that the Beetle had experienced with the use of swing-axle rear suspension. And the air-cooled twin cylinder engine from a Citroën 2CV was a temporary substitution for the as-yet-incomplete planned Villiers power unit. Being such a prototype, the Slug was in a constant state of evolution. It had many striking features, several of which showed its designers to be aware of trends in continental thinking, especially in the area of aerodynamics and the need to maintain a low coefficient of drag when powered by what was for the UK public a ridiculously small engine. The car's large glazed area, in particular its deep curved windscreen, gave the Slug a contemporary feel that seems more reasonable today than it did to the astonished Rootes Board's eyes of the late 1950s. Of the designers' principal objectives, most were matched. Unfortunately its spartan interior revealed all too obviously that it would be a cheap car, and although posterity has not passed on how much fun it would be to drive, it certainly had a low top speed. Bearing in mind that Rootes cherished a reputation for cars that were a notch above those of its competitors, this prototype was far too aligned with the cheap and cheerful bubble- or micro-car concept, and the board of directors reacted to it in an all too predictable manner – it went off to the Rootes styling department, acquiring as it went the official codename, Apex. Two running prototypes of this more expensive, but less utilitarian, machine were built with bodywork fabricated by Pressed Steel. It was at this stage that Ron Wisdom made his first contribution to the shape of the Apex: the more futuristic, quasi-bubble-car front took on a squared-off 'proper-car' shape. While being removed from the merely conventional, it reveals a type of thinking reminiscent of the solutions that continental firms like DAF were adopting.

Styling Then?

Readers who are acquainted with the design and development of today's cars might be forgiven for not realizing how different from today was the world of design during the gestation of the Apex/Imp. Even at this time, however, a difference between engineering design and styling, which was still in its infancy, had emerged. Following the author's conversations with Saward and Wisdom, the principal two stylists responsible for the way different variants looked, Bob Saward contributed the following succinct thoughts:

> It is important that readers differentiate between engineering and styling or design. The two often work closely together, but are also independent. Stylists/designers are not necessarily engineers. The early stylists were trail-blazers; no one before them had been titled in such a way.

Today, the Royal College of Art has a thriving Automotive Design course, as has Coventry University and numerous others. These places produce the designers of the future – interior, exterior, colour and trim.

In the early days Bob Saward was able to be involved in all aspects of the design of the Imp; now, of course, times have changed, and 'the team' is an integral part of any car design. Saward cherished the autonomy of the Humber Road styling department and clearly rejoiced in the experience of taking a car from pastel sketch to reality: such a unique opportunity as Bob was offered will never come again.

The usually retold tale of the development of the Imp portrays the relatively small team as progressing within an atmosphere of unstressed harmony. But like any harmonic progression that is not purely anodyne, it possessed its tensions and resolutions. Where a team comprises engineering-designers who expect the fruits of their toils to be adorned by the styling department, the evolution might be more uncomplicated, but with Parkes and Fry, the Apex project had a test engineer and one with strong views on styling. After all, Parkes was becoming known for his prowess in racing circles, and Fry was working as a consultant providing the styling of the body of the Elva Mk. 4 sports-racer (Peter Knott, Fry's brother-in-law, designed the chassis).

From Slug to Butterfly?

Because of the wishes of the Rootes family for a small car that would resemble what they thought their customers would recognize as a proper car, unrelated to micro-, bubble-, or kit cars, Rootes brought in Bob Saward from Ford to oversee the exterior and interior body styling – to be finical, Saward was brought in to strengthen the emerging Rootes styling department, as the assistant chief stylist to Ted White. Although not expressly engaged because of the Apex, it was he who was the progenitor of what we instantly recognize as the Imp saloon, and he also took sole responsibility for the evolution of its styling. It has to be said, however, that Saward believed that 'the Slug certainly lived up to its nickname'. The Rootes Group's styling studio was part of the Humber factory, and this was where Saward and Wisdom did all the styling of the Imp while engaging in mutually enlightening exchanges with the research department at Ryton-on-Dunsmore about the ramifications for each other occasioned by developments.

Starting with the Slug idea and Wisdom's suggested alterations, Bob Saward commenced on the Imp in the manner that was the traditional approach at Rootes – making the side-view basic drawings and pastel sketches. The popular misconception of a seamless transition of the styling from the Slug to Apex ought to be clarified. Saward had seen the Slug, and was aware of the earlier attempts of others at the Apex; he had also talked to Wisdom about its various features, as well as being familiar with the planned engineering ideas of Parkes and Fry. It should be realized that Saward started the styling from scratch, while incorporating vital dimensions (even if these were to change) and design features. While this is a plausible description of events, there is one piece of extant Rootes evidence

that is perplexing – a book of proposed Apex pressed-steel parts. These are dated, some with updating, from 1960 on, and incorporate many features that only emerge in the latter stages of Saward's photographed 'clay' stages. From the earliest stages, such drawings were made, mostly by the Pressed Steel Company in Cowley, with an eye to the production-engineering phase, and the majority of these drawings are concomitant with Saward's styling chronology. The only way this sequence can make complete sense is to presume that they were kept up to date with the emerging Apex, but the drawing office was less than fastidious when it came to appending the dates of modifications. To give an example, these drawings contain precise information about the opening rear-window lock long before anyone thought of having an opening rear window.

Once Bob Saward's side-view drawings had produced a likely-looking concept, the next stage was to embark upon a three-dimensional realization. Bob Croft then engaged the services of a model-maker, probably Eric Ingram, to make a ⅜-scale clay model – an American proportional size – through applying the clay to a wooden buck, or former; the clay would then be scraped to produce the exact shape portrayed in the drawings. Plasticine had been the usual material, but this was more difficult to work and had been replaced at Rootes. Ron Wisdom retells a serendipitous tale of using plasticine when redesigning the Sunbeam Rapier's rear fins: having got these looking 'just right', the car was taken outside on an extremely hot day. The plasticine slowly changed shape, and much to the joy of the stylists it was decided that this was an even better shape and adopted for production!

The Apex styling project then moved on to the first full-sized clay model. Saward and Wisdom remember realizing the detailing of this, and subsequent clay models through wielding 12in metal rulers purchased from the nearest Woolworth's store, and scraping the clay to modify the car's contours. According to

Bob Saward

Robert W. Saward was born in December 1928 and educated in his native Croydon. Leaving school, Bob progressed to the Croydon College of Art before working in art studios producing cinema commercials, where he gained some expertise in airbrush work. In 1946, Bob entered the *Daily Star* competition for a 'Car of the Future'. This led to the Ford Motor Company wishing to employ him, but the Government had other ideas, and he was 'called up' for obligatory military National Service.

On demobilization from the services, he availed himself of Ford's previous invitation, and worked for them between 1950 and 1958. Bob was a stylist for general vehicle design, which meant occupying the corner of the drawing office and making sketches of general design, the art-work for badges and many other 'artistic' aspects of car design. When Ford's styling studio became a central part of its design process, thanks to George Schnider, Bob rose to the position of senior stylist in both the exterior and interior styling studios. It is at this point that Rootes Motors employed Bob as assistant chief stylist 'to "sort out" the Apex styling – both exterior and interior, and to be solely responsible for the Imp body design'.

On completion of his Apex/Imp work in 1963, Bob returned to Ford as its design studio manager, working on large- and medium-range vehicle design.

He went back to Rootes/Chrysler (UK) in 1968 as the design manager in charge of advanced car and truck projects, including the new Avenger and the in-house student-training programmes with the Royal College of Art, London – he had no formal connection with the Imp at this stage. Bob became the design manager of Chrysler's new initiative, Euro Design, a contract design service that catered for both product and commercial design. When this office closed in 1977, he became the design chief responsible for exterior vehicle design, a position he retained under PSA Peugeot-Citroën until 1984. Like most of his colleagues, Bob declined the company's offer to transfer to France when many areas of work were relocated there, and remained in the Midlands as a freelance designer.

Bob's various projects since have included designs for Eurounion Ltd, Devon (plastic go-kart body, worldwide hotel plastic clothes-hanger, urban litter-bins and children's pedal cars and bicycles), Python Ltd, Birmingham (engineering tools), System Floors Ltd (integrated suspended ceiling system), Shakespeare Trust (interior design and development of catering and refreshment areas) and Myatt Design (body-shell for Eagle kit-car, graphics for a rally car body, modular generator enclosures, instrument housing and cowls for tractors).

the extant personal photographic archive of Bob Saward, this initial full-sized model was followed by four modification and viewing stages, during which the clay model become 'see-through', culminating with the 'final viewing' model – which patently was not the end of the tinkering with details. It would be discovered later that had the designs that located the cabin air intake been retained at the base of the windscreen, then a better pressure differential, and consequently flow of air, would have been maintained between the intake and the stale-air vents above the rear screen. For the all-important final performance, the model would be treated to the clay being sealed with shellac, primed and a top coat of light-blue paint applied. The intermediary stages would receive the board's inspec-

tion either in the styling studio, which was equipped with a turntable to rotate the large model, or it would be taken outside onto a flat roof. The final viewing model would be taken to the adjoining playing fields for the family inspection. Added perspective was given to the car through it being displayed on a field that had a trunk road running alongside; it could therefore be seen against a background of varied real traffic.

Once the full-size model was finalized, it was copied in hollowed-out wood, but this time with opening doors so that people could sit inside the model. This was a peculiarity with which the Rootes Group persisted, as it gave people a much clearer idea of the emerging interior of the vehicle. Both the final clay version and the wooden one were delivered to

Engine in the Boot

The following fourteen photographs are selected from Bob Saward's record of the seven 'viewing' stages of the Imp's styling from first scale model to 'Final Viewing' full-size clay model. The increase in the wheel-base and length took place later, during the prototype stages.

There is only one (offside) front side and indicator light at this scale-model stage; the question whether to use two or a combined unit will change several times during the Apex's styling. The overall bonnet shape has been laid down, even at this stage.

Note the square metal placeholders above the rear wheel for the name, and the indented roof at the rear. The rear-quarter-pillar, thick at the top and thinning as it goes down, will receive further consideration. The idea of the bumpers merely being a more durable addition to the bodywork has been considered at this point.

It is now entitled 'Apex'. There are different front headlights and indicators fitted to each side. The strengthening flutes on the bonnet have become functional as scoops leading to the cabin air intake. Unusually, white-wall tyres are not used on this and subsequent full-size model stages. Even at this stage, these models were taken to the adjoining sports field.

From this stage, the car becomes 'see through' and fenestrated, with a base over where the seats will be. Real exterior fitments are used on the clay models for verisimilitude. The roof is now a flat panel and the number-plate becomes oblong. Saward has placed the lights higher 'because it tied in with the side feature – possibly better how it ended up'.

The next stage is still Apex, with sealed-beam headlights and door handle decided, but side lights and indicators still asymmetrical. These shots were taken on the flat roof outside the styling studios in Humber Road.

This picture shows the louvred engine cover with different styles of rear light. Ron Wisdom recalls working on the number-plate and its light. Like many of the photographs in Bob Saward's Apex development album, there are indentations on the surface of the photograph, indicating that tracings were taken from it: in this case they suggest different rear-quarter-pillars, rear of roof, rear wheel-arch, and door shapes.

The fourth stage. Now it is a Hillman, returned to trying a rectilinear front side-light for comparison. This asymmetrical car has a tapering rear-quarter-pillar and pointed trailing edge to the side rear window from this side. There is a deeper bonnet fluting to the air intake, and the hinges are becoming a feature (that is matched at the rear).

From this side, however, it has a thicker rear-quarter-pillar, diagonally cut off trailing edge to the window and a suggested position for a round badge next to this. These models use real wheels and tyres.

With the fifth stage we see a wide, continuous air intake on the trailing edge of the bonnet and a fussier front bumper, although the characteristic side panels are taking shape. Now, round sidelights and indicators seem to be favoured.

They are clearly still trying to finalize the rear lights — vertical or horizontal? — even the ones close to the eventual design will be much more styled into the bodywork of the rear wing. The parallel rear-quarter-pillar and the diagonal corner of the rear side windows are getting close.

At the next stage, the air intake moves to above the bumper line and the bumper regains its straight simplicity, but below the fresh-air intake.

The vertical rear lights win, set in a more restrained sculpted rear wing. The rear window, not yet opening, reveals the inclusion of the concept with a suggested left hinge and rotational operating handle. The engine cover louvres disappear in favour of ventilation slots above the number-plate.

This 'final-viewing' stage, but is not yet the final form – although now painted! In addition to growing 8½in (216mm), there are numerous detail differences between this and the final Imp: clearly, the bumper line will rise above the front side- and indicator-lights, which themselves will revert to earlier stages in the styling, and further exterior trim and quarter-lights will be added. The final design of the badging will also be later.

Pressed Steel at Cowley so that they could start planning the production of the component pressed-steel panels. It is difficult to ascertain today how many versions of the Imp's development were officially classified as separate stages, but when the factory at Linwood was under construction, it was referred to as being for the Apex Scheme 10. The quasi-hatchback opening rear window might have been much commented upon (and who could forget that token lady loading her suitcase?), but it did not enter the styling discussion until late in the full-size-model stage of the design.

The ⅜-scale model was completed in 1959, with the full-scale one receiving Saward's attention in 1960. Along with the special 'MIRA model', it was this latter clay model that was subjected to night testing in the wind-tunnel of the Motor Industry Research Association. The timing of these tests was not for security purposes, but the energy drain on the national grid at Nuneaton from the huge fans was only advisable during times when the general population was asleep. The evaluation was done through attaching wool tufts to the entire exterior to reveal the airflow patterns

The opening window and lock have been finalized, but the cabin-ventilation slots have yet to be developed. The earlier door handles will be reverted to, the engine cover hinges will be rethought and its handles will be changed to pointing outwards. The roof gutter still requires extending and the rear wings have not achieved their final form – but it is recognizably the Imp rather than an Apex.

and using smoke to show up planar and vortiginous airflow. The aerodynamicist would make suggestions based upon the wind-tunnel observations, and Bob Saward suggested that 'we would try to accommodate them'. In reality, there were very few changes to the body shape during the Apex development, as it was, fortuitously, a very efficient shape – rather more so than the later coupé form. There were small changes to the roof's rear overhang and the body round the rear window which, as well as being æsthetically more pleasing to the designers, probably improved the flow of air over the body. Not part of Bob Saward's sequence of styling models was the rather more dynamic ¼-scale model, incorporating items like the suspension, produced by the model makers for more accurate predictive testing of Apex's aerodynamics. This 'MIRA model' is still owned by them.

On the Inside

When a driver sits in a car, the main three things that impinge upon his or her consciousness, other than the comfort of the seat, are the ease and positioning of the control pedals, a steering wheel that has the function its name suggests, and the look, functionality, and feedback of the instruments. The norms of the day were not difficult ones to surpass, so it is of little surprise that the size and distribution of these vital controls were aspects of design that did not engage the minds of the designer for too long! With an eye to those allegedly typical Rootes customers, the production car would have acceptable pedals. Even so, the author would have appreciated having a trifle more room between the base of the steering column and the pedals for his size eleven shoes – something that various testers have commented upon over the years. The steering wheel was round (the triumph of styling over function of the Austin Allegro's 'quartic' wheel had yet to be presented to an unreceptive public), and the mechanism it was

connected to did not enjoy the comfort of power assistance. Through having the weight of the engine over the rear wheels and not having to contend with the front ones being driven, this car could naturally have light and precise steering without occupying much of the available space with a large steering wheel. Taste dictated that expensive vehicles had large wooden dashboards, while sporting and cheaper cars adopted metal ones, whose elegance was in direct relationship to the eventual cost of the car. Either way, the controls and instruments were scattered over the width of these dashboards, frequently achieving their harmony through the symmetrical placement around the car's centre-line. When space was at a premium, such as was the case in the lowest-cost micro- and bubble-cars, a simple binnacle with few instruments would be mounted on the steering column.

It is unclear who proposed that the Apex should sport the binnacle that is so characteristic of the earlier Imp, and in the words of its stylists, 'Everyone was trying binnacles at the time.' Parkes and Fry designed one version, as did both Wisdom and Saward, none of them being identical to the Imp as it appeared in production, and the pre-Saward Apex had a primitive form of it. The metamorphosis of the Apex into the Imp retained the idea of the focus of a binnacle in front of the driver, but one that gave the driver lots of information from its multiple gauges and warning lights, with the minor controls being operated via protruding stalks – a luxury that even British manufacturers such as Rolls-Royce were only starting to incorporate. Interestingly, when this feature was later to be 'improved', it received censure from the motoring press. Typical of the reception of this feature on the launch of the Imp, *Cars Illustrated* opined, 'The instrument panel is extremely well laid out, with the minor controls in a binnacle immediately in front of the driver: the entire unit is a model of simplicity, convenience and sense.' Whereas, once this was modernized, we find *Motor* lamenting its passing.

The interior was styled separately by the same stylists led by Bob Saward. There was talk that an interior-designer friend of the Rootes family, the Hon. John Siddeley, would coordinate the colour schemes and interiors of the Imp, but following a débâcle over his interior-design work for the factory (*see* page 51), the idea of his involvement with the car was quietly dropped. Areas like the final format of the facia would experience several dashboards, complete with instruments, being displayed along the studio wall. For the original facia, the dashboard's specification would be agreed by all, then the stylist would set about realizing it. It was traditional to obtain as many proprietary items from the West Midlands' parts bins, then set about designing and styling those that would be particular to that model. Naturally, requests for items that the stylist had to accommodate percolated through from the designers in Ryton. One such was extremely simple, but has been appreciated by many owners since: the very tall Mikes Parkes specified that there

should be two location points for bolting the front seats to the floorpan. Although it involves the inconvenience of the owner resorting to a spanner, because the locating points are a couple of inches apart, the Imp has an uncommonly large range of fore-and-aft front-seat adjustment for a small car. Time has drawn a veil over the level of vigour with which the passenger accommodation was discussed between Ryton and Humber Road, but Parkes and Fry (who was of substantial build) were determined that those in the front would be comfortable, with thoughts of 'sod the people in the back'. Like the rest of the Rootes range, the Imp used the modern Imperial Chemical Industries' fabrics – durable Vynide for the seats and breathable Vynair for the headlining. The stitched-panel effect on the seats was in the fore–aft plane on most models, but a transverse effect would also be used from time to time on models like the Singer Chamois.

If Bob Saward enjoyed the styling autonomy that was offered to him at Rootes, it

Every dining table should have one! This is the special ¼-scale model from the Motor Industry Research Association (where it is normally to be found) that was built to assess the aerodynamics of the Imp. MIRA's records reveal that at a prototype stage after this model was tested, the overall length of the Imp increased from 130.5in (3,315mm) to the final 139in (3,531mm).

seems that Ron Wisdom relished the performance aspect of presenting their progress to selected members of the Rootes board. Wisdom recalls that even the artistic margins of Rootes – which was how the styling department was viewed – had a dress code that would not have been out of place in the Civil Service: an artistically flamboyant tie had to be exchanged for a more sober one before a Rootes family visit, which was truly an inspection of the troops. Like many the author has spoken to, the personnel of the styling department are still generous in their praise and liking for 'Billy' Rootes, commenting upon his ability to communicate with all levels of the company and his apparent interest in what each member of his staff was achieving – perceived clearly as a 'toff', but with very much the common touch. One opinion proffered on Sir William when something or someone was less than ideal is 'swearing, kicking, and shouting in a posh accent – brilliant leader, anyone would follow him anywhere'!

Meanwhile, Back at the Ryton Research Ranch

Sporting its intended Villiers engine, the transitional Apex project car was ready to be put through its investigative and appraisal paces. Some of the Parkes and Fry innovations and ingenious touches would progress forward into the production vehicle, albeit with some modification. In these still-prototype stages some others would fail for reasons various: a great idea possibly, but it either did not work or the available expertise could not make it do so with any prospect of longevity. The two other common reasons for the deletion of a characteristic idea were the frequently encountered ones of the difficulty of transferring the concept into production, or just simply that it would be an idea that no potential owner would cherish as much as the designer had! Parkes and Fry were aware of the progress that the rival British Motor Corpora-

tion was making with its Mini as they frequently socialized with its designer, Alec Issigonis, and Alex Moulton, who was further developing his rubberized suspension ideas, this time for the Mini. Unlike the Imp, the earlier Mini had started life as a reaction to the Suez Crisis, and commenced with a similarly minimalist concept, although the two vehicles ended up being quite different manifestations of the small-car concept. Parkes knew Issigonis while the latter was busily designing the V8-engined sporting luxury car with rubber suspension for his father – alas, Alvis could not afford to put it into production and the prototype was dismantled. The oft-told tale of Fry drawing the still-secret Mini's suspension arm for Issigonis over one of their frequent meals is true. Being a man of the old school, Issigonis rather thought that Parkes was a bit of 'a waste of space as a designer as he could not draw'. When asked about industrial security and how they could all have known about each other's projects, Fry replied that 'things were just like that' – it was a small world indeed, and, of course, Issigonis was one of the first outsiders to experience, and praise, a drive in the pre-production Imp. Alexander Arnold Constantine Issigonis had commenced his automobile career as an employee of Rootes Limited at Humber Road prior to designing the Morris Minor, of which he left a prototype front-wheel-drive version at Cowley before briefly transferring his allegiance to Alvis.

Of the interesting experiments along the way, even if they were to wither on the vine before becoming incorporated into the prototype, the wheels, deleted at an early stage, are worthy of mention: they were designed merely as rims for mounting the tyres, and were bolted to the aluminium brake drums – an elegant solution to keep the unsprung weight down. Experimental features did survive into production: for example, the ingenious speedometer drive that resembled the after-market speedometers that were used on pedal-bicycles, and the short-lived pneumatic throttle of Dunlop manufacture. It was one of those borrowed assessment cars that caused the pneumatic throttle control to be adopted. While trying a Renault Dauphine on a fast drive up what existed of the M1 from London to Coventry in deep winter, Parkes lifted his foot off the accelerator pedal, but the Renault continued flat out. The already high-friction cable had stuck as moisture inside the outer cable had frozen solid.

Thus the Apex project positively bristled with innovative thinking, much of which was transferred to the production Imp, but although the management board of Rootes was now convinced that a new small car would be required in the near future, it was going to be more of the 'proper' car everyone had been working towards with the evolution of the Apex, and it would no longer frighten their extant customers. The board, probably correctly, feared that the earlier schemes *would* have frightened them. In an interview with the Henshaws for their book, Tim Fry reports that the board of Rootes Motors expressed the opinion that, rather than the Apex, it wanted 'something which is more like a proper motor car', and he admits it was probably correct, as Parkes and Fry's 'thoughts had been set at too mean a level', and they 'were trying to make a cheaper and simpler equivalent to the Citroën 2CV'. The Rootes board knew that the highly conservative British car-buying public were hardly beating a path to purchase the Slough-built products of M. Citroën, so why would it favour one from a home-based producer? Apocryphal though the suggestion might be, it was commonly rumoured that Lord Rootes would not entrust his life to even riding in the Apex! Looking back and ruminating on this period of rapid change in society and what it meant for automobile producers at the time, Lord Rootes' son, Geoffrey, opines:

> In our case this all happened at a very crucial time. We had decided that, if we were to survive in the world motor industry at a time of increasingly fierce competition, we

needed to have a volume-produced small car. We had therefore developed the Hillman Imp.

The British motor industry of the 1950s is portrayed as lacking the innovation of many of its mainland-European competitors; whilst the majority of the evidence would testify the truth of this assertion, the separate companies frequently did contain talented engineers of enormous ingenuity, but the failure to exploit most of the more speculative approaches to designs must surely lie at the door of the tastes of the great British public. It seems hardly fair to criticize companies for not exploiting the ideas of their brightest engineers, when to have done so would have resulted in their financial ruin. Not that Lord Rootes was faultless when it came to assessing the taste of the public: in addition to his earlier underestimation of the potential of the Volkswagen, when Austin launched his Seven with the promise that it was 'a decent car for the man who, at present, can only afford a motor cycle and sidecar and yet has the ambition to become a motorist', Rootes opined 'that the public just will not stand for it'.

Interesting as the more extremist aspects of the Slug/Apex might seem in today's more environmentally friendly times, it is understandable why Parkes and Fry acquiesced to the wishes of the board for a proper car – and in the thinking at Rootes, this also meant four proper seats and a conventional 4-cylinder engine that was water cooled. The thinking was clear: however space-efficient the passenger compartment was, four full-sized seats with sufficient legroom would equal a larger vehicle, and this would necessitate a much larger engine – even if Panhard was rather proving the opposite on the other side of the English Channel, with their commodious and quick cars with small and efficient engines. Bob Saward was busily fulfilling his styling brief, and it was at this juncture that the adoption of a water-cooled engine with probably four cylinders became unconsciously accepted by all as the obvious solution. Many references to the earlier stages of the Imp's evolution make reference to its minimalist concept. The author is comfortable with this term when considering the 'process-type' musical compositions of, say, Steve Reich, but believes there is a whole raft of confusions when it is applied to automobiles. It was heartening, therefore, to encounter the following typically thoughtful passage of L. J. K. Setright in his *Drive On!*:

What is minimalism? The word is now commonplace among musicians, as it has long been among architects; but what does it mean in the context of the car? We habitually talk about small cars, light cars, cheap cars. As often, we confuse these terms so that we use one to mean another. As always, principles lead us in one direction, practicalities in another.

In 1960, Rootes Motors announced what had been common knowledge to the motoring press for some months: that it was about to build an entirely new small car in a new, but unspecified, factory.

3   The Road to Scotland

Why a Scottish Imp?

As the Emperor Hadrian found on his visit nigh on two millennia earlier, the road to Scotland is not an easy one, either literally or metaphorically. At the commencement of the 1960s, the 'Town and Country Planning' regulations – backed by the Board of Trade – required that prior to any substantial development taking place, an 'Industrial Development Certificate' had to be obtained in order to build a factory. If the proposed development infringed either local or national interests, then the envisaged site was frequently designated part of the country's 'Green Belt' – this being offered up as the official reason for refusal. For those readers not well-versed in

the archaic and arcane intricacies of the Home Civil Service and Government departments, it should be pointed out that the seventeenth-century Board of Trade, or to give it its correct title, the Committee of Privy Council for Trade and Foreign Plantations, had met only once since 1850. In 1942, it acquired control of the location of the country's industry, a situation that remained until the establishment of the new Ministry of Technology in 1969 with Mr Anthony Wedgwood Benn as its Secretary of State. Development certificates became far less burdensome during the 1970s and were eventually abandoned during the 1980s. Phenomenally successful in the short term, they failed to engender long-term revitalization of deprived areas.

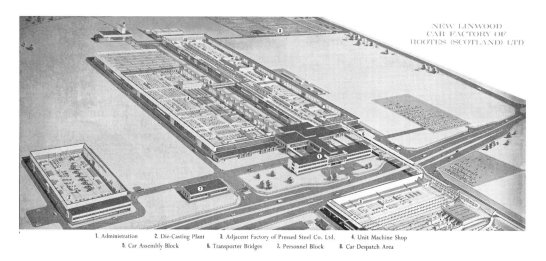

NEW LINWOOD
CAR FACTORY OF
ROOTES (SCOTLAND) LTD

1. Administration   2. Die-Casting Plant   3. Adjacent Factory of Pressed Steel Co. Ltd.   4. Unit Machine Shop
5. Car Assembly Block   6. Transporter Bridges   7. Personnel Block   8. Car Despatch Area

This early artist's impression of the Linwood complex is looking westwards. Following the closure of the factory in 1981, the drawings, plans and much-photographed architectural model of the whole complex were destroyed.

The obvious way of putting the Imp into production would have been to mop up some of the spare land on the south-east of the Rootes ex-shadow factory at Ryton-on-Dunsmore. By 1960, however, the Rootes Group was not in robust financial shape, and the building of an extensive new facility was not to be taken lightly. Should the necessary permission be denied for this expansion, then the board of Rootes had prepared a contingency plan. A few years earlier, a new commercial facility had been established for Commer and Karrier vehicles at Dunstable, and the Imp factory could form part of an extension to this complex. Alas, neither proposal attracted official approval.

Rootes Securities' usual financial guarantor, Prudential Assurance, was not involved in this instance. The reason for this is likely to lie in Rootes Securities' ability, albeit reluctantly, to interlock with the official policy of the Conservative Government of Sir Harold Macmillan, and rather more informal discussions between the Premier and Lord Rootes were held, either on the grouse moors of each other's Scottish estates or during conversations over the post-prandial port.

The Board of Trade had been working with the Government to establish 'Development Areas' (later, 'Districts') scattered throughout the land to address the problem of outdated, failing industries through industrial regeneration. These areas included parts of northern England, south Wales, and the 'Central Belt' of Scotland. Every motor manufacturer received the Government's attention: Ford succumbed to new facilities at Halewood, Liverpool, and later Bridgend, South Wales; Rover on the eastern outskirts of Cardiff; Vauxhall at Ellesmere Port, Cheshire; Standard-Triumph (as it later became) at Speke, Merseyside; and the British Motor Corporation at Bathgate, Scotland. The reason for governments using the automobile industry as part of their macro-economic policy is easy to see: between 1954 and 1966 9 per cent of economic growth was attributable to motor vehicles, which approx-imated to 7½ per cent of all manufacturing production; if the suppliers and associated trades were included, some estimates suggest that the industry as a whole accounted for a third of the country's economic growth. From the late 1950s for several decades to come, the Government would continue to cast its long shadow over the motor industry – but rarely with the detailed understanding that might contribute to a betterment of the industry. Both autocratic and corporate owners alike, and of course their unionized workers, felt that policy decisions were effectively centralized.

Like the Prime Minister, Lord Rootes had a soft spot for Scotland, so the Central Belt appeared more attractive than the other development locations. Unfortunately, the eastern side of the country, where his Glenalmond estate was, enjoyed even worse communications southwards than did the west – there being no convenient airport, poor through-routes to the main Rootes centres of production and not even the distant promise of an upgrading of the railway. Viewed from the Prime Minister's perspective, North Lanarkshire, to the east of Glasgow, had once been, and with national and local government encouragement was about to become once more, an important industrial area, and to aid its prosperity a vast steelworks was under construction at Ravenscraig, Motherwell. This was an expansion of David Colville's second steelworks, the nearby original Dalzell works stemming from the nineteenth century, which led to the nickname of 'Steelopolis' for Motherwell. Ravenscraig would be blessed with a steel strip-mill that was half-a-mile long and could produce miles of coiled thin sheet-steel suitable for pressing into car and truck bodies. At the start of Imp production, however, the 'Colcrest Steel Coil, Cold Reduced, Extra Deep Drawing Quality' coils of 32in × 0.031in (813mm × 0.8mm) for the majority of the bodywork came from Colville's Gartcosh Sheet Works, some miles north of Ravenscraig.

Scotland and the Motorcar

While the Imp was the most numerous model to emanate from Scotland, with the unique St Magnus of 1910, produced by W. R. Tullock of Kirkwall, Orkney, being the rarest, the Scottish motor industry had enjoyed a short, but highly successful period at the outset of private motoring. There were early manufacturers based in Granton or Leith (not then part of Edinburgh), with other entrepreneurs basing their enterprises further north round Aberdeen. It was, however, the industrial south-west of the country that attracted this fledgling industry, with ventures starting in Glasgow and, if viable, moving out to a ring of industrial satellites around the city. There had existed well over seventy or eighty different firms, with the leading four interrelated companies being Argyll Motors, Arrol-Johnston, the Albion Motor Car Company, and Beardmore Motors. By the time Rootes (Scotland) Ltd was established, there had been an interregnum of three decades.

The Albion Motor Car Company, in various guises, survived into the twenty-first century, although it ceased car production in 1913. Formed at the end of the nineteenth century by Thomas Blackwood Murray and Norman Osborne Fulton, it soon moved to its Scotstoun, Glasgow, factory on the Clyde, where it produced cars up to the First World War. It prospered through the manufacture of commercial vehicles and buses until it became, in 1951, part of the acquisitive Leyland Motors, which continued with vehicle production and assembly in Scotstoun until 1972, when it became Leyland (Glasgow) and changed to being a component supplier. In 1987, becoming a subsidiary of the Dutch Leyland-DAF, it continued with component production, but following a management 'buy-out', Albion Automotive restored its obvious heritage. Detroit again played a part in Scottish motoring through the purchase of Albion by the American Axle & Manufacturing Company – ironically, the type of component supplier that was envisaged to agglomerate round Linwood.

Locomotive engineer George Johnston enjoys the distinction of having designed and built the first British car that was not merely an assemblage of continental parts. By doing so in 1894/5 he narrowly pipped Dr Frederick Lanchester to that distinction, enjoying the benefit of a rather more sympathetic backer – Sir William Arrol, architect of the Forth Bridge. With the assistance of his cousin, Norman Osborne Fulton, and Thomas Blackwood Murrey, he founded the Mo-Car Syndicate, initially with a factory in Glasgow, but soon to move to Underwood in Paisley, Renfrewshire, to become the first automobile producer there. In 1905 the firm received the secure financial backing of the foremost Scottish industrialist, Sir William Beardmore (later Lord Invernairn). Concomitantly, the manufacturer adopted a name change to The New Arrol-Johnston Car Company. Arrol-Johnston's most renowned vehicle of the period was the air-cooled special they built for use in Antarctica as part of Ernest Shackleton's expedition, also backed by Beardmore.

This is a cautionary tale. Arrol-Johnston, by now a successful producer, moved just before the First World War to a new, purpose-built factory at Heathhall, Dumfries, in order to enjoy better communications with its main market, England. This new 'daylight', American-style, early modernist factory, fenestrated with huge expanses of glass, was the first example of ferro-concrete construction in the United Kingdom. After the demise of this period of the Scottish industry, the factory would have another life in the hands, from 1946, of the manufacturers of rubber products, originally the North British Rubber Company, now the Gates Rubber Company. An interesting social first for Arrol-Johnston was the rehabilitation of their wartime aero-engine factory at Tongland, Kirkcudbright. It produced the Fiat 501-based Arrol-Johnston Galloway, the factory being run by Dorothée Pullinger, the daughter of the company's general manager, with the staff, remarkably for the time, being mainly female.

With an eye to the English marketplace, and following an amalgamation with the Aster Company of Wembley, London, the Arrol-Johnston & Aster Engineering Company also produced the Arrol-Aster range of cars, which remained available into the 1930s. Before ceasing production in 1929, the company's last claim to fame was to build, at Heathhall, the Napier-engined Arrol-Aster that secured, in 1928, the land speed record of 206.96mph (333km/h) for Sir Malcolm Campbell at Daytona, Florida.

Arrol-Johnston's spectacular factory at Heathhall was not the only pre-Linwood, purpose-built factory: the phantasmagoric Argyll factory, built in 1905 at Alexandria at the southern end of Loch Lomond in the Vale of Leven, was certainly the most palatial. If the Heathhall factory was a brave modernist style, then Alexandria was in the Victorian 'neo-everything' pastiche style. The Argyll car started life in 1899, being produced by the Hozier Engineering Company at Bridgeton, Glasgow. Its driving force was the self-made Alexander Govan, no stranger to the dispiriting poverty of industrial Glasgow. Govan had the fortune to find a skilled backer, William A. Smith, vice-chairman of the National Telephone Company, a director of the United Alkali Company and Bryant & May (of safety-match fame), who also held the British rights to such new-fangled inventions as gramophones and telephones. Govan visited the USA and appears to have been deeply impressed by what he learned about mass production and the possible benefits that might accrue to Argyll through standardization – the new Packard plant in Detroit was particularly influential.

The opulence of the Alexandria factory, with its hand-wrought red sandstone façade, incorporating Argyll cars in the detail, and large gilded dome and clock-tower above the entrance, was predicated on Argyll's continuing success. By the time the new factory was opened by the motoring pioneer Lord Montagu of Beaulieu, in 1906, Argyll was the largest European car manufacturer, allegedly runner-up to Henry Ford on the world stage. Argyll's annual production approximated to a week's output from Linwood, but it was considered grand enough to sustain a central-London showroom off Oxford Street, with its own driving school for lady motorists – the instructors also being female, of course.

Among the more ostentatious aspects of this factory were its Italian marble grand entrance hall and staircase, modelled on the Paris Opéra, the managing director's neo-Georgian suite and the neo-Elizabethan boardrooms, with a lecture theatre that doubled as a concert hall. On a more practical level, the grounds housed Argyll's own test track while also making an unusual social statement for the time: a mini-garden-suburb to house the workers, full dining facilities within the factory and the provision of comprehensive ablutions with hot and cold running water.

Even as Europe's largest producer, the mass-production concept was still a long way off, and the idea of standardization of components was never realized. Govan's untimely death at thirty-eight in 1907 meant that the dream that was Alexandria never reached fruition, and following liquidation in 1914 the company returned to its Glasgow factory. It continued in Glasgow until ceasing production in 1932. Interestingly, two of the apprentices employed by Argyll were the television pioneers Oliver Hutchinson and John Logie Baird.

The Alexandria factory survives today as a retail outlet and a Motoring Heritage Centre (which includes a Singer Chamois and Chrysler Sunbeam 1.0), following extensive renovations that restored the façade and entrance. The building's history has

included being a munitions factory and the Royal Navy Torpedo Factory, but during the stewardship of the Plessey Electronics Group (in the round of Government regional financial inducements after that of Linwood) and a London-based property company, the fabric of the building fell into disrepair and much of the site was redeveloped as a small industrial estate.

Sir William Beardmore, Arrol-Johnston's major shareholder, also produced motor cars at three factories in or near Glasgow in his own right. Starting within the heavy-industrial manufacturing sector of Clydeside industry, Sir William established Scotland's largest industrial empire, which embraced being a significant armaments supplier (including tanks), a shipbuilder (warships, luxury liners, cargo vessels, submarines), a maker of aircraft, railway locomotives and rolling stock, steel, and even the R-34 airship that achieved the first double-crossing of the Atlantic. The enormous Beardmore Glacier in Antarctica is named after Sir William.

Beardmore's motor company was not established until 1919, and it is probably best remembered today in London for its eponymous taxi-cabs. These were manufactured in the former Arrol-Johnston Underwood factory in Paisley, and were produced as three sequential models between 1919 and 1932, when a management buy-out rescued the Hackney Carriage part of the business, moving it to Hendon in northwest London, where it continued as an English business until 1967.

The seeds of the decline of the antiquated heavy industry in the area that would lead post-war Governments to inject ineffectual, but gigantic, sums into the region, and of which the Hillman Imp is one of the most infamous examples, were sown in the 1920s, and were clear for all to see long before the Second World War. The fall from fortune of Beardmore's industrial conglomerate is a typical exemplar. The Bank of England, in 1930, backed the establishment of the National Shipbuilders' Security 'to assist the shipbuilding industry by the purchase of redundant and/or obsolete shipyards, the dismantling and disposal of their contents, and the re-sale of their sites under restrictions against further use for shipbuilding'. One of their first actions was to purchase and close one of the foremost employers on the Clyde – Beardmore's Dalmuir yard. This action alone removed more employment than the Linwood complex would restore thirty years later. The final link of Beardmore with Linwood was its munitions and railway-wagon shadow factory that was reconstructed as the Pressed Steel plant in 1948 – what became the most compelling justification for siting the Rootes complex at Linwood.

The other pressing industrial Scottish matter on Macmillan's mind (or SuperMac as the political sketch-writers preferred) was the old munitions shadow factory on the northern side of the A761 at Linwood. This former Beardmore factory became in 1947 an outpost of the Pressed Steel Company, which used it more as a railway wagon works that produced a small amount of pressed steel to contract rather than as a major supplier of panel-work. Because of the undue haste of the Government's 'dieselization' programme, this wagon works remained profitable to the end of the 1950s, producing the high-density Derby-design of Diesel Multiple Unit, the Class 117 Pressed Steel 3-car set, for use at Paddington, Reading, Bristol and the West Country. What the Premier knew was that these suburban and branch-line trains would not be required in profusion as Dr Beeching's reduction of the network was implemented, and customers would be required for the produce of the Ravenscraig mills. It is impossible to establish where the idea of Scotland for their factory came from, but it is known that the Rootes brothers were assessing sites in Renfrewshire from 1958.

The official records are enlightening. The Government's documents (some of which still remain embargoed) at the start of 1960 refer to discussions of 'Pressed Steel inter alia in Scotland', with the Board of Trade writing to Prime Minister Macmillan in March:

Thank you very much for your minute about Pressed Steel's expansion plans. This is not finally in the bag yet and will not be so until the Rootes expansion plan in Scotland is settled. But negotiations on this seem to be going ahead quite well . . . I am afraid this area [north-east England] and Scotland are going to prove very difficult problems and I am not confident that we shall be able to solve them, particularly the problem of Scotland.

By June, 'Yours ever, Billy' [Rootes] had written to 'My Dear Harold' [Macmillan] from his private apartment in The Towers at the Waldorf Astoria to tell the Premier about the 'greatest possible success' of the New York Exhibition and the Duke of Edinburgh's visit there. Lord Rootes continued, 'I am leaving for home immediately after its [the exhibition's] close on the 28th June, as the Rootes project for the development of a new motor car factory in Scotland has become bogged down.' Within days of receiving this, Macmillan sent a minute to the Board of Trade to enquire about the 'factory in Scotland', and stated that he believed there to be a big difference between Lord Rootes and the Board over the part Rootes might play in this scheme. The Premier received an immediate reply, stating that the Board's Advisory Committee was aware of the Government's

Background to Linwood and Development

Linwood, four miles to the west of the Renfrewshire town of Paisley, and some twelve miles south-west of the conurbation of Glasgow, would now be thought of as Strathclyde, but in the 1960s would have been referred to as Clydeside. It was an underdeveloped place, with the under-utilized former shadow factory as its only potentially considerable employer. However, it was very convenient for Glasgow's airport and railway line south. The Clydeside area was part of the West Coast heavy industrial belt, internationally renowned for its shipbuilding but less known for its equally heavy industry – munitions and railway paraphernalia. With all of these in terminal decline, it offered a great incentive to a government with a concerned eye upon soaring unemployment to try to engage in social engineering. Governments have rarely been successful at dealing with the ramifications of such complex social jigsaws, but to do nothing is tantamount to a public admission of impotence – not to mention all those lost votes, something no government finds an acceptable prospect.

Clearly, making Linwood a Development Area had some immediate benefit for the beleaguered Government of Sir Harold Macmillan, although it is doubtful that he could have been hoping to harness many votes for his own Conservative Party from those who might be employed in manual labour in this traditionally Socialist part of Scotland. However misguided it might seem, with hindsight, to believe that unemployed heavy-industry workers could be rapidly trained to become skilled car manufacturers, it was probably no more misguided than the later attempts of successive governments and local authorities to establish domestic electrical manufacturers or high-technology and telecoms industries in Scotland. It is arguably the task of governments to take on the huge social problems and fund them accordingly.

In far too many significant ways for this brave piece of social engineering to work, it had built into it fatal flaws that might have suggested prudence from all concerned. In addition to justifying the revitalization of the Pressed Steel factory and providing a nearby major customer for the new Ravenscraig Steel strip-mill, it was envisaged, both locally and nationally, that this venture would encourage component suppliers and ancillary industries to establish manufacturing plants in the area, as was the custom of the British motor industry. The Imp would require significant quantities of aluminium alloy, and although the Highlands of Scotland could hardly have been considered nearby or convenient to Linwood by anyone north of the Scottish border, this northerly outpost of British industry had a long-standing tradition of aluminium-smelting. Linwood consumed 100 tons of aluminium a week.

So what was attractive to either the Rootes Group or the Government about this location? The investment required for Linwood was in excess of £20 million, with half of it being funded by national or local government grants or incentives. For this expenditure, four thousand jobs should have been created directly at Rootes (Scotland) Ltd, fifteen hundred at the expanded Pressed Steel factory, and potentially huge numbers of permanent and fixed-term jobs at expanded ancillary suppliers and building companies. This was all predicated on the plant eventually producing about three thousand vehicles per week – a volume it did occasionally, briefly touch, but for a variety of reasons was never able to sustain.

There were problems assembling a workforce despite the good intentions of locating the new factory in Renfrewshire. There might have been unemployed workers aplenty in the area, but they were unskilled when it came to the monotonous and repetitive daily tasks of the 'blue-collar' workers in a car factory, and the skilled personnel who might train them had to be recruited and relocated from the West Midlands. With the exception of a small, but significant, group of fully trained expatriate Scots, it was difficult to bribe the better-paid Midlands workers to relocate somewhere where the new estates of houses, shops and so on had yet to be built, when their jobs in England seemed to be completely secure. The estates of Linwood resembled the early days of the more official 'New Towns', but without the careful planning. Linwood did experience accelerated development in terms of number of residents: the population in 1961 was 15,000, whereas it grew by 47 per cent in a mere five years – alas, without the infrastructure of suitable shops, community centres and all those facilities that might cause the inhabitants to rejoice in living in a particular place and establish a sense of community external to the workplace. When it perpetuated its assertion that the whole region was about to be an immensely prosperous one, it is unclear today whether the complicit Renfrewshire Council believed its enthusiastic propaganda with its promises of the forthcoming land of plenty – for the Utopian future – or whether it was just local officials doing what came naturally and justifying their own decisions with wishes about how wonderful the locality might become.

It was not only local government, but all involved with this industrial and social experiment who seemed to be complicit in their tenuous grasp of reality in the hope that the motor industry might provide the employment stability that was no longer offered by the collapsing heavy industry.

views, but thought 'the Rootes family opened their mouths very wide in the first place and have had difficulty in supporting their requests by detailed argument'. The estimated cost of the Linwood scheme was £4.67 million, comprising a loan to Rootes of £4 million and a grant of £670,000, whereas Rootes had lodged a grant request of £1.5 million, which the Board thought excessive. The Board then indicated that at the next meeting 'they will make progress, particularly if the less exuberant and more concise members of the family do the talking', and concluded:

> I will continue to keep in very close contact with all these goings on in view of the crucial importance of the project. I am reluctant to stress this importance too much in conversation with the applicants for Government help, because they clearly intend to screw as much out of us as they can, and I do not want to encourage them too far. But certainly we will do everything in our power to keep this fish on the hook.

As the long summer rumbled on, the Advisory Committee was claiming that Lord Rootes had accepted the proposals, although with reservations, and it pointed out that the company had yet to purchase the necessary land next to Pressed Steel. By the end of the next month it was being referred to as the Rootes/Linwood deal, and the Board confirmed it was not 'going bad' – a curious memorandum as it is appended with the annotation that on the previous day, 29 September, the following telegram had been sent to the Prime Minister by the President of the Board of Trade:

> I think you would like to know that Billy Rootes intends to unveil his new Scottish project at a Press Conference in Glasgow tomorrow morning. It involves the production of an entirely new small car as an addition to the existing Rootes range. The plan is to produce three thousand a week and possibly more later. The bodies will be made by the Pressed Steel Company next door and the total employment involved should be over

The roundabout outside the main buildings, with the sign next to the perimeter fence proclaiming 'Rootes (Scotland) Ltd, Home of the Hillman IMP', is pictured in 1963.

five thousand. This should come as a pleasant surprise to many who have been growing sceptical about the chances of motor industry expansion in Scotland. In particular it will give the Scots what they have been clamouring for, namely a car of their own. Let us hope it will keep them from applying to join the United Nations.

The deal was done and dusted, although it would cost the Government £10 million as its contribution to the eventual cost of £22.5 million, and it did truly appeal to nationalistic pride and sentiment, with a contemporaneous television report proclaiming, 'Scotland starting afresh in this restless time – making motor cars'. Now Rootes could progress with building its Imp factory on the southern side of the A761, with the old Pressed Steel factory on the other side of a proposed short length of dual carriageway. As Pressed Steel would fabricate, paint and trim the completed bodies for the Imp, which became its main customer, an overhead covered gantry would connect the two complexes. Through complex financial arrangements, much of this expenditure would be amortized via the Scottish Industrial Estates Management Corporation. Rootes

also announced the construction of a 'second Scottish factory' for the production of unspecified pressings, which turned out to be the separate die-cast-aluminium block built at the far eastern side of the site – a propagandist announcement at the nadir of the BLSP strike.

An Automobile Odeon?

Many writers have mentioned that new post-war motor-industry factories contain detailing that is reminiscent of cinemas: this is more than coincidence, as most of the factories were designed by the Birmingham-based firm of architects, Harry W. Weedon FRIBA and Partners, whose founder, Harry Weedon, had made his initial reputation producing cinemas for the entrepreneur Oscar Deutsch. Whether one prefers the name's Graeco-Roman origins or as the acronym for 'Oscar Deutsch Entertains Our Nation', both the circuit and the Art-Deco styling became instantly recognized as Odeon, as are many of the factories. The architect entrusted with designing the Linwood development was Allan Lloyd Davies. The Weedon partnership would also design the other new Scottish factory, Bathgate, for the British Motor Corporation.

The Imp and Pressed Steel Factories

Architect	Allan Lloyd Davies
Archtectural Practice	Harry W. Weedon FRIBA and Partners (now Weedon Partnership)
Contractors	Melville Dundas & Whitson
Local Architect	Michael Beal, Senior Assistant at Walter Underwood & Partners
Groundworks	R. M. Douglas
Steel Structure Design	Redpath Brown (Manchester)
Steel Structure Construction	Redpath Brown & Dorman Long
Side-wall & Roof Glazing	Henry Hopes (undertaken by Hopes, Crittal, Mellows and others)
'Well Pack' Doors	Westland Engineering
Interior-design consultant	Hon. John Siddeley (later Lord Kenilworth, third baron)
Design Team:	Fred Carter, Senior Partner and Senior Assistant (Weedon)
	Reg Bidmead, Partner and Senior Assistant (Weedon)
	Don Bayless, Diecast Building (Weedon)
Quantity Surveyor	Bill Young of L. C. Wakeman
Final Consultants	Donald, Smith, Seymour & Rooley (Glasgow)
Subcontractors	Brightside (Birmingham), heating
	Walker Bros (Birmingham), electrical installations and lighting

This aerial view is looking eastwards, showing the transfer body conveyor from Pressed Steel to the Rootes Car Assembly Building across the centre of the shot, which is taken from above the west side of the CAB.

Following Rootes' approval of his initial design of what was still being called 'Apex Scheme 10', Lloyd Davies recalls his first site visit to Linwood. Lord Rootes and he were mortified to discover that an alluvial bed, running diagonally across the site, had been located by R. M. Douglas, the firm awarded the groundworks contract. They soon discovered why the Pressed Steel Company's factory was on the other side of the trunk road: the proposed Rootes site was effectively a floating bog!

The University of Birmingham came to the rescue, employing a technique similar to that used for the Ford factory at Dagenham many decades earlier. The footprint of the entire Rootes Linwood site would be piled, under the direction of the firm of Rennie & Kirkwood. It was an ingenious scheme that comprised the installation of a 12ft (3.6m) layer of hardcore that squashed out the water into strategically placed pits, following which a company called Vibro Piles drove in literally a couple of thousand piles on 20ft (6m) centres to support two 1ft-thick (0.3m) concrete slabs as the firm base of the main parts of the factory that were separated by the central parking area. The archive film footage of this operation shows that the piling machines were somewhat incongruous steam-driven piling rigs from an earlier age. One of the main rafts was to become the car assembly block, while the other supported the machine shop.

The main façade comprised the offices, boardroom, works canteen and welfare facilities and two vehicle display areas at ground and first-floor level. The centrally placed showroom that fronted the southern edge of the new dual carriageway might have been accompanied by a large road-sign that proclaimed 'Rootes (Scotland) Ltd, Home of the Hillman Imp', but the showroom was also used to sell other examples from Rootes' range. This façade, the only part to survive today, was linked via three bridges to the two

In this view northwards from the rear of the incomplete Rootes buildings, the main road runs across the photograph and the Pressed Steel buildings are beyond. The boggy nature of the still remaining fields can be seen. 'Rootes' was painted on the roof panelling, as the factory was in line with the nearby Abbotsinch airfield, later Glasgow Airport.

This late aerial shot of the virtually-complete complex looks westwards. The Pressed Steel factory is on the right with the long transporter bridge leading into the Car Assembly Building, which itself is connected by shorter covered conveyor bridges to the Unit Machine Shop. Fronting the road (from right to left) is the main office building and showroom (with its three short bridges linking it to the main factory), the separate personnel block, and the die-casting plant, which is separated even further from the other buildings.

main production areas, while access to the upper floor was via a central staircase made with reinforced concrete heads, cantilevered off a central steel rib and fitted with stainless-steel handrails. The entrance and vehicle display areas were floored with a Roman mosaic black terrazzo finish that contributed to the modern feel of the whole complex. During the construction period, the Rootes

The executives' offices led off this top landing above the reception area. The commemorative plaque is on the half-landing below, and the aluminium panelling that replaced the proposed stained-glass project can be seen on the right of the staircase.

brothers suggested that both the factory and the car would benefit from the attentions of an interior designer, and they knew just such a well-connected fellow from the eponymous motoring and aircraft family – the Hon. John Siddeley (later the third Baron, Lord Kenil-worth). The relationship was not a fruitful one, alas. Siddeley prepared a colour scheme of magnolia walls and dark brown skirting boards for the offices, and also prepared stained-glass panels to be incorporated on either side of the staircase. The suggested dec-oration and the stained glass were not thought to be in harmony with the building's design, and following the destruction of the glass while in transit, Siddeley withdrew, and alu-minium-clad panels were used on the staircase. His interior-design ideas and colour coordina-tion schemes for the cars pass unremembered, but Siddeley's contributions were regarded as unhelpful. Several suggest that he was more at home as a socialite than being involved in industry – his chosen places for meetings were exclusive London restaurants.

Allan Lloyd Davies's Linwood factory with the rebuilt Pressed Steel building was, unlike the Imp itself, ready on time and potentially fully operative. With the appropriate level of

The directors' dining room, seen here a year after opening, was furnished and decorated in a modern style, but with restrained taste that makes reference to the heritage of Glaswegian design.

pomp and ceremony, the complex was opened on 2 May 1963 by the Duke of Edinburgh – arriving by a Rootes top-of-the-range Humber and leaving in a self-driven Imp. Lord Rootes was never one to miss a publicity opportunity, although it could be argued that, with distant memories of the launches of the Wizard and Minx, he should perhaps have taken the advice of his technical director, Peter Ware, who thought the opening of Linwood should be delayed. The regal opening was clearly of great promotional value to the launch of the Imp, and the car had to be made available immediately to gain sales from the resultant publicity. Lord Rootes was skilled enough in the ways of selling cars to have known that the production vehicles would have to make their own way in the world, so they had to be up to standard. It was clear to all in the company that they were not yet ready to be launched on the unsuspecting public. Some commentators cite this as the most significant reason for the Imp never maintaining its envisaged sales, and while not being in full agreement, the author takes the view that for the older members of the Rootes family to

The ground-floor reception and showroom was used to display both cars and their component parts. It was also used, as here, as an exhibition space for Scottish suppliers to the industry. The majority of completed cars were Imps, but other Rootes cars were also put on show. The foot of the staircase leading to the executive suites is on the right.

The Colvilles' 'Colcrest Steel extra deep drawing quality' rolled steel coils are unrolled and cut before being made into one of the 250-plus stampings or pressings.

have overlooked this flaw, one that was fatal to the success of the Imp, seems astonishing.

The Glasgow Museum of Transport has, as part of its collection, 'Imp 1' and the plaque commemorating the official opening of Linwood which was located on the first half-landing of the main staircase. A number of those working at the factory claim that this Imp was certainly part of the first batch, but their memories suggest the best-looking example was chosen, and this is likely to have been the thirteenth produced. As part of the natural rivalry between Renfrewshire and the West Midlands, the workers at Ryton claimed that the Imp driven by the Duke of Edinburgh was specially made at Ryton, and that this is the one now on display.

Linwood's functional design was a good example of the latter-day modern, rather than aggressively modernist, style that is reminiscent of some continental pre-war practice, but achieved with up-to-date structural techniques. Whereas the communal and reception areas, with their terrazzo flooring, were treated to a version of British post-war modernist style, the directors' area had this tempered through being furnished in a neo-Glaswegian School fashion. Although not quite up to the grandeur of the Argyll factory at Alexandria, Linwood was an attractive factory in which to work, with above-average facilities for the staff. Lloyd Davies reports that at the earliest architectural meetings it was decided that the plan had to incorporate not

The fully painted, glazed and trimmed car bodies arrive at Linwood's Car Assembly Building, having literally crossed the road from Pressed Steel in the covered 410-foot (125m) transporter bridge.

only the usual locker rooms and the normal social amenities, but also copious bathing and medical facilities, while the works canteen was designed in such a way that the kitchens and food-preparation areas were viewable, through two large plate-glass windows, from the main dining area. This last detail had the desired effect upon the cleanliness and tidiness of the kitchens – a characteristic that many have commented upon with reference to the whole facility, which was provided with lots of disposal bins to prevent the accumulation of debris. Jim Pollard attests to Lloyd Davies's success with the canteen, saying that most workers felt that it was more like a proper restaurant – it had, after all, accommodated the official opening celebratory dinner in the presence of the Duke of Edinburgh.

Being a British factory of the 1960s, separate dining areas for more senior management was *de rigueur* – Lord Rootes insisting that a full butler's pantry be added to the directors' dining room for his butler. The Imp might have been classless, but society in the United Kingdom was, in terms of employment structures, slow to change. Lloyd Davies's comment about the pantry at Linwood is not far removed from the Trade Union leader Jack Jones's report of visiting the bombed Singer factory during the war: the factory was a complete mess, with tarpaulins keeping the rain off the cold shop floor, heated by open coke-burning braziers – but he was still treated to an inglorious luncheon served in a makeshift 'directors' dining room', with a white tablecloth on an equally makeshift table! Incidentally, Allan Lloyd Davies went on to purchase four different Imps, from the Deluxe to Sport models, and still speaks highly of them.

For those interested in further information about the entire Linwood project, Robert Allan's *Geoffrey Rootes' Dream for Linwood*, 'a pictorial fantasy about the lives and times of the men and women who built the Hillman Imp', offers a remarkable insight, although Allan rightly concludes, 'Eighteen years from the start of "The Dream" Linwood had become one of Scotland's most notorious graveyards.'

The Working of Linwood's Factory

The body panels for the Imp were pressed by magnificent new machines in the Pressed Steel Company's refurbished factory on the northern side of the A761. The stampings were assembled by traditional techniques into the completed bodies. (A later proposal to press much larger sections of the body as a single pressing was abandoned by Chrysler because of the cost of implementation.) The completed bodies were then painted and fully trimmed, initially with rudimentary corrosion protection, but from 1966 fully under-sealed. Even at these 'Pressed Steel' stages, the model type, market destination, trim level and paint colour was under the control of the ICT 1301 computer in the main Rootes building, but of course, although this was the most modern and highly automated facility in Europe for its time, robotics had yet to be developed to a stage that the manual labour was replaced by digitally controlled machines and the International Computers and Tabulators Limited computer-controlled MTE Control Gear. Linwood was claimed to be Britain's first 'computer-controlled' automotive factory when it opened, with this aspect alone accounting for £1 million of the budget, and ICT issued, by way of a paper, 'Electronic Data Processing in the Service of the Rootes Group', a technical description of this control system. The computer not only gave the specification of each car to the workers, it printed out a sheet about each one at the completion of the assembly. It is instructive to note that some seven years later, when the computer was already obsolete, the far more powerful IBM mainframe was going to cost only £60,000.

The fully trimmed, glazed and painted Imp body was taken by the track within the covered transporter bridge to the Car Assembly Building. Early production was hampered by the rapid wear of this part of the track, but that was something that was easy to rectify with the fitting of respecified fixing pins. The ICT 1301 was also responsible for coordinating and gathering together the various subassemblies and other components, and delivering these to meet up with the painted body-shell in the Car Assembly Building on the main moving-assembly track. This automated facility still required a large input from the thousands of unskilled, semi-skilled and skilled workers on both sides of the dual carriageway – many of whom on the Rootes side were female. At this time, Ferrari would not even allow female visitors into its factory, as Tim Fry's wife would discover.

Whilst in some ways emulating the social provisions of André Citroën's first European assembly-line in Paris, forty years earlier, Linwood did not extend to providing the work-force with crèches. In this age of robotics, it is quaint now to see archive film footage of four men feeding an automatically cut piece of steel from the huge coils from Gartcosh or Ravenscraig into a hugely complex press that would produce the entire floorpan: they then manually lifted the completed part out and passed it on to the next automated stage. Other British manufacturers, even Ford at Dagenham, were to invest large sums over the next few years acquiring automatic transfer machines that could emulate and surpass the automation of the Linwood facility. Two oft-quoted examples that were the pride of Linwood would be the Archdale transfer machine that dealt with the eleven or so machining operations on the rear suspension arms, and the Churchill Link Line used for the production of the final drive units. This automated line comprised nine machines and conveyors.

After the time of Linwood, some of this by-then-outdated technology would be sold at knock-down prices to Far-Eastern competitors. Many of these new machines were imported, leading to criticism of the Rootes Group for spending Government subsidies on what became imports from the Government's balance of payments viewpoint. Numerous dignitaries visited Linwood to marvel at this modern facility. When Rootes' Jim Pollard visited Volvo's new and refurbished factories in Sweden, however, he was amazed to discover that some of their envy-making facilities hailed from the Glasgow region. Rootes had not been aware of this localized supplier. Pollard's visit, incidentally, was occasioned by Volvo investigating the possibility of subcontracting components from Linwood for their 140/160 series; an amusing tale is told about the specimen parts not being the correct dimensions, as Volvo had incorrectly converted metric to imperial measurements on the drawings!

At the end of the car assembly line, all cars were treated to high-pressure water-spray tests, as well as braking and basic operational tests while being driven on rollers. Ten per cent of the cars were offered up to a road test. Scottish cars were transported to Rootes dealers by Commer transporters, whereas those destined for England were loaded onto the 'Imp Special' trains, the railway being conveniently located at the rear of the factory. These same trains were used for the transport of components and the return of engines from Ryton – these had been tested in Coventry, and would be tested again in Linwood.

The Working of Linwood's Factory *continued*

Initially, the factory produced fewer than 1,000 cars per week, and in an attempt to meet demand for the new car the company suggested 24-hour operation of the Linwood facility. Target output was 3,000 Imps per week, but by the end of 1963 the average weekly production was, in reality, closer to 1,000 vehicles, and the envisaged output was moved to being an aim for the following year.

As was common at the time, the 'Completely Knocked Down' (CKD) concept had always been a feature in the costing of the sales potential of the Imp. The CKD car was an idea that originated with Ford in America, as a means to distribute its cars over the enormous distances of that continent. As this had been successful, Ford adopted the same technique for its initial overseas venture, the assembly plant at Trafford Park, Manchester. Rather than assemble finished cars for export to some markets, manufacturers planned their assembly lines so that completed cars, but dismantled and crated-up by a special section of the factory, could be exported overseas for reassembly in their overseas plants. The principal two reasons for

exporting cars in this complex way were political and/or economic – and after all, this is the way continental European manufacturers had originally addressed the British markets. The Rootes Group commenced by concentrating on the Australian market through supplying CKD kits, at the rate of five hundred per week, to the Rootes Melbourne factory. Such was the initial success of this Australian assembly, which was increased by a fifth, that an option was extended to build another factory at Harrisfield in Victoria. For reliability reasons similar to those in the home market, the Australian venture was severely scaled down and disposed of by 1966. Other Antipodean and worldwide markets were targeted in the same way as Australia, including Eire, New Zealand, South Africa, Venezuela, Uruguay, the Philippines, Costa Rica, Portugal, Malta, Japan and Malaysia. (Rootes gave the final three places as local assembly of CKD kits from Linwood, but the author has not managed to reveal evidence of this having occurred.) Completed cars were officially exported to more than seventy countries.

A Good Idea?

Economic commentators often cite Rootes as the first and most obvious victim of the Government's refusal to allow a company to operate on its 'home ground', but this argument assumes that Rootes Securities was in a

far more secure financial position than was the case. It is true that Linwood exemplified how the government of the day still saw the motor industry as the apparently strongest manufacturing sector, which could be relied upon to assist with the resolution of the country's larger

The Scottish-smelted aluminium was melted within the die-casting building in this line of furnaces that were designed to liquefy 3½ tons per hour. The molten aluminium-alloy was pressure-fed or poured into the relevant dies to produce the required casting; here it is being drawn off the furnace.

The Quality Control Area in the Car Assembly Building was where different models were taken from the end of the assembly line to be thoroughly checked and 'audited'.

socio-economic problems. Geoffrey Rootes was later to opine:

> It was the Government's disastrous attempts to make the industry disperse to the areas of high unemployment. It would have made sense if they had offered major inducements, rather than refusal of IDCs; we could have made up our own minds . . . It entailed moving to Scotland where there was no infrastructure and labour was not particularly suitable. We had inevitable duplication of overheads and practically without exception those factories which they forced the industry to have elsewhere in the country turned out to be failures.

It would be illuminating to know where son Geoffrey was located on the civil servant's scale of 'exuberance'; the author doubts that it was the perfervid or over-impassioned one. In his statement, Geoffrey is making two questionable assumptions: that Rootes was in a position to afford to build the Imp factory without financial assistance, and that the company met its obligations to prepare the labour-force and contribute to the establishment of a suitable

infrastructure. Rootes Limited did, admittedly, have to contend with increased overheads, but much of this was self-inflicted, notably because of the many senior personnel who had offices and staff in triplicate in London, Ryton and Linwood.

For whatever underlying cause, it cannot be denied that British industry, even in times of growth like that of the period of the Imp, was blighted by ageing plant and facilities. With investment in industry typically pitched at only a third of that of its continental competitors, this consequence is unsurprising. The facility at Linwood was one of the shining exceptions in Britain, but owing to the multitude of operational difficulties described elsewhere, it would never achieve its potential. With the benefit of hindsight, the Government's 'carrot and stick' approach to regional aid can only be considered an ill-judged interference with manufacturing industry.

Unlike other parts of the Rootes Group and its British-made competitors, the Imp had a high level of standardization of its components, and Linwood's expensive modern automated assembly facilities capitalized on this advantage. Mass-production, however, is

The assembly line, 670ft (204m) long, was 5ft (1.5m) from the ground with forty-one assembly stations along 540ft (165m) of its length to allow the operators to work at two levels.

predicated on a large number of units – something practicable in the huge American home market, but not achievable in Europe. Linwood was designed with modern mass-production in mind, the marketplace had other ideas about its realization. The assumption of growth was a reasonable one, as the number of cars in the United Kingdom had doubled as the 1950s progressed. This number doubled again to over eleven million in the first half of the 1960s, but alas, there it would remain for the second half.

The Linwood facility was always described as almost self-sufficient: the intention was for it to be so, but this was never achieved. Complete self-sufficiency would have required a complete engine plant, but Linwood, none the less, was a remarkable achievement and rather more self-sufficient than the other Rootes factories, where the pressing of body-shells or the production of sub-assemblies was scattered over the south-east of England. The Imp conformed to the norm of the day, and comprised a very large number of bought-out components – approximately 1,600 – and it

The ancillaries are finally assembled before being transported by the overhead conveyor to the Car Assembly Building. Most of each engine had been produced here, and had been to Coventry and back before this stage.

Left-hand-drive Hillman Imp saloons sit in railway sidings on the Portuguese version of the 'Imp train'. These have been locally assembled from exported completely knocked down kits in the new Portuguese factory.

could have done without those engine blocks going to Coventry and back. In later Imp production, a few engines were built at Linwood, possibly in a futile attempt to qualify for further Government grants. A common reason for refusal was that the company had not achieved many of its earlier targets for employment, nor its expansion promises – one of which was the greater self-sufficiency of the Linwood plant, including engine production.

Like the BMC Bathgate factory, also a product of the Conservative Government's regional development strategy, Rootes' Linwood venture failed to establish a local network of satellite suppliers. This was not for want of trying, but Rootes was up against the age-old cultural problem of indigenous manufacturers not trusting the posh-speaking Sassenach incomers. This distrust is more acute than it ever used to be, reinforced by the industrial detritus left by the failed socio-political initiatives that offered so much and delivered so little that was sustainable. Rootes might have claimed that the Scottish content of an Imp was 76 per cent, but this figure should be treated with caution, considering how few suppliers established themselves in the country and how much of the Imp was imported from England. In the engine, for example, the crankshaft and cylinder head were produced in the Midlands, while the die-cast engine blocks might have emanated from Linwood, but were moved to Coventry for machining and assembly before being

returned to Scotland for fitment to the drive train on the assembly line. Most of the completed vehicles, of course, were then sent to England again for distribution – leading to much humour at the time about how many thousands of miles an Imp engine had done before it fired a cylinder!

Like other factories that have relocated to Scotland, neither Rootes Motors nor the Pressed Steel Company became an integral part of the economic and business fabric of the country. While the Linwood complex contributed a quick fix to the unemployment statistics, in terms of developing an expanding community it cannot be considered to have been a sociological success. With the benefit of the revelations contained within Government papers, Scottish cynicism of the time seems to have been justifiable – even if there was some quasi-nationalistic sentiment about Scotland's new small car. It is salutary to notice that as early as 1966, Tam Dalyell, the Labour Member of Parliament for West Lothian, was informing Tony Benn about the unrest in his constituency caused through the British Motor Corporation's redundancies at its new Bathgate factory.

The more numerous Mini was not without its geographical problems either – it was assembled in three different locations, and like the Imp was reliant on many bought-out components. While the Mini might have seemed to be more commercially successful in terms of the number of vehicles built and sold, it would be many years before British Leyland knew the

An 'Imp Special' train. In this case Commer Imp vans are arriving at Luton before distribution to dealers.

true production cost of each car, unlike the carefully costed Imp. BMC had originally priced the Mini to be the cheapest proper car then available, regardless of financial prudence. Although the Rootes Group as a whole has been described as comprising uncoordinated separate empires, with no clear profit plan or adequate cost-accounting methodology, this accusation could not be levelled at Rootes (Scotland) and the Imp.

Successive governments used the fiscal instrument of credit restraint in the form of hire purchase agreements as a fundamental economic regulator. This led to the 'stop-go' policies that not only affected the overall output of the industry, but exacerbated the already deteriorating labour relations within the industry. The Linwood workers' attitude could be summed up as, 'Why work flat-out now when we will be laid-off soon?' This could be interpreted as a smoothing factor, but alas, it was also deleterious to output figures and inconducive to settled labour relations. The Labour Government used the hire purchase/credit agreements as financial instruments to the point where in not much more than the two years leading to the buyout of Rootes Limited by Chrysler, these arrangements had been significantly altered more than seven times.

The 1966 meeting of the National Advisory Committee for the Motor Manufacturing Industry with Government, a group in which Rootes was a principal player, was reported by the Postmaster-General, Tony Benn, as: 'It was a very difficult meeting indeed, as they were extremely anxious about the position in the light of the credit squeeze and particularly the effect of the imposition of a deposit of 40 per cent on hire purchase payments'. Such hire purchase forms of credit were controlled by the Government, not so much by the underlying rate of interest to be added to the repayment of the loan, which fluctuated in the normal market manner, but through the imposition of minimum deposit requirements, along with the maximum term over which the

repayments might be spread. During the first half of the Imp's life, the lows of the earlier 1960s required the minimum statutory deposit of 20 per cent of the cost of the item to be fully repaid over twenty-four and then thirty-six months, whereas the problematic period mentioned above specified a deposit of 40 per cent with the repayments spread over twenty-four monthly payments.

Are the Natives Restless?

By the mid-1960s, industrial relations within the motor industry were poor, for a variety of reasons – this was particularly so for most of the Rootes Group because of a damaging dispute at its British Light Steel Pressings factory in Acton, West London, that had taken place in 1961. Although Linwood was yet to initiate production, this Pyrrhic industrial triumph for Lord Rootes, some say the whole industry, came at a cost to both the company and its employees that, to this author's mind, delivered the fatal blow to the company's balance sheet, as well as to the morale of its founders and employees alike. It would take many years to play out the excruciating end game, but Rootes would never again flourish in its traditional manner.

The UK's largest operator, Progressive Deliveries Holdings Ltd, of Coventry, operates the first triple-decker car transporter. A normal double-decker transporter was used for most of the Scottish deliveries. These Rootes Group Commer CC15 tractors used the extraordinary 135bhp TS3 3-cylinder, 6-piston, 2-stroke engine.

British Light Steel Pressings' Dispute

British Light Steel Pressings (BLSP), a relatively new company, was one of the later pre-war additions to Rootes Securities. Sited in Warple Way, Acton, it was part of the light-industrial and residential mix that occupied much of suburban west and north-west London. The industry was mainly automotive, with coachbuilding a local speciality. Rootes' flagship company Thrupp & Maberly, where the quarter-light is said to have been invented, was only a handful of miles away in Cricklewood.

BLSP housed some of the largest presses in the United Kingdom outside the Pressed Steel company's plants. Most of its production comprised suspension and other sub-assemblies, petrol tanks and a multitude of small pressings to be distributed throughout Rootes' factories, although it did produce body-shells for Sunbeam and some of the panel-work for Rootes' smaller model-runs, commercial lorry cabs and the like.

Industrial relations in this part of the Rootes Group had been poor for some time, but 1961 would prove to be calamitous. The Rootes Group's small factories in London experienced eighty-three stoppages and a devastating thirteen-week strike. The year started with the second twenty-four-hour unofficial strike in recent months at BLSP, with 800 of the thousand or so workforce stopping work because they wanted compensation for their loss of working-time occasioned through other stoppages within the Group. Because the workers were paid on a piece-work basis, stoppages elsewhere meant they did not get paid when they were not working. Two months later, the factory again ground to a halt as a result of an unofficial 'walk-out' by ten door-hangers who were disputing their piece-work rates while working on Commer cabs and Humber Hawks. The local paper, the *Acton Gazette & West London Post*, reported that even the 'shop stewards pleaded with the door hangers to return to work'. A week later, thirty-two workers went on strike for forty-five hours – and so the long year wore on.

By the start of September, the local paper was running the front-page headline: 'Redundancy fears prompt workers to call on TUC: Thousand march out of car factory.' It reported that the workers were 'ordered back to work the first day they stopped', without the Devonshire House management considering the nature of the dispute. Within a fortnight, invective was not in short supply from both sides of this quintessentially 'them and us' dispute; over 6,000 Rootes workers were laid off and all Coventry pro-

duction was halted. The management talked of communist plots from the five separate unions that represented the workforce, while a representative of the Commer cab-assembly workers stated, 'The ideal we are aiming at is 52 weeks' pay a year for all workers in the car industry.' Lord Rootes felt that he was making a stand for the entire industry, and the principals of many other firms offered their moral support. Encouraged by this, he issued his catastrophic 'Return to work by Thursday, or be sacked' ultimatum, followed by 'We regard the strikers as ex-employees.'

As October and November progressed, the story was kept alive in the media through descriptions of marches and mass meetings (including a report of a striking assembly worker, who earned £20 a week, being fined £3 for breaking a Rootes' Social Club window), 'human interest' interviews with strikers' wives, the 'Red Plot' to overthrow society as it was known, the involvement of Members of Parliament, and statements by other local employers about the shortage of skilled labour in the area. Things looked more hopeful at the start of November when the workforce voted at a mass-meeting to return; the local paper reported: 'In and Out – That's Rootes!' When the workers arrived at the factory, they changed their minds and the strike continued. With the propaganda accompanying this brinkmanship, Rootes Securities issued a press release that appeared in the press alongside descriptions of the strike: 'Rootes Announces second factory in Scotland.' It transpired that this was the die-cast block at Linwood, and another press release was hurried out by way of assurance that this second Scottish facility was not to replace the Acton factory. By the end of November, seventy workers had reapplied for their jobs, and 680 had indicated their willingness to return to work, leaving 570 not intending to do so.

After thirteen weeks, the strike petered out. The board of Rootes Securities had won the dispute, but at an estimated cost of £3 million and more than 50,000 lost vehicles. The loss included £500,000 spent on paying those fortunate workers at other plants who did enjoy a guaranteed-wage agreement. To place this figure in perspective, during the Rootes Group's profitable years, annual profits would rarely exceed this sum. Along with the discontinuation of the Humber Hawk and Super Snipe in 1967, the highly problematic factory was closed, along with the coachbuilding arm, Thrupp & Maberly. The outputs of many other smaller outposts of the Rootes Group

---

British Light Steel Pressings' Dispute *continued*

were relocated within an extant facility. Later in life, Geoffrey, the second Lord Rootes, was to write of this period:

> My business life began to get rather more difficult as we entered the sixties. We had a very serious strike at our body plant, British Light Steel Pressings, at Acton, which affected us seriously from a financial aspect. We stood out as a matter of principle against communist infiltration and influence, but in retrospect we might have been better to compromise to some extent . . . I therefore felt it important to stand firm against communist influence at a particularly crucial time. My father and my uncle both felt the same.

The author considers that this strike, which was concomitant with the building of Linwood and the final stages of the development of the Imp, was very important, as it marks the commencement of the decline and fall of the Rootes empire. At no point during Imp production would the company again be in a robust financial position – not a good point of departure for the single most important car that might have caused Rootes Motors to flourish once more. Of subsidiary interest, from both extant written evidence and the comments of those in or close to the boardroom, Lord Rootes might have been triumphant, but he had lost a discernible spring in his step and would seem to seek consolation from his dispiritment through throwing his undoubted enthusiasm much more into his rural estates than his Scottish factory.

Miss Norma Miller, who worked in the die-casting plant in 1963, is seen here modelling the new female white overalls, trimmed in turquoise. Seven designs were modelled and voted on by the 300-plus female workers. Norma was voted 'Miss Imp' and this design was adopted for all the female workers.

Many of the newly trained workforce in Scotland had memories of their previous rather militant industrial-relations practices. Linwood was a meld of these memories and the newly acquired culture in which the workforce found itself. The immediate future saw a remarkably low number of instances of the withdrawal of labour by the Scottish workforce, at least on the Rootes side of the road. Those that did occur were classified as 'unofficial action', as they did not have the official backing of the relevant unions or, surprisingly, the shop stewards. These minor disputes were dealt with in the traditional Rootes manner of the striking workers being dismissed. The mutual trust that the company was attempting to foster at Linwood was only slightly dented, but over the next few years the workforce became anxious and very much more militant, as its experience was to become one of real or threatened redundancies, short-time working, and a high level of insecurity about future employment. These problems were being experienced by the whole motoring production sector, but they were writ large at Rootes/Chrysler, and at Linwood in particular. It did not help that the majority of the workforce had already experienced similar treatment as heavy-industrial workers.

The Linwood Workforce

The majority of the Linwood workforce was recruited and trained locally. For a year or two before the factory opened, however, Rootes Motors (Scotland) placed local advertisements for potential staff, both trained and untrained, the latter to receive their training in the converted Singer Motors factory in Coventry, which became the Rootes Motors training college. Much to the chagrin of the Scottish commercial-vehicle builder, Albion, a number of its staff showed an interest in joining the new car production venture.

Two managers at the ex-Singer training college, Jim Pollard and Garth Vaughan – the former to return to Scotland to become the factory's vehicle assembly and test manager, with the latter being made the original production manager at Linwood – assessed the newly recruited trainees for their potential in either a future management structure or as shop-floor engineering managers. Close on twenty English recruits were poached from Midland firms to join nearly eighty who were recruited from Scotland. Because history is traditionally portrayed in this way, most of the extant photographs of Viscount aircraft disgorging their passengers in Glasgow feature prominent dignitaries and visitors to the Linwood factory, but there was a fortnightly service provided by Rootes for the Scottish trainees to return home from Coventry for the weekend. At the end of their year's training, they were ready to return to train the locally recruited workforce that would assemble the Imp.

It is unknown who devised this scheme before the time of 'human resource professionals', but it was a masterstroke. The returning trained managers understood the culture of the new, unskilled recruits they were having to train. Despite having worked in heavy industry, the new recruits required a thorough preparation. As one manager stated, 'They needed to be taught how to put a screw on a screwdriver.' The one aspect of automotive production the managers were unprepared for was the dispiriting effect of the mind-numbing repetitive tasks that were the essence of many of the new assembly jobs. This greatly contributed to the fractious nature of the workforce, particularly after the Detroit take-over.

In spite of the integration of the two halves of the factory, they were under separate ownership and control until 1966. On the Rootes side of the road, Geoffrey Rootes was the official chairman over five successive managing directors – the first had a background with aluminium and was charged with ensuring the die-cast plant worked. He was followed by a 'specialist in personnel matters' – it is revealing that no one the author has spoken to can remember his name – who was rapidly followed by Bill Garner, a 'vehicle man' whose name everyone cites. The oft-referred-to Jim Lauder was the chief metallurgist for the Pressed Steel Company, which did not have a local quality manager. As so much of the Imp would be completed on that side of the road, Lord Rootes insisted that someone at Pressed Steel (Linwood) should be responsible for the quality of what was being delivered over the transporter bridge: Jim Lauder became that person, with his former assistant, Peter Griffiths becoming the managing director of Pressed Steel. Following Rootes' ownership of both parts, Griffiths became the managing director of the entire facility.

Linwood's workforce was mainly Scottish, with only a few trained in Coventry. The managers found that improving efficiency meant changing the whole workplace culture, since the workforce presumed that the speedy completion of a project would only serve to hasten their inevitable redundancy, as was the custom within the heavy-industry sector. The rest of the Rootes organization operated a piece-work system of long standing that had been used throughout the industry, but this was replaced by the 'measured day' in 1966. This scheme assessed a base of 75 per cent proposed output, with a greater output resulting in staged increases in payment for the worker concerned. A piece-work system had never been part of the Rootes part of the Linwood way of working, although it was the basis of remuneration at Pressed Steel. The system Rootes employed for the hourly paid operatives was close to the 'measured day' system that was later applied across the company. A frequent piece-work clause in parts of the industry was that when a model's component part was altered for a later design, the agreements for all the unrelated jobs on that model

Future Linwood engineering and management staff are seen outside the Brabloch Hotel in Paisley. The Coventry team chosen to start up the Linwood factory and train future workers were flown up with their spouses to view the area.

had to be renegotiated. Whilst the 'measured day' was a more satisfactory system for the workers, and an improvement on piece-work, at Linwood it suffered from the enduring custom of working hard at the start of the week, after which each worker would operate his or her own phased shutdown in preparation for the forthcoming weekend. It is easy to see how the British term 'Friday-afternoon car' was coined to describe any unreliable or poorly assembled vehicle.

In designating the Central Belt of Scotland an industrial development area, the Government assumed that it, like other chosen areas, would offer firms the possibility of paying lower wage levels than were usual in the more prosperous centres of manufacturing. This might have been true of Scottish hydro-electricity and aluminium-smelting projects in the traditionally rural Highlands of Scotland, but the unemployed workforce of the Central Belt expected the same financial rewards as their previous heavy-industry employment –

not exceptionally high, but quite well paid and strongly unionized, whether the worker was skilled or unskilled. This was a very different background from the expansion of the 1930s in Oxford, Birmingham or Luton, where the industrial wages seemed beyond the dreams of avarice to the newly industrialized migrant agricultural workers.

Jim Pollard, Linwood's former Vehicle Car Assembly and Test Manager, confirms that, unlike the Pressed Steel part of the complex, 'where there were always disputes about pay levels', there were very few industrial relations problems at Linwood until the full take-over by Chrysler – and certainly it had a far superior record to most of the other Development Area/District factories. He remembers an early strike over 'Coventry Parity', which lasted until the workers were paid the same rates of pay as others in the Rootes Group, and only one early 'lay-off' through the car assembly workers downing tools. This dispute had the potential to escalate into a typical

Jim Pollard

James Arthur Pollard was born in April 1923 in Cupar, Fife, and educated at Aberlour, Banff, Scotland, followed by King's Lynn Technical College, Norfolk. Jim joined the Royal Air Force in 1941 and saw service at home and abroad, including the North African and Middle-Eastern deserts. On his demobilization in 1947, he worked for the General Electric Company in Coventry before moving in 1952 to the Humber Motor Company. During his following nine years of experience of managing vehicle assembly, finishing and testing, Jim availed himself of the management training provided by Rootes, as well as later inputs from Chester and Strathclyde Business Schools.

Once the decision to build the Imp at Linwood was made, as a project engineer in 1961 Jim was officially attached to the team that would set up the Linwood factory, and assist with the training of the new workforce. He was also to find himself driving the early Imps during the testing programme. Once production was under way at Linwood, he was the vehicle assembly and test quality superintendent, and subsequently the quality assurance manager. Finding himself out of sympathy with the cost-cutting, to him quality-reduction, ethos of Chrysler (UK), he went into business on his own account in 1970, becoming the owner-manager of the Eastwood Toll Garage in a residential suburb of Glasgow.

By 1975, Jim found himself attracted back to improving production quality, this time for the Singer Company in Clydebank, but the 'other' Singer: as the quality engineering manager, he helped the directors achieve major improvements in the quality of their three sewing-machine factories, and in doing so visited the factories in North America and Canada. Before enjoying a well-earned retirement in Scotland, he returned to what was now the Talbot Motor Company in the role of dealer development specialist. His task was to advise the new board of directors on the assessment and monitoring of their newly acquired UK dealer network, and to make suggestions for business improvements.

In retirement, Jim lives close to where Chrysler might have built their own car factory, and visits Linwood frequently – the shopping centre constructed on the old Pressed Steel site.

One of the many female staff clocks-on for work through taking her time-card from the wall-rack and getting it stamped by the official time-clock at the works to establish a record of her time-keeping and working hours.

confrontation, as the assembly workers who were taking 'unofficial action' were immediately dismissed; what was unusual, and unheard of elsewhere, was that the workers' union shop stewards and the managers combined to keep the car-assembly 'track' running until the protesting workers returned to work. Only a 'few militants' were not re-engaged. More typical of the popular perception of the labour-force is the comment of one of the principals in the factory: 'There were unemployed shipbuilders to master bakers; we built them this new factory and the buggers went on strike for parity with Coventry wages!' An early example of insensitive management following the Chrysler take-over was the immediately imposed penny-pinching: the 'Quality Control Inspectors' were renamed 'Viewers' and their wages were cut as the visiting Detroit management could not see why such a small and inexpensive vehicle could justify such care over its build quality.

While Linwood was still in the hands of the Rootes family, the firm did try quite hard to produce an agreeable working environment for the staff. As well as the superior amenities at Linwood, there were competitions, works outings and even a continental motoring holiday costing approximately three to four weeks' salary per person – not something that many of the workforce would have experienced before.

The approach of the Rootes family might seem positively beatific compared with the discovery of the young Geoffrey Rootes when being taken to Vincent Bendix's grand house near the American Bendix Corporation's facility: 'I was astonished to see by the entrance two pillboxes with slits for machine-guns', which were for defence in case of attack by the work-force during strikes! Later in the 1960s, the interventionist Government of Harold Wilson would bring together the management and unions of the automobile industry and present them with the finding that, in the United Kingdom during 1965, the abysmal labour relations accounted for the loss of six million working-man-days in the industry, but as has been observed by Industrial Tribunals, there is a long tradition in the United Kingdom of a 'manager's right to manage – however badly he does it'.

Some economic commentators will produce a 'but' argument at this juncture. Minor industrial disruption was with the complicity of owners and managers, since this situation could act as a type of smoothing operation, smoothing the resultant exigencies of supply and demand. Although such complicity is plausible in terms of a reaction to three decades of the indigenous, governmentally inspired 'stop-go' cycles of the country's economy that amplified the market-driven periodicity, none of the managers the author has spoken to would offer any credence to this theory, as the hypothesis is promoted by those who have not endured the experience of dealing with the resumption of production after such stoppages.

There were constant disagreements between Jensen, which assembled the P1800, and Pressed Steel, which manufactured the panels, as to where responsibility lay for the recurrent failure to meet Volvo's quality standards. Jensen assembled some cars with the Linwood panels without rectification, marking the pressings' errors.

The Pressed Steel Company at Linwood

When the Pressed Steel Company took over the ex-Beardmore shadow factory after the war, it mainly concentrated on being a railway wagon works that produced a small amount of pressed steel. With the demise of the mass rail system in the United Kingdom, presided over by Dr Beeching, and the increase of contract work at Pressed Steel's main Cowley factory, near Oxford, the expanded Linwood Pressed Steel factory, involving an £8.5 million Government loan, concentrated on what its name suggested it did for a living – mainly cabs for British Motor Corporation and Ford lorries, and certain smaller jobs for home and overseas manufacturers. The main automobile job for the former was the P5 top-of-the-range car for Rover, while the latter comprised the bodies for the 'English' Volvo, the 1800 series – a contract that stemmed from 1959 for their 'sports touring' car. Not having sufficient capacity in their own plants, Volvo's original approach to have the bodies assembled was to Bristol Cars, then Jensen Motors of West Bromwich. The lucrative contract was to produce 5,600 P1800 bodies at Linwood, with painting and final body assembly and trim being carried out at Jensen. Following severe quality problems and a vacant line at Volvo's Lundby assembly plant, after 1963 the 1800S bodies were shipped directly from Pressed Steel to Sweden. The 'P' prefix for *Personvagn* (private car) was dropped in favour of the 'S' suffix for *Sverige*. As Volvo and Chrysler could not arrive at mutually agreeable terms for the pricing of these bodies, the pressing tools were moved from Linwood to Olofström during the winter of 1968/9, and the contract lapsed.

In 1965/6, the British Motor Corporation took over the Pressed Steel Company, mainly for the factory at Cowley, Oxford, that was adjacent to its own complexes and made bodies for many third-party manufacturers, including most of the Rootes Motors' bodies used at Ryton – it was quoted to the Government that 40 per cent of Pressed Steel's output was for the Rootes company. As its first rationaliza-tion, British Motor Holdings reduced its body-pressing facilities to four subsidiaries in six locations under the single company, Pressed Steel Fisher Limited. The locations it retained were Fisher and Ludlow at Castle Bromwich and Llanelli, Nuffield Metal Products Limited at Washwood Heath, Birmingham, Pressed Steel Company at Cowley and Swindon, and Morris Motors Bodies Branch (the old Coventry Body Plant that virtually hand-made the Minor Traveller).

By this time, Linwood comprised four main pressing areas. The old building (still often referred to as 'Beardmore') produced the Volvo and Rover bodies, a trailer for the RAF and railway wagon subcontracts, which continued in a much reduced way. All of these were profitable. The adjacent building produced pressings for Rootes, Ford, and BMC commercial cabs, while the 'K' building produced Ford and BMC cabs. The large 'L' building, to which the overhead covered gantry was connected, was where the Imp bodies were processed. Having little use for their Linwood outpost, BMC welcomed an immediate approach from Rootes Securities to purchase the facility. Following prolonged funding negotiations with the Government and eventual clearance from the Monopolies Commission, Pressed Steel (Linwood) became Rootes Pressings (Scotland) Limited. From the start of 1966, Linwood would augment its existing work with pressings for its own Hunter, Minx, Sceptre, Singer Vogue and Sunbeam Rapier models. When the remodelling of Ryton-on-Dunsmore began in February 1967 – two years before the launch of the Avenger model – the new integrated body-building, painting, and final-assembly line was planned based upon the body panels being pressed at Linwood and being taken to Coventry by rail. At the time, this was considered a strange way of doing things, but by the end of the century the Ryton facility (now in the hands of Peugeot) was sourcing all its pressed panels, with a few minor exceptions, from outwith the United Kingdom.

Some commentators attribute Rootes' eventual demise directly to the Imp, especially those who think that Rootes were plodding along nicely with well-proved and trusted products. To adopt this position is to ignore the changing marketplace. Had the Imp been a reliable, properly built car from the outset, the opposite stance is more appealing: the Imp would have represented such an attractive part of the company, it alone would have caused

Rootes to survive in some form. And without such a car, which would address the changing tastes of the population, the Group would have suffered a slow demise of a thousand lashes, as most of the range would appear to even the most loyal customer as a progressively ageing series that was not responding to either the tastes or the aspirations of its customers. The Imp, through being a small, sporty, and fun-to-drive car, was more than capable of holding its own between the smaller and more spartan Mini and the larger and decidedly 'non-fun' family saloons. Looking back on the period from a purely motoring perspective, L. J. K. Setright postulates:

In the early 1960s it looked as though, after repeated and sometimes disastrous failures by Renault, Hillman might have done it [rear-engined drive] with their sweet and stable Imp. Sadly, it was too heavy and too badly let down by minor faults; and so the front-drive Mini, which . . . had beaten it to the marketplace by a couple of years, but had not yet taken hold, was suddenly seen as the exemplar of the right way to go.

4   Finalizing, Testing, Proving, Adjusting . . .

Whose Engine, Though?

The use of an in-house Rootes power unit of the time would have resulted in an outdated side-valve engine of enormous weight. Such a solution would have pleased the Rootes directors, but would have produced a truly ghastly vehicle with such a lump of cast iron in the tail. As the original minimalist concept was slipping away, Parkes applied some lateral thinking and looked for a lightweight, but powerful, small unit. The engine designer, Coventry Climax, still an independent company, was developing an interesting lightweight engine that used an aluminium alloy for the engine block, cylinder-head, pistons, and various ancillaries. Coventry Climax had a long-standing relationship with Rootes, and Mike Parkes was well known to them through his familial and racing connections. A number of the smaller British manufacturers had used such an alloy for some components, and Reliant and DAF were working on die-cast aluminium-alloy engines, but no mass-producer favoured this material as extensively as Coventry Climax. It would not be until 1960, for example, that even the giant General Motors would unveil its mass-production aluminium-alloy V8, and the Renault R16's alloy engine was still a long way off. Admirers, not to mention Rootes' copy-writers, would suggest that the Hillman Imp was powered by an engine with a racing pedigree, whilst detractors would be able to claim it was merely a fire-pump engine – and both would be correct!

The FW, or Feather Weight, series of engines commenced its varied life as a lightweight fire-pump unit, and would spawn, via the Feather Weight Automobile engine, successive generations of sporting power units that would find favour with Lotus and Cooper cars before, in V8 guise, it would become the standard fitment of many a successful Formula-One car. The version developed for sporting marine use, the FWMA, would form the basis of the unit that Rootes' deputy chief engineer, Leo Kuzmicki, would develop and redesign as the power unit for the entire Imp range. An émigré Pole, Kuzmicki had arrived at the Humber division via racing-engine development work for Norton motorcycles and Vanwall racing cars: optimizing the efficiency of an engine was his speciality. Kuzmicki was the lead author of a fascinating paper detailing the development of the Imp's engine which was delivered at the engineering soirée, 'Design of Small Mass-Produced Car Engines', and repeated for the Automobile Division of the Scottish Mechanical Engineers. In 1963 this was what would now be described as the leading edge of this type of engineering, in stark contrast to the A-series engine for which BMC had found a new home in the Mini.

The Imp was nearing reality, albeit with some significant changes yet to be made. The Rootes board expressed a commitment to the project's continuation, and ordered the final restyling of the package described above until the Apex would become the acceptable car that could be offered to the world bearing the imprimatur of one or more of the group's

Coventry Climax Feather Weight Engines		
FW	1,020cc	Original stationary-engine design for fire-pumps
FWA	1,098cc	Feather Weight Automobile, the initial automotive application
FWB	1,480cc	Long-stroke racing version used in Cooper racing-cars
FWBP	1,480cc	Fire-pump version of FWB engine
FWC	744cc	Unique engine produced for Colin Chapman's successful Le Mans car
FWD		Unique diesel marine version
FWE	1,216cc	Used in the Lotus Elite
FWM	653/745cc	Feather Weight Marine: stationary and marine engine
FWMA	741cc	Competition auto version of the FWM, used as the basis for the Imp engine
FWMB	741cc	Occasional nomenclature for Imp version within Coventry Climax
FWME	1,216cc	Occasional nomenclature for FWE version within Coventry Climax
FWMV	1,475cc+	V8 competition version eventually used in Lotus Type25 and Formula 1 racing
FWMW	1,475cc+	Occasional nomenclature for V8 competition version
FPE		Original Coventry Climax V8 specifically developed for racing
FPF	1,475cc+	4-cylinder developed for Formulas 1 and 2, Coventry Climax's true racing engine

marques on the bonnet. Some commentators think it was at these incremental restyling stages that the Imp gained rather too much weight; while this is certainly true when measured against the earlier ideas of the designers, if the Imp was ever to be the second small British car in the marketplace, it was necessary for it to be demonstrably superior in a host of ways – accommodation being one.

As far as the engineering development of Apex was concerned, Parkes and Fry had many changes yet to make. The largest concerned the rear of the vehicle, which was getting jolly crowded with the new Coventry Climax 4-cylinder, water-cooled engine, which now required a radiator to dissipate the heat from its coolant. Necessitated through its height, the engine would be canted over and the radiator could be accommodated alongside it, after the style of the Fiat 600. Fry admits that had the project started with the idea of this engine, then the layout would have incorporated its transverse mounting. It was quite early in the twentieth century that the American, Walter Christie, proposed that having the engine's crankshaft rotate in the same plane as the driven wheels removed the power-consumptive transfer of the drive through 90 degrees – Issigonis's models would enjoy this in-built advantage, but alas, the Imp

did not. There would be numerous other small changes, few considering this was an entirely new model, and these would have to wait until endurance testing revealed peculiarities that development and rig-testing had not. One such was a result of the ingenious idea of canting the engine at 45 degrees. The engine had been designed to run horizontally or vertically, but not in between; and so there were some shortcomings concerning the draining of lubricating oil from the cylinder head. Using valve-stem oil seals on the input valves and changing the number of drain holes was an immediate answer, but the engine was provided with better draining arrangements to ensure the lubricating oil found its way back to the sump, rather than into the cylinders.

Because of the airflow through the engine compartment (something that was not fully understood at the time) and the matrix of the radiator's cooling fins, the cooling system was, and remains, of marginal ability to cope under all conditions. It was possible to use a large remote fan to make the air pass either way through the radiator: forward was the chosen direction, something a new owner might find counter-intuitive. Any fan capable of functioning in this way will be of a size that will contribute noise to the engine bay and be a drain on the useable power of the engine. Several designs of fan were used to strike a balance between cooling efficiency and generated noise. Polypropylene was the chosen material for the fan after extensive testing without any failures occurring. The fan was assessed through over-speeding tests for a constant twenty-four hours at 12,000rpm, followed by a similar period at half this speed.

The envisaged gearbox was changed to suit the output of the new engine. A space-saving solution of combining the gearbox and differential/final drive into what is called a transaxle was designed in-house, with aluminium alloy being used in an attempt to keep down weight. Although the use of a transaxle was not uncommon among European continental manufacturers, this gave the Imp another innovative feature with regard to other British makers. This gearbox was another of the outstanding features of the car; uncommon for the time, it possessed synchromesh on all its forward gears, complemented by a precise and light gear-change that would become much praised – as late as in *Motor*'s group test of 1968, the Imp's synchromesh on bottom gear was still worthy of a special mention. By contemporary standards of five-speed gearboxes, the indirect top gear might seem rather low when cruising at the car's limit, but the Imp would be thought to be highly geared at the time. Depending on the tyre fitment on the normal 12in wheels, the standard Imp achieved just over 15mph (24km/h) per 1,000rpm of engine speed, and the Rally version a fraction under 14mph (22km/h) per 1,000rpm.

The connection between the power output of the transaxle and the driveshafts was via flexible Rotoflex couplings. Manufacturers such as Lotus also employed these couplings, but they were an untried solution in a mass-produced car, and caution was exhibited over their use for the Imp. They offered one huge advantage: when the wheels moved up and down with the suspension, these Rotoflex couplings obviated the need for the driveshaft to have a sliding splined joint. An early quirk that remained good practice was that if one of these rubberized couplings had to be removed, it was refitted in exactly the same orientation to the components either side of it – even better practice, of course, would be to fit new ones.

Many rear-engined models had a frightful reputation as far as their handling was concerned. Because of this, along with the

This shows the driveshaft connecting the transaxle to the road-wheel – the Rotoflex coupling at one end and a universal joint at the other.

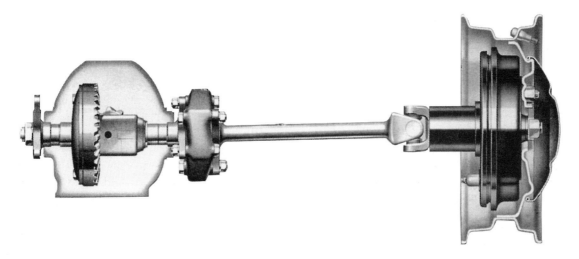

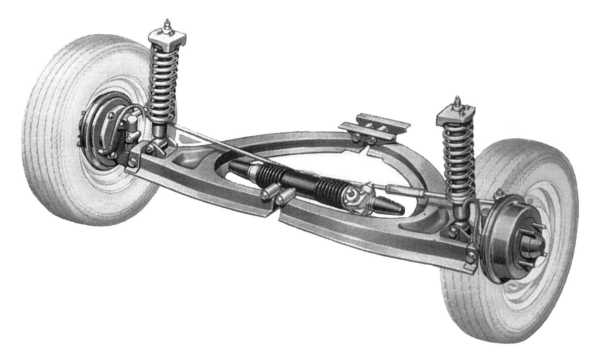

The front part of the all-independent suspension of the Imp was a simple swing-axle. The steering rack is between the two arms.

The trailing-arm rear suspension is viewed from the front, with the engine behind.

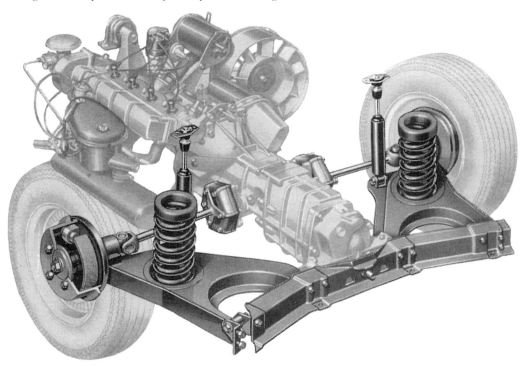

designers' wish for this new car to be fun to drive – and not from the aspect of it being frighteningly fun – much thought was given to the behaviour of the rear under all driving conditions. The weight-saving measures described above were mainly with this view in mind, but Parkes and Fry, while retaining the simple swing-axle front suspension, took advice on equipping the Imp with a more sophisticated trailing-arm suspension which was duly developed. After all, even the efforts of Ferdinand Porsche, with his appropriation of the swinging rear suspension of the brilliant Czech engineer and designer of the Tatra, Hans Ledwinka, had fallen short of ideal and had required rectification following the dissatisfaction of many owners. It was the thoughts of the antics of earlier KdF Volkswagens and Auto Unions that strengthened the resolve of Parkes and Fry to design a rear suspension that would be exemplary under all conditions. Not only did this overcome much of the public's resistance to a car with the engine at the 'wrong' end, but it was to be showered with plaudits by reviewers and road-testers. This success formed the basis for salesmen to stress to customers that the suspension was 'perfected only after exhaustive development', and that it 'introduces a remarkable combination of three most forceful selling features: namely, superb riding comfort, first-class roadholding and precise, responsive steering'.

In the 'Confidential Facts for the Salesman' that Rootes produced to educate the salesmen in its dealers, the message of the wonderment to be found in the rear suspension is amplified: 'Rear-end breakaway on corners, usually associated with rear-engined cars, is precluded by an inclined roll axis converging towards the ground at the rear. This greatly increases the slip resistance of the more heavily loaded, rear tyres.'

Various small wheels would be tried, and 12in ones were to be standardized for the Imp range, partially for cosmetic æsthetics, but mainly for the practical reasons of allowing decently apportioned drum brakes and a rea-

sonable life-expectancy for tyres. The front bumper-line was raised from that of the 'final viewing' to lie between the side/indicator lights and the headlamps. The initial prototype cars were like Bob Saward's final model. It is thought that the rectilinear side- and indicator-lights, and the raising of the bumper, occurred at the same time as the wheelbase increased from 79 to 82in (2,006–2,083mm), and the overall length grew from 130.5 to 139in (3,315–3,531mm). According to one of the early testers, this transformed the handling, whereas Tim Fry claims that the original length produced the same results. When asked about this, he then returns to the topic of the longer springs and the height of the car's front causing side-wind problems, as explained below. Unusually for such a vehicle, the bumper was more robust than many such fitments – a point that *Which?* magazine would praise when testing the commercially available Imp.

Coventry's engine climax

The Apex was now approaching its form that would be a recognizable Imp. The Featherweight engine still required to be developed into its final, standardized manifestation. Leo Kuzmicki readily acknowledged the assistance his team received from the engine's progenitors, Coventry Climax. The original engine capacity was 750cc, and the envisaged sizes that would be made available to the different variants of the Imp were 800cc, 875cc and 1,000cc. The initial pre-production units would be of the smallest size, and a small quantity of the largest units would be made available for sporting applications, but for reasons of engineering production costs and reliability, the median capacity was standardized across the range with detuned and higher-tuned versions accommodating the various performance demands of the different models of Imp. This decision might have been a sensible one, but it imposed a constraint with which competitors like the Mini did not have to cope. The inflexibility of not having a range of different capacities for this new engine made the future introduction of more sporting variants more problematic, even if it did refine the tuning skills of mainly third-party developers. Revitalizing the public's interest in the Imp when sales started to flag, by the simple expedient of slotting in a larger-capacity engine, would not be available to Rootes. It was discovered that the largest capacity the standard engine would reliably tolerate was 948cc, but alas, without more development, neither it nor the later-envisaged 928cc unit was used.

The standardized 4-cylinder 875cc aluminium-alloy engine is of the type described as 'over-square' – meaning that its 67.99mm cylinder bore is wider than the distance of its piston stroke of 60.375mm. The engine employed a simplex-chain-driven single overhead camshaft for operation of its valves – the idea of an inexpensive toothed-belt to transfer the rotational motion of the crankshaft to the camshaft was not introduced until 1963 (by the German Glas firm). The application of this form of camshaft, which lies above the cylinders, being mounted in three white-metal-lined bearings directly in the cylinder head and operating the valves directly, was uncommon in the UK. When it is compared with the then much more common pushrod-operated valve layout, even if often accompanied by a forest of rods, it is not difficult to appreciate why British customers did not care for this unnecessary complexity. Checking the 'valve clearances' might have turned into a once-in-a-flood operation, but it required greater precision and a level of skill and understanding that many a do-it-yourself owner-mechanic or local garage did not possess, and in production it was found that some of the under-trained engine-assembly staff also lacked the necessary skills. The valve-gear comprised camshaft, tappets, adjusting shims and poppet valves. The original valve diameters were inlet 1.064in, exhaust 1.01in; these would increase in the Mark II Imp to 1.202in and 1.064in respectively, with the Sport engine reaching 1.276in and 1.064in.

The designers realized that this engine possessed the potential for being used at high revs, and recommended that owners restrict themselves to 6,000rpm – figuratively 'red-lining' it at this speed. Double valve springs were incorporated in the original design to ensure that 'valve bounce' would not occur at high engine speeds, to be dispensed with when it was discovered that this was unnecessary under 7,400rpm. This left plenty of room to fit valve-stem oil seals, so when the engine's oil consumption was thought to be excessive under certain conditions, this state was easily resolved.

Kuzmicki had the idea of dispensing altogether with valve springs to close the valves and to achieve this mechanically – revealing his racing motorcycle background. Like other manufacturers who have thought about using desmodronic valves in anything short of a competition engine, it was quickly realized that the advantages were heavily outweighed by the disadvantages of complexity and cost.

When designing the cylinder head, there were two principal considerations – thermal efficiency and production efficacy. Using a wedge-shaped combustion chamber with a compression ratio of 10:1 to achieve a good surface-to-volume ratio, and combining this with an appropriate degree of turbulence of the incoming fuel/air mix, Kuzmicki achieved an efficient engine, but one that could be run on 95 octane (RON) petrol without the risk of pre-ignition or 'pinking/pinging'. Putting more of the heat from the burnt fuel to the useful work of driving the engine also assisted the excellent fuel consumption. A lower compression-ratio version of the engine, usually 8:1, was supplied to some overseas markets and fitted to more utilitarian versions of the Imp.

At every stage of the engine development, considerable cognizance was paid to the ease of production from both machining and casting standpoints – this was for good engineering principles as well as keeping the production costs to a minimum. An example would be the machining of the combustion

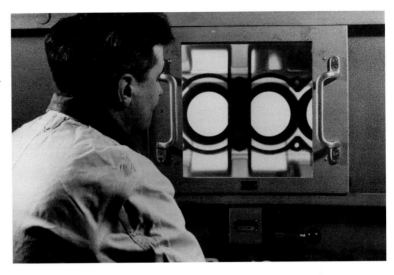

Prior to the integral iron liners being machined in the cast aluminium-alloy engine blocks, they were checked both visually and through using X-rays. Here, the operative is looking down on the engine. The Siamesing of the pair of liners on the right can be seen.

chambers: the shape had to be such that a single traversing tool could machine the chamber, with a minimum of divergence between the four capacities in the final cylinder head. The production cylinder head would be produced by a gravity die-cast process that used sand cores for the water galleries and head-ports. The cylinder head would not be cast at the die-casting division of Linwood, but in Birmingham by Aeroplane & Motor Aluminium Castings, who made other aluminium-alloy cylinder heads for other, newer engines in the Rootes range.

Engine experiments included casting the cylinder head in three separate parts and, after machining, literally gluing them together – alas, the adhesive technology of the time did not promise a long life for these. Another experiment was to equip the pistons with iron piston-rings that could run directly in the aluminium-alloy block. Various aluminium-alloy recipes were tried, and this concept was more successful than it might at first seem, the limiting factor proving to be the level of precision required in its manufacture.

Some features of the engine were highly conventional, for example the three-bearing, four-throw steel forged crankshaft (which was made near Coventry). Abandoning the idea of the pistons running directly in the aluminium-

alloy engine block, cylinder liners that were centrifugally cast in iron were used, and to save space the two pairs of liners would be 'Siamesed'. The initial four prototype units had their liners pressed into a sand-cast alloy block, but the ingenious technique of die-casting the liners and the aluminium-alloy oil gallery tube *in situ* ensured a more reliable fitment of these 'dry' liners (that is, they were not directly surrounded by the coolant fluid). Following research, the production liners were externally finished with circumferential grooves so that they stayed firmly in place as well as efficiently dissipating the combustion heat into the alloy block.

The original idea had been to use high-pressure die-casting for the manufacture of the engine, including the casting of the engine block. This high-pressure system, unsurprisingly, uses high pressure to force the molten metal into a die that is manufactured from a tough, high-quality steel. Using an aluminium-alloy type called LM24, the bearing caps, timing cover with integral engine-mounting bracket, and tappet carrier on the cylinder head, were die-cast by this high-pressure method. It was decided, however, to use LM9 alloy injected at low-pressure for the main body of the block. This transition from high to low pressure was accomplished with

Jim Pollard tests a pre-production Imp in his native rural Scotland.

relative ease once adjustments to the design were made to allow for certain increases in machining tolerances. From an accounting standpoint, the low-pressure system was irresistible, since, for the added cost of having to produce a greater number of dies for this slower process, these dies were markedly cheaper because they did not require to be anything like as rugged. As far as the engineering and production considerations were concerned, there was a small negative feature to overcome – the molten metal flow into the die at 16psi was slower through the reduced velocity, and temperature differences could lead to early solidification and resultant possible porosity of the block. Once these difficulties were accommodated, many benefits were apparent: the principal one was most helpful during the empirical phase of development – the dies were made of an easily machinable material, offering a greater facility for experimentation.

Some attempts to increase the size of the engine continued. It was discovered that replacing the 'dry', cast-in cylinder liners of the 875cc and 948cc versions with 'wet' ones would substantially improve its reliability. A larger-capacity production engine was not thought practicable – this 998cc engine would become a popular choice for the latter-day owner. The bored-out dry-liner version would remain of interest in sporting circles where longevity is not the hierarchically most prominent requirement. The alternative of increasing the capacity through lengthening the stroke, rather than the bore, was also investigated, but the necessary taller engine blocks and different crankshafts were thought to be too expensive. Ironically, the last incarnation of the standard Imp engine would emerge after the time of the Imp: the awkwardly named Chrysler Sunbeam of 1977 would be available with a modified, bored-out 928cc implementation, some of these being reputedly made in Scotland. This unit had been proposed as early as 1964 as part of the investigation into the possibility of furnishing the car with a semi-automatic or fully automatic gearbox – all models were intended to be fitted with this engine for the 1968 revision.

In addition to the Asp sports-car, which will be dealt with later, the Imp might have had a big brother, the Swallow – a rear-engined replacement for the ageing Minx. It would have used a 1,250cc engine related to the Imp, with which it shared ideas like the pneumatic throttle and remote water pump – but this time with a front-mounted radiator. Because of early Imp-related problems, the idea of replacing the core Hillman vehicle with another untried idea caused too much apprehension at Rootes, and the idea withered on the vine other than to feed the basic body shape into the Hillman Hunter. This was a sensible decision, for the Hunter went on to become Rootes' most profitable vehicle.

Time was spent eradicating the Imp's various sounds and vibrations, as well as wind and water ingress. Some of the former were trivial, but irritating, while others required a more comprehensive rethink. Keeping an Imp properly sealed is still a challenge for any owner, as it had not been properly solved by the production stage. Remedial action improved it and today's owner has more sophisticated products with which to tackle this shortcoming.

In a close-up of what would become the vehicle's Achilles heel, the radiator, fan, and (closest to the camera) the problematic water pump, are seen to the left of the engine on this Mark I car. With elegant attention to detail, the owner has replaced the distributor cap with a period Lucas item.

Time to Provoke the Worst

By 1961, the extensive testing of prototypes commenced concomitant with the design and building of the Scottish factory. The Hillman Imp, as well as its component parts, became the most tested and modified car of its period. Whilst blurring the prototype and pre-production testing of the Imp, the Scottish documentary film, *Young at Heart*, put it thus:

> A life of agony for every one [component] before it can be passed as fit for big-scale production. In the test-rig shops, individual components are given a lifetime of strain in a few months. Even details like trafficator switches have to be fit for brutal use, or even misuse . . . The whole car must be tested in what the engineers laughingly call 'realistic conditions' — endless high-speed thrashing is only the beginning of the course at the test grounds. [Shots of MIRA testing ground and ambitious handling tests] But the real testing has only just started, this car has got to be fit for any road in the world — so that is where they take them. First to France, on the old military roads — the Italian autostrada — the cold passes of the Dolomites — the German autobahn — and then, far south to the African Bush. From Africa to the Arctic Circle . . . now they have done everything except drive her under water, and at the end of the day — they know they have a *car*.

With the composer Anthony Hedges' busy fugal accompaniment, film footage of all of these — including African wildlife — captures the urgency and determination of these proving stages. Not only would the customer be convinced of what he was about to consume, but so were many at Rootes Motors. The prototypes coped well enough with these tortuous mountain climbs, but a question-mark was raised about its ability to maintain its coolant temperature within safe limits during high-speed cruising. Like others, Rootes was grateful to the Government for providing them with an unrestricted high-speed test track — the M1 motorway. The barely adequate radiator was mounted alongside the engine, and for a long time the developers did not really understand the airflow through it; this was probably the reason for these early cars' marginal ability to keep a cool head — literally. That was not a problem the Scandinavian testers experienced, as there they wished Rootes had fitted all the prototypes with a heater — driving there in winter was 'sheer Hell'!

The other cooling problem was that the company might have identified the heterodox water pump as problematic during early testing, but despite addressing its shortcomings through constant rig-testing and tinkering, no real resolution was achieved. This would prove a very costly oversight once thousands of these cars started to experience this failure. For reasons of bringing the Imp to full production in too hasty a timescale, there would be many unknown deficiencies that would come to light as the public tested the new model over a far greater range of operating conditions than those of Rootes' endurance-testing. The deficiencies of the water pump and its ability to pump the coolant efficiently round the engine, while not being prone to leaking it all over the new owner's boots as he or she vainly stared at the engine to find out why the temperature gauge was reading alarmingly high, was not one of those deep and dark problems that were waiting to be revealed by the luckless owner — this is assuming the owner had paid extra for this essential 'accessory'. The water pump was an identified problem that for unknown reasons seems not to have received the attention it deserved. What made it a peculiar design is that the seals round the impeller shaft had to prevent the coolant from seeping into the bearings fore and aft of it.

These cooling-system weaknesses seemed as nothing when compared to the multitude of other problems revealed during the pre-production stages. Like all pre-production cars, the problems of the Imp were virtually hand-

Rootes' Routes

The extant test-route maps make interesting reading: London Route (50 miles [80km]): Marble Arch, Oxford Street, Cheapside, London Bridge, Kennington, Chelsea, Kensington, Marble Arch, Euston Road, Shoreditch, Tower Bridge, Peckham, Trafalgar Square, Oxford Street, Piccadilly, Oxford Street, Euston Road, Oxford Street, Shepherd's Bush, Fulham, Marble Arch.

These maps have a note about care being required, as there are 'experimental' one-way traffic schemes in London.

Birmingham City Route: Coventry Road, Bull Ring, then fifty miles [80km] of leaving and returning to the city centre along most arterial roads.

Both of these tests rather belie the notion that the Imp did not experience congested traffic.

Continental Route: 2,405 miles [3,870km] from Calais, via Brussels, Cologne, Stuttgart, Salzburg, Bolzano, Andermatt, Viareggio, Modane, Chaumont, and back to Calais.

Scandanavian [sic] Route (325 miles [523km]): Pitea in Sweden, Luleå, Boden, Jokkmokk (within the Arctic Circle), Kabdalis, Arvidsjaur, and Pitea.

The railway connections are marked on this map – in case of need?

Scottish Route (A9, 236 miles [380km]): Invergordon (A836), Brora, Latheron, Thurso, Wick, and back via Tain.

The Swedish Route caused a story to appear in the *Motor Trafik* section of the *Dagens Nyheter* on 9 February 1963, about '*Nytt tillskott från England i Europaklassen*' [The new addition from England in the European class] and '*Baby-Hillman provas hemligt i Norrland*' [Baby Hillman test in secret in Norrland], complete with photographs of the unbadged. but uncamouflaged, Imps in Gällivare. The paper reported: 'The test drivers refused to speak of the car and they were not pleased when the photographer of *Dagens Nyheter* took the pictures.' It thought 'the lines of the body are rather original', although it spotted a 'Ford line' to the roof. The Rootes internal memorandum about this incident still refers to the Apex cars.

made in the new Linwood facility. Not only was the new model going through its 'snagging' paces, but so was this ambitious factory. By the middle of 1962 it was realized that few of the Imp's components had actually been driven very far – the oft-quoted example was the realization that the brand-new transaxle had not been driven further than a motorist might cover in the first year's ownership. The gearbox worked rather well, but it was still exhibiting an excessive level of mechanical whirring.

Truly Testing Times

The initial plans were for a substantial number of pre-production examples to be evaluated over five endurance routes that would encompass continental European mountainous terrain, the tortuous Scottish A9 trunk road north to Thurso (which was even more perilous in those days than it is now), and a few cars devoted to sitting in the congested Midlands (which was far less severe than those that one now associates with bypassing the area) and London. Because this was less than a year to the public launch of the car and arrangements had been made to open officially the Linwood plant, urgent, followed by panic, testing methods were employed. Testing on such an indiscriminate scale meant that feedback data were incorrectly assessed. No one realized that this was an inadvisable decision, but one that legions of 'professional' pen-pushers would also overlook for generations to come – reports and appraisals form a nugatory exercise if no one ever reads or acts upon their findings – in the case of the Imp, lots of reports, but little coordination of their revealed findings. The sole purpose of this testing was to accrue a series of cars, with high mileages, to see what failed. Like 'Africa to the Arctic Circle', little did, leading to a false sense of security about the reliability of the new model. It is understandable to see why Rootes was so confident about its new baby, and consequently so flummoxed when it was put in the hands of Mr and Ms Joe/Jo Public, who

Pre-production car 'L1', virtually hand built, demonstrated the inherent strength of the Imp when it was rolled over many times in an incident involving an inexperienced new tester.

A 'weekend' test car passes the O'Connell Bridge in the Highlands of Scotland.

Tests are carried out with apprentices at the incomplete Forth Road Bridge.

Alex Wise, who drove an Arrol-Johnston in the 1912 French Grand Prix, sits at the wheel of WHS 171, the early-production endurance test car that was driven round the clock in shifts until it completed 128,000 miles in a single year. Other than an early transaxle failure at 15,000 miles, it remained a trouble-free car. Wise had been retired before joining the test programme.

When Jim Pollard went on another Scottish tour, the 'L' plate was necessary as he was teaching his wife Friede to drive!

proved to be a much stiffer test of their gleaming pride and joy, with failures to the front, rear, and centre. A plausible reason that is offered is that the test cars were literally driven night and day and prepared for each shift, though, as one tester describes it, 'only dipped for oil and water between runs'. It would be the boring stop/start plodding to work through urban traffic that would bring the Imp to its knees as far as the public's perception of its reliability was concerned.

Because of the exuberance of some of the drivers exploring the excellent roadholding and high top speed of the Imp, there were a number of substantial collisions, the perilous A9 in Scotland taking its usual toll. An unexpected area of feedback from these unplanned destructive tests was how little injury was suffered by the occupants of cars that were thoroughly written-off. The Imp's reported performance started to cause consternation in the Rootes boardroom. The larger relative, the Swallow, was not going to see the light of day, so the staid Minx range would occupy the next step up from the Imp. This was a serious consideration in the days when there remained a significant level of brand loyalty upon which every manufacturer could rely. How could the company allow the cheapest car in its model line-up to possess far superior performance to the more expensive models? Also, with half an eye on the classification insurance companies would determine for the Imp, the economy car of the marque, Rootes detuned the engine, making small changes to its engine breathing – at a stroke, both reservations were attended

to while leaving the Parkes/Fry fun-quotient largely intact. Several testers have confirmed that this is more than Imp mythology: the prototypes were noticeably faster.

By the start of 1963, the production engineers had completed their stage of getting this show on the road, and the production of vehicles for sale to the public was commencing. Rootes' 'Set Delivery Schedule', circulated to all in November, planned 5,231 built-up Deluxe Imps and 312 Irish CKD kits ready for the launch. The developers hoped the major problems had been satisfactorily resolved, or, as in the case of worries like the pneumatic actuation of the throttle, if it continued to give problems, remedial plans had been made for its rapid replacement with the conventional cable mechanism. The cooling and water-pump problems were still bubbling away just under the surface, if not always under the engine cover; the inside became too damp through water ingress various as those sealing problems were only just contained, but it looked hopeful.

A last-minute problem changed the aesthetics of the stature of the front of the car. It was discovered that the front sidelights did not conform to the Construction and Use regulations as they did not meet the minimum height from the ground (it was not, as is sometimes cited, the headlamp height). The indicator lenses were much larger than the norm of the day and the datum point for measurement was the centre-line of the lens. Tim Fry suggested a half-inch blanking strip on the bottom of the lens – a sort of durable Duck

The odd and unkindly called 'knock-kneed' look of the front wheels of the early cars, caused by raising the front with longer springs, can be seen on this car, which is undergoing high-speed stability tests. Note that the bumper is in its final position.

tape – so that the centre-line of the operative part of the lens would be raised, but this would cost more than respecifying the spring length. Redesign of the front bodywork was out of the question, so the Imp became legal through the fitment of longer front springs. Problem solved, but the poise of the car lost and this is where the previous wind-tunnel tests went out of the window and the Imp acquired its twitchiness in side-winds.

What of the tame banshee in the gearbox? It is difficult to tell during the dramatic retelling of its rectification if it was the Rootes family, test engineers, or the transaxle that screamed the loudest, but it had to be silenced. Jim Pollard recalls that a theoretical mathematician, Andy Nicholson, from the Isle of Skye was attached to Rootes at this time. He was investigating working in industry, but his real passion was salmon fishing – which eventually won the battle for his attention – and he theoretically proposed a change in the helix angle of the gear. This was tried with great scepticism from the experienced engineers: silence. Pollard, who was helping to add Scottish miles to Imps, having already taken one

The first Imp built in Eire from completely knocked down kits was built by Dublin Motors. The badges remain covered as this predates the Imp's announcement.

Some of the initial batch of Imps built by Dublin Motors are seen here. Eire was the first country to receive CKD kits from the special division at Linwood that dealt with their building, dismantling and export.

across Europe, often took his wife with him on his long drives on the A9, and she complained that the car no longer sounded like an Imp!

Linwood had been producing a cache of finished cars for six months, and these would be used the day following the ceremonial opening of the factory, when the Imp officially went on sale to the public. Many commentators have argued that if the opening of the factory and launch of the car had been delayed by several months, the Imp would not only have been the stunning design that all recog-

nized, but it would have been a far more reliable object and would not have acquired its initial frightful reputation. It is certainly beyond dispute that this collection of early stock-piled cars was of varying quality. Whether this cache comprised the reported 116, or some claims of several times this number, there were just far too few cars to ensure that the dealers could hope to meet their customers' needs even to view, never mind buy, one. Rootes' production had fallen very far short of the intended 'Set Delivery Schedule' of the previous November.

Jim Pollard and Neddy Lucas (of Sales and Marketing) demonstrate the Imp's abilities in Scottish snow for the press.

Like the Slug becoming the Apex, no one today can be definite about when this car irrevocably became the Imp. Ron Wisdom recalls that Timothy Rootes was nominally attached to the styling studio, and for Timothy one of the many advantages of being a Rootes was that when he was entertaining and impressing a young lady, he could take her on a tour of the Humber Road styling studios. On one such occasion, the current focus of his amorous attentions, an American lady, thought the Imp, which she seemed to like, was 'a real Honey of a sedan' – a name that he then proposed to the extent that metal badges were made up for assessment purposes – but Uncle Billy's taste prevailed and the Imp became definitive.

Ever the marketing-man at heart, Lord Rootes augmented the publicity of the factory's official opening through introducing the Imp to an interested public via a stage-managed presentation at the Daily Express International Trophy Race meeting at Silverstone. This event incorporated most of those who were involved with the car's development. They drove sixteen new Imps round the circuit, each containing a Kodak publicity girl. At each corner, and anywhere else the public had gathered, the cars stopped for the girls to parade with the car. All of the drivers had spent weeks being trained in circuit racing, so that a demonstration race could take place after this display. It was planned so that Mike Parkes, the only true racing driver, was not in his car at the start of this mock race; once the rest of the field had rounded the first corner, Parkes ran onto the track, jumped into his specially prepared racing version, and set off in hot pursuit of the rest of the Imp development team, cutting through the pack as he reached them. To quote Bob Saward: 'The "race" got out of hand, everyone got competitive and started to enjoy themselves.' Parkes succeeded in achieving the leading position, but rather than it being the planned set-piece drive, he had to race the over-enthusiastic amateurs who were proving that the Imp was fun!

Pollard and Lucas again demonstrate the Imp on a snowy local corner. After several high-speed runs, the press required 'more action', which was what they got: alas, the car crashed just out of this shot! Lord Rootes, always the salesman, was unperturbed by this, as the resultant photograph was used all round the world at the Imp's launch.

5 On the Town

On Sale at Last

The ceremonials were over, the Kodak girls had returned to what they did as the daytime jobs, the sales literature, films and other wonderments to boost the spirits of the dealers had been posted – the Imp was in town, if not on the streets yet. There were nowhere near enough Imps to satisfy the curiosity of an eager public. Lord Rootes had partially done his job: this launch and the exciting new factory had been carefully planted with motoring writers for them to trail for some years. The public were keen, eager and still highly chauvinistic: the Scots felt a sense of pride (encouraged by films that showed 'Arrol-Johnston Paisley' on the hubcap of a suitably ancient specimen from the country's heritage), and the rest of the land could experience a warm glow of satisfaction about the most English of the volume manufacturers – Rootes Motors. Everyone knew this family-run firm produced trustworthy and reliable cars. Oh that the marketing juggernaut had heeded Peter Ware's concerns; had the board paid cognizance to his Cassandra-like pleas, then the public could have pressed its sticky-fingered patina on the high-gloss finish of the metal while it eased its backsides into those accommodating seats.

The documentary film, *Young at Heart*, which has already been mentioned, opens on a West Coast Highland scene with the happy couple driving their Imp past a defenestrated and roofless deserted croft – this probably looked quaint then, rather than the dispiriting

Typical of the media message is this production still from the 1963 film, Young at Heart, *a documentary featuring Elizabeth Yuill, the young Bill Simpson (an archetypal Scot after the television adaptation of A. J. Cronin's* Dr Finlay's Casebook*) and the Hillman Imp.*

This is just the sort of Scottish terrain over which much of the domestic testing took place and through which the Imp was so good at progressing at a decent speed. Interestingly, the film makes quite a point of the female driving, while the production-stills feature Bill Simpson as the driver.

common sight of today – and the voice-over proclaims:

> They call this *Tir-nan-Og* – land of the young in heart [actually, land of the ever-young is better], a remote fairytale land, it now offers its magic to the traveller . . . a new age in an old, old country. The small car is the symbol of this new revolution to delight in their heritage.

Two versions were offered as 'an inspiration in light car design' and stated to be 'Made in Scotland' by 'The Hillman Car Co. Ltd – Division of Rootes Motors Limited'. The Saloon at £508/1/3d (£508.06) including purchase tax, and the Deluxe Saloon at £532/4/7d (£532.23). Rootes Acceptances Limited offered 'easy terms' for the higher price of £106 deposit and £14/5/0d (£14.25) per month. This form of 'never-never' credit was popular with the Imp's target stratum of society. Few of the purchasers of an Imp as their first new car would have been on sufficiently familiar terms with bank managers to negotiate a loan for such an inessential. Following a relaxation on credit restrictions, advertisements for 'the amazing Hillman Imp'

proclaimed 'An Imp for £3/3/0 per week' (3 guineas, or £3.15), stating the conditions as 'Cash Price (Ex. Works) £508/1/3 [£508.06], Initial Payment £101/12/3 [£101.61] and 36 monthly payments of £13/16/7 [£13.83]', which meant the buyer would pay over £600 in total, but have a shiny new car for a sixth of this. Recalling how low interest rates were, this was an expensive way to purchase one's Imp, and of course the buyer was not the owner until the final monthly payment had been made – the car would be repossessed if a payment was missed.

Such were the pricing conventions; 'ex-works' meant just that, not that anyone at Linwood would expect the buyer to call to collect the car, with additional payments added at the point of sale. Such payments comprised 'delivery', number-plates, seatbelts, and any accessories, whether you had requested them or not. No wonder there were cries of protest when some importers, mainly Japanese, changed the expectations of the public once their cars, replete with 'extras', appeared and were priced with all these included – they even threw in a radio.

Once the decision to produce the Imp was made, it was also decided that it would be

Irresistible Imp

Rootes Motors told its customers:

Here's full-size family motoring with real performance, reliability and <u>superb</u> <u>economy</u>

And followed this with the same six frequently used points:

★ **Takes four without squash, fuss or effort**
IMP's a roomy car. Easily takes four adults – with luggage – in extreme comfort. Lift the back window and fold down rear seat for estate-car luggage facilities. Wind-up windows and wide visibility add to IMP's overall comfort and safety.

★ **Outstanding fuel economy and low service costs**
Touring consumption of 40–45 m.p.g. (higher still with careful driving). Motoring costs down, but ROOTES high standards of quality maintained. IMP needs no greasing; routine service once every 5,000 miles.

★ **Superb traction under all Road Conditions**
Get an IMP on ice, and you'll soon see what light-weight rear-engine advantage really is. Balanced weight distribution over all four twelve-inch wheels. No slither, no drag. First-class roadholding.

★ **Acceleration that puts others in the rear-view mirror**
875 c.c. From a standing start to 50 m.p.h. in 15 seconds (even a Grand Prix racing driver wouldn't scoff at that). Up to 80 m.p.h.

★ **Safety in Suspension – safety in Braking**
IMP independent suspension provides the most secure and comfortable ride you've ever come across. And with it, big brakes which take the strain of hard braking without any sign of fade.

★ **Aluminium Overhead Cam engine, all-synchromesh gears**
IMP's engine was designed to give really high performance, economically, and to take punishment without wear or whimper. Effortless control at all speeds and 4-speed all-synchromesh gearbox for fast, smooth changes.

To inform the buyer of the Deluxe's appointments: IMP de Luxe has heater and unique 'thru-flow' ventilation, screen-washers, opening quarter lights, four stowage pockets, fully-carpeted floor, twin sunvisors, safety belt anchorage points all included. Whitewall tyres, over-riders and wheel trim discs available as extras.

The sectioned view of the Mark I
Hillman Imp Deluxe is seen here.

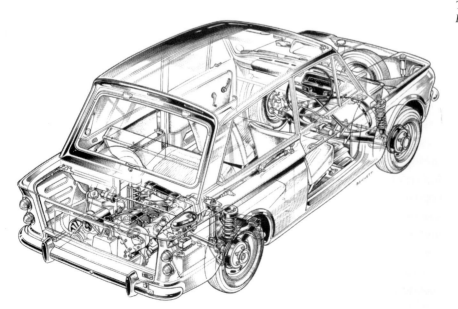

The ageless quality of Bob Saward's styling made the Deluxe Imp an acceptable car for daily motoring. This well-preserved example is going to have to have a new sticker in the rear window to change the 35 to 40, as this photograph was taken at the Imp's fortieth birthday.

marketed under the various Rootes marques, with the separate car divisions being represented by the type of Imp that was most suitable. Hillman, Singer, Humber, Sunbeam, and the commercial Commer were to wear the Imp imprimatur for the different body styles, levels of trim and performance. There would be the basic three-box saloon/sedan shape, an estate, van, pick-up, fast-back or coupé, and a sports car; with some of these further refined for special purchase, such as fleet and police cars (of which two did go into service in the Highlands of Scotland). Humber would not adorn an Imp, and the sports car and pick-up never matured beyond the prototype and concept stages respectively. Perhaps the cancelled automatic gearbox might have been used in a Humber, although they were intended for the Sunbeam Imp Sportsedan, which was the wrong image to offer the North American buyer of a 'four-on-the-floor' – even if all four gears were equipped with synchromesh. All the variant models of the Imp would be in the future; the corporate minds had been concentrating on launching the Hillman Imp.

The truly basic Imp was the Saloon: tech-nically, without a heater, screen washer, passenger sunvisor, opening quarter-lights, side stowage pockets, the air extractor above the rear window (advertised as 'thru-flow' ventilation) and having to make do with rubberized flooring, rather than carpeting. On the earlier cars, headlamp flasher and safety-belt anchor points were only advertised as fitted to the Deluxe, with whitewall tyres, over-riders, and wheel-trims being available as extras. Theoretically at least, one had to buy the Deluxe version to get most of these, and this model was frequently delivered with essential 'extras' such as a water temperature gauge and heater-blower fan. Because of overheating problems, later examples would have the oil-pressure warning light also serving duty as a warning of overheating, through a temperature switch fitted next to the thermostat housing, activated if the temperature reached 106°C. The thinking was that if the warning light came on, the driver needed to stop quickly, then establish the malfunction. The author would cite both the heater fan and the optional coolant-temperature gauge as essential, but *Car & Driver* thought the latter 'not a bad investment'. The basic Saloon was more of a marketing exercise than a reality: those that were produced were usually fitted with many of the extras – for example, those who worked in the car assembly block cannot ever recall assembling a heaterless car. These basic models were advertised to stress their value for money. When the buyer was to tread down the pile of the car-salesman's office carpet, he would be presented with an invoice that had under 'consideration' the separately charged extras (inbuilt at the factory, along with the car). Should a customer want to be obstreperous and insisted purchasing a model without the extras, then an unacceptably long time for delivery occurred. The heater was an optional accessory for the completely knocked down kits of the Australian market, and it is reported that most Imps were assembled without. The admittedly somewhat better-equipped Saloon that was reintroduced in 1969 was sold, for £570, under the banner of 'Rootes Value Year – 1970', making it the cheapest British family car.

So, What's It Like?

The press reception was rapturous applause, with many plaudits being handed out to both designers and manufacturer. A group of journalists went to a Glenalmond Imp preview,

enabling them to augment news stories about the factory with impressions of the car. Typical was that of *Motor*, for whom the Imp

> aroused nothing short of enthusiasm among most of our staff, those who drove it farthest being the most enthusiastic . . . From the driver's point of view the Imp is a most attractive car. All the major controls are remarkably light and precise and the gearchange is perhaps the best we have ever tried.

The magazine assuaged its readers' prejudices about rear-engined cars and stated that 'the Imp is extremely safe and will corner at speeds which are altogether unusual by saloon car standards without exhibiting any vices'; it also reported that at a constant 30mph they achieved a remarkable 62mpg.

Car & Driver's international perspective on the Imp was, 'The hitherto reactionary Rootes Group . . . has been responsible for launching some pretty lacklustre cars, but has more than redeemed itself with the aptly named Imp.' While not being over-impressed with the 'kerb weight', *Car & Driver* attributed this to the gauge of the panels, continuing: 'The whole shebang [engine], complete with accessories, weighs 170lb [76kg] (the Volkswagen's is almost 250 [112kg]). The transmis-

The engine compartment of the Mark I Imp is seen here, with the radiator, water pump and dynamo (top) on the left-hand side, and showing the inclined fitment of the engine; further to the right are the carburettor (here with pneumatic throttle), air cleaner and the battery on the far right.

It is interesting to compare the rear of the Mark I Deluxe Imp here with Bob Saward's 'Final Viewing'. The opening rear window and lock are clearly similar, although more elegant hinges were finally used. The three ventilation slots are now above the rear window and the final version of Saward's engine ventilation is above where the number-plate will go. The operating handles for the engine cover have been rotated through 180 degrees since all model stages, and the hole in the bumper is for the small starting handle.

Jim Pollard hands over to Chief Constable John (Bob) Allan of the Dumbartonshire Force the first of two police Imps for use on its Loch Lomond patrols. These had their rear seats removed to enable the patrols to carry the necessary rescue equipment. They were also the very first Imps to be fitted with an alternator, which charged a very much larger-capacity battery.

sion weighs only 65lb [29kg].' It concludes, 'Whatever its destiny, it is certainly the best car Rootes ever made, a Great Leap Forward from their old-fashioned 1,600cc cars, and a veritable mechanical miracle at a time when their designs were in danger of stagnation.' These views concurred with *Road & Track*'s opinion of Rootes: 'Although doing well in export sales, [they] were really oriented towards the middle-class home market. They are . . . about as English an automobile as one could find.' These accorded with early conclusions from Britain; with a fallacious final opinion, *The Sporting Motorist* thought, 'The Rootes Group deserves admiration for putting its head into the lion's mouth and congratulation for the manner in which it has done it. It remains a matter for speculation as to whether the head will be bitten off: we believe not.'

Small details apart, revealing foibles of individual cars or testers, the reports were glowing

for the Imp's innovative features, and in concordance with Jim Pollard's view that there was 'more of interest on that little car than any other I have seen'. Could anything go wrong after this superb reception? The one enormous problem not apparent to testers being wined and dined by Lord Rootes was: where were the cars for the public to buy? There was a shortage, but Linwood was attempting to manufacture as many as it could – dangerous with a new model. Linwood could produce a new Imp every two minutes, and Pollard claims this could have been one a minute. As if the quality control was not difficult enough, there was that dangerously large amount of bought-out English components.

Cars were finding their way to the dealer's forecourts or higher – larger outlets presented their new models on the garage roof, to be seen by passing motorists. This was not a new ploy, as the first post-war new car in Orkney

When advertising its new Hillman Imp, a Rootes dealer, the Phoenix Garage in Vale Road, Sutton, invites passing motorists to 'Take it away and test it!' It is not clear whether or not this is separate from the self-drive Rootes Hire business it also advertises. It is some time since a BP filling station could confidently advertise its service and supply 'Everything for the Motorist'.

In an age before the hatchback format, additional to getting the luggage-capacity message across to the public, Rootes had to try to educate the potential purchaser of the advantages of opening a window that had been traditionally fixed. I know a female owner today who cannot load bags behind the rear seat of her Imp without thinking that she is acting out this advertisement!

was from Rootes and arrived by helicopter. The cars were available, the excellent Rootes publicity machine accelerated, the partisan motoring press had eulogized, success must now be guaranteed. Michael Young (later Lord Young of Dartington), a sociologist whose academic work was well recognized, also realized society was changing in egalitarian ways and was ploughing ahead with the Consumers' Association and its members' magazine, *Which?*. This was the period prior to motoring journals like *Car* having test vehicles withheld from them because they had written a critical review of another model from the withholding manufacturer. The disinterested *Which?* magazine had a supplementary issue, *Motoring Which?*: this was to compare a very early example of Imp (£538) against alternative cars – Ford's Anglia (£556) and the British Motor Corporation's Super version of the Mini-Car (£493). The results of its comparative test were published in the October 1963 supplement. These novel comparisons would not have been as influential had they only been read by the membership; however, the tests were reported in Radio 4's morning broadcasts.

Motoring Which? found the Imp praiseworthy, and it proved to be the fastest of the trio, with good roadholding and the best-handling

car on test, as was its gear-change, and economy – an apologia for the designers and the testing/modification regime. The top speed was 85mph (136km/h), described in the article, with their normal oblique, but laconic, style: 'The manufacturer's claim of 75 mph [120km/h] was refreshingly modest'! The car was easy to drive with 'light and positive' steering as 'The Imp . . . needed an effort [for parking] of only 15lb [6.7kg] – one of the lowest figures we have recorded.' And the pedals were certainly far superior to 'the small cramped controls in the BMC Mini-Car', with 'This set of dashboard controls was one of the best of any car we have tested.' On the move, *Which?* expressed the view that the ride was 'as good as some of the large cars we have tested' and the car was equipped with 'one of the best gear-changes we have tested'. This test picked out: 'The de-luxe model came with a heater as standard equipment, but you have to pay £5 6s [£5.30] extra to get a blower fitted', although it did appreciate the luxury of the carpeted interior at no extra cost and thought the optional starting handle at £2 2s 6d (£2.13) a useful extra and the automatic choke intriguing. As one might expect, the review contained some minor criticisms: the Imp was more affected by side-winds than the competition, it found the brakes light enough from

93

speed, but too prone to fading and heavy when it came to gentle application, and thought that no lockable 'glove box' was out of character with the rest of the interior. *Which?* also alerted its readership to the warning in the handbook to turn off the air intake in traffic.

Alas, buried among *Motoring Which?* magazine's far greater-detailed test than one might find today was a consumers' report on the products it purchased: which car was the best value for money and could it recommend it to its readers? Its answer to the former suggested the Imp was the best car of this test, but then, with more empathy with the manufacturer than *Which?* was noted for, 'It would perhaps have been naïve of us to have expected completely trouble-free service from a car of new design, made in a new factory. And we certainly did not get it in the first 6,000 miles, the most important replacements being two gearboxes and two replacements of most of the throttle linkage.' Following this rectification work, the test car proved to be reliable, but *Which?* was puzzled at the disappearance of the coolant for no apparent reason. *Motoring Which?* even summed up with praise for the way in which Rootes Motors was dealing with its warrantees: 'What conclusions can we draw from this? It is really rather difficult to say anything except that the car had weaknesses and the manufacturer is trying to do something about at least some of them.' It was admitted that the Imp was superior to the competition in acceleration, top speed, hill climbing, some internal dimensions, handling, ride, driving controls and load-carrying versatility, but it found itself unable to recommend the Imp, with the damning sentence:

We wish we could be more enthusiastic about the immediate prospects for its reliability . . . But if these disadvantages do not deter you, the Hillman Imp seems to us to offer pretty good value for money as a practical small car which is pleasant to drive and gives unusually good performance, economically.

Autocar and *Motor*, both having dropped the definite article from their titles, treated the Imp to long-term tests. They did not experience greater reliability, but were kinder in their published findings – *Autocar* saying that, despite the number of faults, it still liked the Imp, and praised Rootes for dealing with the multiplicity of problems. Both these test Imps were 1963 cars, but ones that incorporated some of the immediate improvements following the welter of problems that might not have been evident to the bystanding giraffes of Africa, but were becoming recognized by Mr or Ms J. Public in suburbia. *Autocar's* list of maladies with its Imp could be said to be many and various, but seen in the light of the emerging pattern of warranty claims, they were predictable. Overheating, of prominence in *Autocar's* recounting of its Imp ownership, caused its car to be dispatched to Ryton for inspection and the replacement of radiator pressure cap, engine head-gasket, camshaft tappet block, water pump, carburettor, ignition coil, transaxle, clutch, dynamo and radiator. No other cooling faults occurred, but yet another gearbox was fitted. Interestingly, despite Rootes increasing the height of the front, the front headlights were found to be ½in (12mm) below the legal minimum height of 24in (610mm). The remarkably few negative aspects were not unlike those mentioned in other tests: the brakes were described as 'only fair', similar to *Motor's* 'can best be described as unobtrusive', the ultra-light clutch proved too sensitive, and the versatility of the opening rear window was let down by the vast quantities of water it shipped – water ingress would remain one of the unresolved complaints of owners and testers.

Motor's long-term test car also exhibited early Imp failings concerning coolant loss, the automatic choke and unpredictable performance; once modified parts were fitted, the car continued to be fortuitously reliable. Alas, in the general public's mind, the damage had been done and it would take a very long time for people to be dissuaded of their prejudices against the Imp.

There were attempts to make the Imp more Swinging-Sixties chic. History has been kind and not passed on the interior designer's name for this matching luggage with door and under-dash trim idea.

Here we see another car with a similar style of door trim. A similar concoction of flower power was tried on the whole interior fabric.

Easier as being the first small British mass-produced car, the Mini was perceived as being synchronous with the *Zeitgeist*, having a functional simplicity that offered the purchaser a classless chic air; and as the 1960s progressed, there would be no shortage of minor celebrities who would be seen in their trendy Minis. Semiologists might suggest that 'mini' was a far more powerfully persuasive message to the 1960s – on a technological level, small was new and beautiful, while on the more frivolous level, when combined with 'skirt', thanks to Mary Quant and Courrèges, it conjured up the idea of young and beautiful! (The Imp has escaped such semiological attentions, but the mind boggles as to what conclusions feminist semiologists came to with regard to the Minx!) All manner of 'muttering-rotters' could hone their journalistic skills with well-argued cases for why the Imp was the more interesting, better performing, and more useful car, but this was to fly in the face of fashion – and fashion and being fashionable was the profundity that was the 1960s. Under headlines like 'New Imp is ready to do battle', the *Australian Motor Sports* could propose, 'If you think the Mini is an amazing little car, just wait until you see the Hillman Imp.' Their readers did – then went and purchased the Mini; after all,

celebrities drove one when their chauffeurs had the day off and the exotic vehicle was being repaired.

Getting it right

The Quality Control department at Linwood was in its infancy and required fine tuning; it achieved a high level of build with commendable speed, even giving function tests and inspections to entire cars and dispatching assemblies to Ryton for assessment. This was essential if the cost of warranty claims was not to dwarf the carefully calculated profits that the Imp was realizing. What was becoming apparent was that the problems of controlling the quality of the many bought-out parts was more difficult than rectifying shortcomings in the quality of those of Rootes' own manufacture. The bought-out components did not reflect well on the suppliers. One such problem concerned the brakes: swarf had not been cleaned from the brake master-cylinder body – easy to rectify, but it caused over six thousand cars to be recalled.

The pneumatic throttle activation was wonderful, but when it did not work it was extremely troublesome. Its main point of failure was leaks when the plastic pipework touched hotter items near the engine. Before the decision to replace it with the conventional was taken, a whole series of new problems was traced to its supplier, Dunlop, having simplified the activation units for cost reasons and without consultation. Pneumatic control was developed to overcome problems associated with cable runs to the rear of the car, and the replacement Bowden cable offered the designers an apologia for their concerns: it obliged though remaining far from unproblematic. Transfer from pneumatic to orthodox control was achieved, without hitch, overnight.

Not all the changes were caused by production difficulties, whether within or outwith Linwood. The automatic choke was deleted and replaced with a conventional Bowden cable. Through operating this from a floor-mounted lever in front of the handbrake, at least some of the more tortuous layout from the dashboard was circumvented. Those who have seen the archive film footage of the electromechanical indicator switches being abused by the testing rigs might deduce that if these switches survived this maltreatment, then they would outlive any car – but this proved far from true. This could be said for the sealed-for-life PTFE or Teflon kingpin bushes – frequently their lives were unacceptably brief. The Ryton testing regime had nearly perfected other parts, but service in the real world would reveal the need for further development. The transaxle was starting to develop a reputation for general fragility: the selector forks required more surface hardening than they received, and because of the generally imprecise assembly of the casing, the lubricant had a tendency to seep out. The gearbox baulk rings proved to be too fragile, and the specification of some gearbox bearings fell short.

There had been a lot of development concerning the durability and aerodynamics of the huge engine fan. The durability was impeccable, but development work continued to both the stator and rotor blades to increase the airflow and reduce noise. Multitudinous small changes were made in the light of experience:

The canister sticking downwards from the underside of the Solex carburettor is the still-functioning Dunlop activator unit for the pneumatic throttle of Imp 669 KOE. However, the automatic choke operation has given way to a Bowden cable.

the brake-linings were considered too harsh and noisy, a stiffener and two small stays were added to the body-pressing to alleviate the instrument-panel shake, and fitting an under-tray between the sump and the silencer was necessary. Other small modifications included preventing the carburettor flooding through lowering the fuel level, rejetting and eliminating some of the troublesome 'flat' spots at the expense of reducing the potential performance at full throttle. The following year, *Motoring Which?* was to complain, 'The performance of the Imp, remarkably good when we tested our first car, has been reduced by modifications, particularly to the carburettor.' It was presumed it was the varying gas-flow in the different cars that caused different reviewers to publish disparate performance figures. The clutch, thought beautifully light by many, but far too sensitive by others, was enlarged.

The three main Imp body styles: Ron Wisdom's coupé Sunbeam Stiletto and estate Hillman Husky with Bob Saward's original saloon Deluxe – Frosty the horse looks on.

Hillman Husky late Mark II. The large windows and higher roofline make this a very light and airy Imp as well as being an extremely versatile workhorse.

Commer van Mark I being put to its intended agricultural use. The traditional financial prudence of the small farmer extends to the sack truck in use here!

Sunbeam Imp Stiletto – the top-of-the-range coupé version that offered performance to match its looks.

An early Mark I Hillman Imp Deluxe that is tastefully restored and in use. The unadorned simplicity of this period, with only a single trim strip along the waist-line, adds to its appeal. The wing mirrors are a period accessory but the wheels painted in this way are original.

The original Mark I interior displays the successful compromise between the original minimalist concepts of Parkes & Fry and the later thoughts of practicality. This car, which still has an operational pneumatic throttle, benefits from the optional water temperature gauge and has had auxiliary switches fitted to the painted dashboard. The parcel shelf is completely open.

A metallic blue Imp Deluxe Saloon, one of the last from the final year of production. The Dunlop alloy wheels were an optional extra and Tim Fry of Smallfry contributed to their design.

The Sport saloon gained quadruple headlights with metal surrounds (the owner has had these chromium plated). The fragile hubcaps are original as is the red embellishing strip between the double waist-line trim strips (black on lesser models).

The profile of the Singer Chamois Coupé Mark I reveals the lower roof line and altered angle of the front windscreen. The car has the usual Chamois fittings, including these wheel embellishers.

INSPIRATION IN LIGHT CAR DESIGN

HILLMAN
IMP

ROOTES SERVICE

BUILT BY ROOTES (SCOTLAND) LIMITED

Typical of the art-work and illustrations of the period, as applied to the Mark I Imp; both red and white are Deluxe examples.

The five stainless-steel strips that were first used on the Chamois which greatly increase the functionality of the opening rear window. Items can be placed on these prior to loading without them scratching the paintwork.

The badging of the original Commer Imp van. Its commercial ancestry is reflected by the two set-screws at each end of the name badge that are utilized to affix it to the bonnet.

The final version of the Sport badge. Some cars only displayed one of these on the rear off-side wing.

Close-up of the gold pentastar that reveals the involvement of Chrysler. This only appeared on the front nearside of most cars. As well as the difficulty of the fragility of these hub-caps, they are held in place with strong springs that scratch the painted wheels.

Front panel of the Sunbeam Stiletto, revealing its swivel badge that gives access to the key-operated bonnet lock. All cars with protruding front badges operate in this way, others with flush badges have the bonnet release connected to a Bowden cable that runs into the passenger compartment.

A contemporaneous tourist picture-postcard from Orkney of Churchill Barrier No. 2 looking north-easterly from Glimpsholm towards Lambholm that also featured a locally registered Imp.

The same barrier forty years later; the sea of the Pentland Firth has moved many of the stones and armco barriers now prevent this local Singer Chamois from taking a dip.

The Mark II Singer Chamois dashboard, a combination of high quality walnut veneer, vinyl and painted metal. It has a lockable glove box, oil pressure gauge (the adjacent badge is a blanking plate for a clock) with the heater/air distribution controls below, and the rubber windscreen washer bulb can be seen to the left of the steering wheel.

entirely new in conception and design

NEW HILLMAN IMP

Bright red seats with rather thin backs furnish this early Mark I Imp. The extra luggage room behind the rear seat can be seen, as can the fore and aft oddment bins.

THE WORLD'S MOST ADVANCED LIGHT CAR

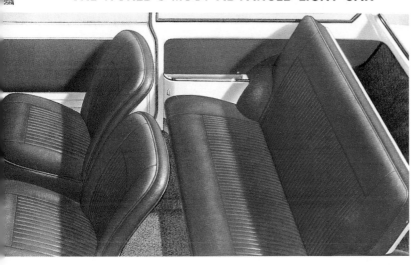

The final stages of building the Imp: cleaning, polishing and detail rectification on Linwood's 'car finishing conveyor'.

Imp bodies, resplendent in their new paint and already glazed, advance on the Pressed Steel conveyor to the Trim Shop.

The most northerly British Imp in daily use, a Singer Chamois Mark I seen on the runway of Westray airport on the first day of the new millennium. The original pastiche radiator grille is deeper than on later variants – whichever way up it is used.

To appropriate Alan Bennett's title, Forty Years On! *A selection of the many Imps that returned to Humber Road for the fortieth birthday celebrations of the Imp Club on 3 May 2003.*

Also following customer reaction, the hand-brake lever was given more clearance.

The cooling system was a real Achilles heel of the Imp, with little margin of safety. The slightest coolant leak would deplete the system sufficiently for serious overheating to occur, and as sure as night follows day, the owner would experience comprehensive damage to the engine. Raising the pressure of the coolant system through fitting a higher-pressure radiator cap to increase the coolant's boiling point might have alleviated the problem of the coolant boiling, but this also increased the engine's proclivity for finding weaknesses in its continence. Increasing the number of blades on the fan assisted the engine's cooling, at the expense of adding to the noise it made and the power it absorbed. The sealing of the cylinder-head gasket was frequently problematic, especially as an aluminium-alloy engine and head were more prone to distortion when mal-treated, but it was the water pump that again was the main culprit. How had this survived the snows of Canada and the heat of Africa? It did not leak at high or low engine speeds, but at just over 2,000rpm it frequently exhibited a small dribble – unfortunately, this represented town-driving speeds. Rootes did inspect pumps that had failed under warranty, and it was not short of exhibits, which led to an improvement in this troublesome part. This revised water pump had small holes at each end of the body so as to allow any coolant that seeped past the impeller shaft's seals to leak away before bathing the shaft's bearings in coolant. The seals were assisted by dished washers on the inner side of the bearings, but the constant evolution of the cooling system, and the water pump in particular, would feature for years in the company's Service Bulletins. The new dual-purpose warning light was added to the display to warn of trouble.

Through the CKD outlets and other exports, Rootes gained feedback of the specific problems of individual markets. Most of the warranty claims from overseas were all too familiar to Linwood, but one that led to changes for 'dusty' markets was first discovered in Australia: over unsuitable terrain, certain driving conditions could provoke a positive sandstorm for the carburettor to inhale. The resolution of this problem was to place the air intake on the side panels immediately behind the doors, and a car that is found with this today is revealing its original birthplace.

Both the public in general and many garages were unfamiliar with aluminium-alloy engines or overhead camshafts. This would lead to the car's already poor reliability being exacerbated. It was a new idea for the owner of a mass-produced car to check that an antifreeze was compatible with the metallurgy of the engine, and it was novel to use this during the summer months. The anti-corrosive additives in the antifreeze were essential to the engine's longevity, and the resultant accelerated corrosion from the lack of these additives led to an even higher rate of head-gasket failures. Those more familiar with today's cars have probably forgotten how regularly one had to top up the coolant on all cars of the period that were without sealed overflow or expansion tanks.

The other problem that was self-inflicted on the car's reliability by owners who did their own repairs and some garages was the lack of use of a torque wrench when tightening up bolts. To many, this was seen as being over-fussy, as how much force to apply to a bolt was part of the black art of getting the 'feel' just right. This might have been sufficient when working on iron blocks and cases (and it is certainly not far wrong when using standard imperial spanners with BSF threads), but it is disastrous with lightweight alloys. The do-it-yourself motoring magazines quickly tried to educate Imp owners in the peculiar ways of their cars, but if anything this only contributed to a perception that the Imp was just a difficult car. There was also a pretty steep learning curve when it came to adjusting the valve clearances on the engine, even if this task had become an infrequent one. The owner or mechanic had to measure both the clearance and the operating shims very accurately and

The Singer Chamois would be the last launch of any Rootes Motors car where the entire family would be present. This photograph, taken at Devonshire House, is also thought to be the last of the assembled family. Left to right: Geoffrey Rootes, Sir Reginald, Lord Rootes, Timothy Rootes and Brian Rootes.

then have a stock of these shims in different thicknesses – the temptation to leave well alone was overwhelming for some.

From Hillman to Singer

Leaving aside a consideration of the general financial well-being of Rootes until the next chapter, the company remained solvent and would further develop the reliability of the Imp along with investigating other versions of it. Through default, all of the pre-September 1965 Imps would be classified as the 'Mark I' model – which like a composer's symphonies, only becomes thus entitled retrospectively on the appearance of Number 2. Rootes felt confident enough to launch the first of its planned derivatives on the original theme – the Singer Chamois. It still had the format of the three-box saloon, but this time it was a more upmarket version – like many first variations, the theme was receiving delicate ornamentation, rather than structural development. The

Singer Chamois of October 1964 was an attempt to address a market slot that had been created by similar upmarket minis – the Riley Elf and Wolseley Hornet – greatly surpassing either of these.

At £581 11s 3d (£581.56), this mountain antelope might be 'the new light car in the luxury class', but it was not cheap. In addition to targeting this stratum of the market it also addressed some of the reservations of the more traditional Rootes customer through persuading him or her that a less racy and somewhat more sybaritic motoring lifestyle could be enjoyed in an Imp if it were behind a Singer badge. In addition to the added comforts of the Deluxe model, the Chamois offered the driver the consoling comfort of walnut-veneered cappings to the doors as well as the dashboard, and it now came with the requested lockable glove box – for a car in this price bracket, the matched veneering was of an extremely high quality, something that should be taken into account when planning

today to restore it to its original appearance. The Chamois also offered its buyer somewhat more commodious seating that was thicker, lower-mounted, and trimmed in 'two-way stretch, fusion-blown p.v.c.' (usually with transverse quasi-fluting), as well as using more sound-deadening material. To enhance the feeling of well-being, coolant-temperature and oil-pressure gauges assured the driver that the engine was not misbehaving, and a standard heater-blower dealt with a driver who was underheated – again, something that was not apparent during testing, but without the ram effect of spirited driving, little air entered the cabin. The positioning of the Imp's heater controls below the centre of the dashboard was devised before the wearing of static seat-belts became a statutory requirement, and to place the oil-pressure gauge in a similar place was hardly ergonomic, as was the blanking plate for the optional clock. To borrow a phrase from another manufacturer, the walnut veneer was 'real tree wood' – although this situation would not endure to the end of the Chamois' run – curiously, leather seats, that other great comforter of the English gentleman, were never offered as an option. It is not known if this is where the idea emanated, but as early as 1963 *Autocar* was carrying advertisements to 'Add to the magic of your Imp' through fitting a number of accessories, including a 'walnut-veneered dashboard with a glove compartment lid and door fillets, etc.'.

The Chamois name would continue to be used to indicate most of these features on later types of Imp.

From the outside of the Chamois, the Joneses next door realized one had eschewed the ostentatious with a car that was offered in more sober colours, and sported an imitation front radiator grille, over-riders, wheel trims, and a double stainless-steel coachline-trim with a light-painted flash in between. A touch that enhanced the functionality of the opening rear window was the addition of five stainless-steel trim strips to the rear-engine cover, allowing shopping to be placed on the engine cover prior to loading. The standardized engine, running gear and suspension were utilized, although revised. Most Chamois models were supplied with modern Dunlop SP41 radial-ply tyres – although these were usually fitted to the half-inch wider wheel rims of four and a half inches with a 'J' profile. The Singer Chamois rewarded Rootes through being a popular choice with buyers, and it accounted for almost a third of Imp sales in the following year – was this the traditional middle classes raising their cheque books, if not their heads?

Most of the reviewers spoke favourably of the Singer Chamois, but when testing a later version of the car, *Motoring Which?* felt it incumbent upon itself to warn the middle classes not to be parted from their wealth. It was only worth the extra expenditure if the reader wanted the walnut, otherwise 'on its current reliability form, the best buy in the mini class is the Hillman Imp' – though only if the extra was paid for the optional radial-ply tyres. Probably because it eschewed such thoughts itself, or because it felt that the consumer required re-education, *Which?* seems to have overlooked the reality of selling cars – visual opulence sold well. *Speed World International's* reviewer, before making the positive statements quoted elsewhere about the Imp replacing the Mini as the smart car to own, laments his experiences with his early Chamois, which he loved driving, while not being responsible for its upkeep, although he goes on to opine: 'For my money the Imp is still the only small saloon that has ever made the rear-engined arrangement work.'

Other Ideas

In addition to the development of the Imp which was necessitated by urgent remedial measures, a number of ideas were being investigated to broaden the model's appeal. Some of these would reach fruition, while others would become moribund for various reasons – usually because of ongoing development costs or the realization that the company was not sufficiently awash with spare cash to fund the high production-engineering cost. One of the most interesting – and its failure to reach realization would affect both European urban sales

and the North American market – was an automatic transmission saloon. There is a 'Project Intention' of May 1964 described as, 'The origin comes from a request from Lord Rootes for a cheap automatic transmission for the Hillman Imp for the USA market', and this should not be confused with the later project which became known as the 'Ferodo Imp'. This project intention expressed an optimistic timetable: pre-production within two months and production by October. Time was of the essence, as the rebadged Imp, the Sunbeam Imp Sportsedan, was being targeted at the American market and Lord Rootes knew the dollar-riches that could be generated there.

The ingenious proposal was to use the standard 875cc engine, but to couple this to the transmission through either the novel Smiths Industries electromagnetic, powder-type coupling or the Borg Shift hydraulic servo clutch made by Borg-Warner. In the case of the latter type, the engine's oil pressure would operate the servo mechanism. (Five years earlier, the Rootes Group had claimed that the Minx, fitted with a Smiths Industries Easidrive electromagnetic system was the first and smallest British car to be offered with automatic gear-selection.) The gearbox was a modification of the standard Imp unit. The synchromeshing of the gears was achieved either through the development, with Borg-Warner, of its own system or the adoption of a Porsche-type. The

Jim Pollard borrows (officially 'tests'!) the first production Singer Chamois to come off the Linwood assembly line.

Looking like the specification of an NAS (North American Specification) car, complete with over- and under-riders, these cars were sold as Hillman Imp 'Spring Specials' on the home market – thereby using up some of the NAS Sunbeam Sportsedan parts.

intention was to make this a fully automatic gearbox operated by a rotary switch and/or push buttons, but there was discussion as to whether it also should have the option of manual control via a self-centering [*sic*] 'flick' lever. The rear suspension cross–member required modification to provide more space, otherwise no changes were anticipated other than 'a script will be required to denote the car is "Automatic"'. In addition to the general design, development and testing by Ryton's Engineering Division, three cars were to be prepared – a 'Porsche conversion', 'IMP conversion with Smiths coupling', and 'IMP car with . . . "Borg Shift" coupling'; this last car was to be supplied and prepared by Ryton for Borg-Warner. It remains unclear today which, or how many, of these prototypes were produced. It is assumed that at least one version progressed as far as a working prototype, as there are a number of tales surrounding someone of importance within the company finding himself marooned with an example that could not be moved – a parking pawl had

been added, and this could jam if the car was parked in a confined space.

With the accompanying blaze of publicity, but without the automatic gearbox, the American market was targeted with its rebadged Imp. Citing its first American customer, the expatriate actor Cary Grant, Rootes hoped that the Sunbeam Sportsedan might enjoy the almost cult status that Volkswagen's Beetle was achieving. Imp production had now doubled to two thousand per week, with half of this going for export. The American reviews of the Sunbeam were a mixture of ecstatic and bewildered – the concentration being on the former. Although not difficult to surpass the American norm of the time, reviewers and test drivers alike responded to all those attributes that Parkes and Fry had fought to preserve in their fun car. While the Sportsedan was not without American support, it fell far short of the hoped-for sales, with Linwood not completing later orders but finishing them for home consumption to be sold as bargain Spring Specials. By 1966/7, the demand had

Bob Saward (left) and Ron Wisdom, soberly dressed, await a Rootes family viewing of the Sunbeam Asp full-scale model in open form. The smaller-scale model in the background has the hard-top fitted. Many Humber Road styling studio photographs also feature the 'No Way Out' door to the lavatory and the electric radiator (just visible above the engine compartment)!

atrophied, and so, combined with proposed American safety and environmental legislation, this market no longer possessed the attraction it once had for the company – perhaps it would have done had the Asp ever gone into production.

A two-seater sports car, code-named Apex-B2, but better known as the Asp, was based upon the Imp and was one of the variants that reached the prototype stage. Following the successful completion of the pre-production stages of the Imp, Mike Parkes had left the Rootes Group for the sunnier climes of Italy, whilst Bob Saward would move on to Ford, and the design of the embryonic sports car was in the capable hands of Tim Fry, with Ron Wisdom taking care of the final styling touches, which had been virtually completed by Saward. In the manner of many of the third-party Imp-based sports cars, the Asp was of light weight and good aerodynamic shape, and had it gone into production, would probably have used a glass-reinforced-plastic body over a steel frame. It would appear that A. Craig Miller, the chief engineer, initiated discussion of this variant before the Imp testing was complete and the possibility of Jensen Motors manufacturing the Asp had been assessed. As well as the Volvo P1800, Jensen assembled the Sunbeam Tiger for the Rootes Group – it appears that the consultant

designer, Tom Killeen, was involved from the Jensen Motors side, as he was with Fraser's Imp-based K-9 sports car.

Saward and Wisdom produced clay models of both convertible and hard-top versions before a prototype steel-panelled body was fabricated by Williams and Pritchard, North London; this was open-bodied, but with a substantial hard-top. This firm also received the commission to produce the glass-reinforced-plastic moulds that would be needed for the future bodies, but whether it progressed that far is a matter of conjecture. The Imp's suspension was retained and the car was furnished with vacuum-operated pop-up headlamps of Fry's design. The prototype Asp was powered by the 998cc linerless experimental engine in which the pistons ran directly in the aluminium-alloy cylinder bores, and not only did this prove to be fast, it also did not experience the rapid wear that had been anticipated. With large air intakes on the bonnet, the Asp was taken by many to have the engine mounted in the front, whereas it was the capacious radiator that the front housed, the engine being in the conventional rear. Tim Fry reports that it had a top speed of 105–06mph and really did go 'like a rocket', and handled very well indeed. Having spent several years developing this outstanding small sports car, in the words of Fry: 'The Yanks came in and said, "What do you want to make a silly little car like that for?" That was the end of it. The Americans went on to buy thousands of Spitfires and Midgets – it would have sold well.' It is often cited that the body moulds were disposed of to the Alan Fraser racing team, who were going to produce further versions, but this is to confuse the Asp with Fraser's K-9 and his CUB project – it seems unlikely that any moulds were produced for the Asp. Rootes only made the one, all-steel prototype that is said to survive and has reputedly been seen on the Iberian peninsula. Fraser Racing went on to make at least one glass-reinforced-plastic version of each of its cars which were known to have been tested from 1967 by Ray Calcutt, taking it on an official trial the following year – Alan Fraser has little recollection of these events. Fry also proposed a forward-control van based upon the same frame as the Asp. This type of vehicle might be common now, but at the time Fry never managed to persuade Rootes Motors to progress the idea beyond its conceptual stages.

Another interesting prospect that did not go into production was the Zagato-bodied Imp, the Zimp, that was exhibited at the 1964 Earls Court Motor Show by the British concessionaires for Zagato of Milan. Some enthusiasts, and the author is among their number, think that these three cars are exceptionally appealing, but the board of Rootes Motors did not. Zagato used the Imp floorpan, suspension and running gear, then clothed this with a Super-leggera system of tubular body-frame with aluminium panel-work in its traditional manner.

Just when both the production engineers and the public were hoping that the reliability problems of the Imp were in the past, *Motoring Which?* bought another Mark I Imp to see how it fared. The long-term report was not published until after the model had been superseded by the Mark II, but this January 1966 supplement would scupper any rebuilding that had occurred in the public's mind as to the reliability, finish and durability of the Imp. Unfortunately, the car that the Consumers' Association compared with the larger Vauxhall Viva Mark I predated Linwood's remedial measures, and the history of the experience of its members was drawn from the earliest Imp production.

The dynamics of the car were praised to the

The final full-size model of Apex-B2, or the Asp, is seen prior to construction of the prototype steel-panelled open body with substantial hard-top. The stylists frequently rolled the full-sized clay models out onto the flat roof of the styling studios in Humber Road to compare them with contemporaneous putative competition. Here, the Asp compares more than favourably with a Triumph Spitfire, itself considered rather stylish.

skies: from the 'light and high-geared' steering and the gear-change and transmission, which received its finding, 'By any standards, both were superb,' to the handling, which 'was highly praised by our drivers. Drive the car how you might, it was virtually impossible to lose wheel grip on a dry road, and very difficult to do so on a wet surface.' It was not without detailed criticism of its Imp. There were complaints about road shocks getting through to the driver and the Imp's ability to cope with strong side-winds, it thought the

Described as a 'wide rear seat' by Rootes, both this and the front seats, especially the thickness of the seat backs, would become more sumptuous as the model progressed through its different variants.

If employed as a twin-seat car and the folded rear seat space is utilized, an Imp can carry an astonishingly large amount of luggage. Any owner today will be lucky to find intact the stretch-rubber seat retainers to stop the folded seat back bouncing up and down. The back-projected seascape of the photographic studio is typical of a lot of Rootes photographs of the period.

brakes somewhat lighter this time, but repeated its caution about brake-fade and thought that the headlights did not supply sufficient illumination for the car's performance. After mentioning a few other minor points concerning the heater controls, thinking the sole lock on the driver's door and the lack of underbody protection miserly features, the review identified a persistent problem that Rootes had known about, but had not resolved. 'There was a tendency for exhaust fumes to be drawn into the Imp through the ventilating slots over the back window when the front windows were opened to help ventilation.' After testing Imps at the Motor Industry Research Association's wind-tunnel, the 'Confidential' report of 1964 from Rootes' Experimental Department includes:

The worst condition was found to be, heater closed and vent windows open, when the car is slowed down rapidly. The vent windows being open create a depression inside the car which sucks the exhaust fumes in. Leaks occurred in the following places in order of severity. 1. Opening back-light lock. 2. Rear air extractors. 3. Back-light surround – rubber seal. 4. Door seals on lower edge. 5 Front heater intake.

A larger flow of smoke could be detected passing through the back-light lock. The non-return flaps on the rear air extractors were not functioning correctly. These extractors are wrongly positioned to effect extraction . . . It was noticed that the engine cooling fan sucked the exhaust smoke forward, which brought the exhaust fumes in close contact with the lower edge of the doors and the heater intakes when the car speed is reduced quickly.

It was not the ingesting of exhaust fumes that set the seal, it was the essentials of *Motoring Which?*'s reliability report: here was the evidence that its earlier suspicions had suggested, and it was gathered from 118 members – not at all the sort of broadcast message that goes down well with the morning coffee and

Because it was an unaccustomedly small car for the British market, Rootes went to some length in its publicity shots to show how much luggage could be accommodated – as in the front compartment here. Notice also the white cover (on the front right of the car) of the siamesed reservoir for the brake and clutch fluid and the black petrol filler cap in the corresponding position on the other side. The spare wheel can be extracted without excessively disturbing the luggage.

cereal. 'It is seldom that we have quite such overwhelming evidence of a defect from our members. No fewer than 80 . . . reported water pump failure, and these members have between them gone through 103 pumps . . . so it is no surprise that ours did.' The review continues, 'Our car had some quite severe engine trouble, and faults in the heater, rear brakes and fuel system – including two broken throttle cables.' The members had troubles with poor bodywork, especially the hanging of the doors and rainwater leaks, and they 'also suffered badly from clutch troubles, engine oil leaks, stiff or seized kingpins, and gearbox faults. Nearly half reported failure of the turn indicators.' Rootes had attended to the most pressing shortcomings of the model, but it was difficult to persuade the buying public of that

Reinforcement of the Imp's carrying capabilities has Rootes showing the owner the seven standard items of luggage that could be distributed between the front luggage compartment and the space behind the rear seat. This car has the optional wheel embellishers fitted.

when the history since Day One was being presented in this way. To add insult to injury, *Motoring Which?* produced an inevitable conclusion: 'We would make it a joint Best Buy [with the Vauxhall Viva] if so much had not gone wrong with our car and those of our members.' The populist press was to accuse the Consumers' Association of a bias in favour of mainland European vehicles in its reports, but this does not stand up to investigation. If the Consumers' Association had a 'car agenda', it was predicated on the generally shoddy standards of finish and reliability during this troubled time for all the industry, and therefore the very bad deal British consumers were getting.

Imp Models – Chronology		
Model	*Started*	*Finished*
Hillman Saloon	April? 1963	July 1965
Hillman Imp de luxe	April? 1963	February 1976
Singer Chamois Saloon	July 1964	July 1970
August 1965 Mark II		
(Hillman Imp de luxe Mk II)		
(Singer Chamois Saloon Mk II)		
Hillman & Singer Rally Imp/Chamois	March 1965	November 1965?
Super Imp	August 1965	January? 1976
Commer Van	August 1965	July 1970
Sunbeam Imp Sport	June 1966	March 1970
Singer Chamois Sport	October 1966	December 1969
(Super) Californian	May 1966	July 1970
Singer Chamois Coupé	April 1967	March 1970
Hillman Husky Estate	April 1967	July 1970
Sunbeam Stiletto	October 1967	August 1972
October 68 (Mark III)		
Hillman Standard Saloon	September 1969	January 1976
(Hillman Imp Deluxe)		
(Singer Chamois Saloon)		
(Super Imp)		
(Former-Commer now Hillman Imp Van)		
(Sunbeam Imp Sport)	(Trim downgraded to Super Imp)	February 1976
Sunbeam Sport	April 1970	
(Singer Chamois Sport)		
(Californian)		
(Singer Chamois Coupé)		
(Hillman Husky Estate)		
(Sunbeam Stiletto)		
October 1973		
(Hillman Standard Saloon)		
(Hillman Imp Deluxe)		
(Super Imp)		
(Sunbeam Sport)		
Caledonian	October 1975	February 1976

This press photograph claims to have the rear seat folded to give the customer a better view of what can be placed behind the rear seat, even with it up. It is certainly more than a minor parcel shelf.

William, Lord Rootes, died in December 1964, his elder son, Geoffrey, succeeding to the vacant title. Some suggested that the new Lord Rootes was not sufficient of a chip off the old block. While this is probably so – Geoffrey was too similar in approach to his mentor, Sir Reginald – it is difficult to say that even the old block of William could have done much to resist the overwhelming changes that were overtaking a none-too-flourishing motor industry – Rootes was not alone in its predicament. If I suggested in an earlier chapter that the Rootes brothers rationalized the company far too little and too late, this was certainly the period when the proverbial chickens were coming home to roost – this would continue to blight the Hillman Imp for the remainder of its production, as well as the future prosperity of that brave socio-economic industrial experiment that was Linwood.

Imp Specifications and Dimensions

Model type	Saloon, Coupé, Estate, Van (for individual fitment to models and years, refer to the text)
Layout and chassis	Two-door; four-seater Saloon, Coupé, Estate, and two-seater van; unitary (steel monocoque) construction

Engine

Type	Rootes, based on Coventry Climax Featherweight design
Block material	Aluminium alloy with cast-iron cylinder liners ('dry' liners in most applications, 'wet' in later 998cc units)
Head material	Aluminium alloy
Cylinders	In-line, 4-cylinder
Cooling	Pressurized water-cooled, remote centrifugal pump, fan assisted

Bore and stroke

Standard and Sport engine	67.99 × 60.375mm
Rally	72.542 × 60.375mm

Capacity

Standard and Sport	875cc
Rally	998cc

Crankshaft	Running in three bearings
Camshaft	Single overhead camshaft, simplex-chain drive, running in three white-metal bearings
Valves	8 valves

Mk I:	inlet	1.064in (27.026mm)	exhaust	1.01in (25.654mm)
Mk. II:	inlet	1.202in (30.531mm)	exhaust	1.064in (27.026mm)
Sport engine:	inlet	1.276in (32.41mm)	exhaust	1.064in (27.026mm)
Rally:	inlet	1.276in (32.41mm)	exhaust	1.064in (27.026mm)

Camshaft Valve Lift

Standard Single Carburettor, 10:1 & 8:1 CR	0.2467in (6.2662mm)
Standard Twin Carburettor, Sport	0.3114in (7.9096mm)
Rally	0.3114in (7.9096mm)
R15, R17, R20, R22, R23 Performance Camshaft	0.360in (9.144mm)

(Timing and valve-overlap of performance camshafts varies with type)

Valve Timing

(Valve-timing figures are merely representative due to the number of different camshafts fitted as original equipment, the differing bases for measurement, and the later frequent factory-fitment of Sport camshafts to standard engines. From 1974 on, the Sport camshaft was used in all extant models)

	Inlet Open	Close	Ex. Open	Close
Early Standard Single Carburettor	6° BTDC	46° ABDC	46° BBDC	6° ATDC

(Based upon a nominal clearance of 0.010in (0.254mm) at the cam-lobe face)

	Inlet Open	Close	Ex. Open	Close
Earlier Twin Carburettor, Sport §	23° BTDC	53° ABDC	61° BBDC	15° ATDC
Rally §	23° BTDC	53° ABDC	61° BBDC	15° ATDC

(§ Based upon a nominal clearance of 0.014in (0.3556mm) at the cam-lobe face)

	Inlet Open	Close	Ex. Open	Close
Later Standard Single Carburettor★	36° BTDC	76° ABDC	43° BBDC	3° ATDC
Standard Twin Carburettor, Sport★	67° BTDC	93° ABDC	63° BBDC	13° ATDC

(★ Based upon normal specified running clearances)

Tappet Clearance Cold	Inlet	Exhaust
Mk. I Single Carburettor	0.005in (0.127mm)	0.007in (0.1778mm)
Early Mk. II Single Carburettor	0.005in (0.127mm)	0.011in (0.2794mm)
Later Single Carburettor	0.007in (0.1778mm)	0.014in (0.3556mm)
Standard Twin Carburettor, Sport	0.007in (0.1778mm)	0.014in (0.3556mm)
Rally	0.012in (0.3048mm)	0.014in (0.3556mm)

Advised safe engine speed before valve bounce			
	Standard Single Carburettor	6,500rpm	
	Standard Twin Carburettor, Sport	7,450rpm	
	8:1, Low-compression engine	6,300rpm	

Compression ratio

Standard 10:1

Van and some overseas markets fitted with a low-compression engine 8:1

rally   10½:1

Compression pressure   875cc

High Compression	185–200lb/in^2 (13–14kg/cm^2 or kp/cm^2)	
Low Compression	175–190lb/in^2 (12–13kg/cm^2 or kp/cm^2)	

Carburettor — Single Solex downdraft fixed jet (early implementations with automatic choke)

Sport: twin Zenith-Stromberg 125 CD

Rally: twin Zenith-Stromberg 150 CD

Carburettor control — Early Mk. I, Dunlop pneumatic

Later and all other applications, Bowden cable

Air cleaner — Earlier models, oil bath with steel gauze

Later models, paper element,

Twin carburettor, twin paper elements

Max. power (gross)		
Standard Single Carburettor, 10:1CR	42bhp (31.3kW, 42.6PS) @ 5,000rpm
Standard Twin Carburettor, Sport 10:1CR	55bhp (41kW, 55.8PS) @ 6,100rpm
Low Compression, 8:1CR	37bhp (27.6kW, 37.5PS) @ 4,900rpm
Rally 10:1CR	62bhp (46.2kW, 62.9PS) @ 6,200rpm
Rally 10½:1CR	65bhp (48.5kW, 65.9PS) @ 6,200rpm

(Nett figures: 39bhp, 51bhp, 34.5bhp, 58bhp, & 61bhp respectively)

Max. torque (gross)		
Standard Single Carburettor, 10:1CR	55.6lb ft (75.3Nm) @ 2,800rpm
Standard Twin Carburettor, Sport 10:1CR	55.6lb ft (75.3Nm) @ 4,300rpm
Low Compression, 8:1CR	52.6lb ft (71.24Nm) @ 2,800rpm
Rally 10:1CR	59.0lb ft (79.65Nm) @ 4,000rpm
Rally 10½:1CR	62.7lb ft (84.91Nm) @ 3,200rpm

Fuel capacity — 6gal (27.2ltr) (optional Rally, 10.5gal (47.7ltr))

Oil cooler — Tubular oil cooler fitted to some Sport and Rally versions

Transmission (transaxle)

Clutch — Single dry plate, hydraulic operation

  Early cars — 5.5in (139.7mm)

  Later cars — 6.25in (158.8mm)

Gearbox (Standard) — 4-Speed all-synchromesh and reverse

Ratios

		overall ratio	Road speed mph per 1,000rpm (cross-ply tyres)
1st	3.417:1	16.596:1	3.76 (6.05km/h)
2nd	1.833:1	8.903:1	7.02 (11.3km/h)
3rd	1.174:1	5.702:1	10.96 (17.64km/h)
4th	0.852:1	4.138:1	15.1 (24.3km/h)
Reverse	2.846:1	13.823:1	4.4 (7.08km/h)

Final drive — 4.857 (Hypoid)

Rally options — Close-ratio, some 4-speed synchromesh others non-synchromesh 4- and 5-speed

Sample Ratios		overall ratio	Road speed mph per 1,000rpm (radial-ply tyres)
1st	3.417:1	16.596:1	3.7 (5.9km/h)
2nd	1.833:1	8.903:1	6.9 (11.1km/h)
3rd	1.274:1	6.19:1	9.76 (15.7km/h)
4th	0.922:1	4.48:1	13.96 (22.46km/h)
Reverse	2.846:1	13.823:1	4.4 (7.08km/h)

Suspension and steering

Front suspension	Independent, swing-axle, coil springs, wishbones and telescopic dampers
Rear suspension	Independent trailing arm with coil springs and telescopic dampers
Steering	Rack-and-pinion
Steering ratio	14.15:1 (2⅝ turns lock-to-lock)
Standard steering wheel diameter	
	15.72in (399.3mm)

Turning circle

Between walls	31ft 6in (9601mm)
Between kerbs	30ft 6in (9296mm)

Tyres	5.50 × 12 cross-ply or 155 × 12 radial-ply tubeless
Wheels	Pressed-steel disc, bolt-on, 4-stud, 12L × 4J or 12L × 4½ (van 12H × 4)

Brakes

Type	Front and rear 8in (203mm) drum brakes, front with twin leading shoes. Servo assistance on some later models

Dimensions

Track

At kerb weight:

Saloon & Coupé	Front	49.7in (1262.4mm)
Saloon & Coupé	Rear	48in (1219.2mm)
Husky	Front	49.5in (1257.3mm)
	Rear	48in (1219.2mm)
Van	Front	49.2in (1249.7mm)
	Rear	47.5in (1206.5mm)

At fully laden weight:

Single carburettor	Front	50.6in (1285.2mm)
Sport engine	Front	50.7in (1287.8mm)
Saloon & Coupé	Rear	48in (1219.2mm)
Husky	Front	50.4in (1280.2mm)
	Rear	48in (1219.2mm)
Van	Front	49.5in (1257.3mm)
	Rear	47.5in (1206.5mm)

Wheelbase	All	82in (2083mm)

Overall length

Saloon & Coupé without over-riders	139in (3531mm)
With normal over-riders	141.25in (3588mm)
(North American Specification (NAS) with over- and under-riders varies)	
Husky & Van	140.5in (3569mm)

Overall width	All	60.25in (1530mm)

Overall height

At kerb weight:

Saloon (Single Carburettor)	54.5in (1384mm)
Coupé (Single Carburettor)	52.2in (1326mm)
Saloon (Sport Engine)	54in (1372mm)
Coupé (Sport Engine)	51.8in (1316mm)
Husky	58.6in (1488mm)
Van	60.2in (1529mm)

At fully laden weight:

Saloon (Single Carburettor)	53in (1346mm)
Coupé (Single Carburettor)	50.8in (1290mm)
Saloon (Sport Engine)	52.7in (1339mm)
Coupé (Sport Engine)	50.1in (1273mm)
Husky	56.6in (1438mm)
Van	58.2in (1478mm)

Body overhang

Front	All	23.25in (591mm)
Rear	Saloon & Coupé	33.75in (857mm)
	Husky & Van	35.25in (895mm)

Minimum ground clearance

Saloon & Coupé (Single Carburettor)	6.5in (165mm)
Saloon & Coupé (Sport Engine)	6.2in (158mm)
Husky	5.8in (147mm)
Van	7.3in (185mm)

Height of centre of gravity

Saloon & Coupé	23.5in (597mm)

Weights

Dry weight

Deluxe	1486lb (674kg)
Super Imp	1518lb (688.6kg)
Californian Coupé	1516lb (687.6kg)
Singer Chamois	1539lb (698kg)
Singer Chamois Coupé	1525lb (691.7kg)
Singer Chamois Sport	1596lb (723.9kg)
Imp Sport	1538lb (697.6kg)
Sunbeam Stiletto	1566lb (710.3kg)
Husky	1589lb (720.8kg)
Commer Van	1506lb (683.1kg)

Kerb weight

	Front	Rear	Total
Deluxe	582lb (264kg)	963lb (436.8kg)	1545lb (700.8kg)
Super Imp	593lb (269kg)	984lb (446.3kg)	1577lb (715.3kg)
Californian Coupé	600lb (272.2kg)	975lb (442.3kg)	1575lb (714.4kg)
Singer Chamois	613lb (278.1kg)	985lb (446.8kg)	1598lb (724.8kg)
Singer Chamois Coupé	611lb (277.1kg)	973lb (441.3kg)	1584lb (718.5kg)
Singer Chamois Sport	627lb (284.4kg)	1028lb (466.3kg)	1655lb (750.7kg)
Imp Sport	592lb (268.5kg)	1005lb (455.9kg)	1597lb (724.4kg)
Sunbeam Stiletto	606lb (274.9kg)	1019lb (462.2kg)	1625lb (737.1kg)
Husky	565lb (256.3kg)	1083lb (491.2kg)	1648lb (747.5kg)
Commer Van	557lb (252.7kg)	1008lb (457.2kg)	1565lb (709.9kg)

Maximum permissible weight

	Front	Rear	Total
Saloon & Coupé	950lb (430.9kg)	1390lb (630.5kg)	2300lb (1043.3kg)
Saloon & Coupé (Sport)	950lb (430.9kg)	1485lb (673.6kg)	2405lb (1090.9kg)
Husky	950lb (430.9kg)	1580lb (716.7kg)	2405lb (1090.9kg)
Commer Van	842lb (381.9kg)	1624lb (736.6kg)	2285lb (1036.5kg)

Maximum towing weight

Saloon & Coupé	952lb (432kg)
Husky & Van	Unsuitable for towing

Performance

Top speed

Saloon & Coupé (Single Carburettor)	77–80+ mph (124–130+ km/h)
Saloon & Coupé (Sport Engine)	86–90mph (138–145km/h)
Husky	72–75mph (116–121km/h)
Van	69–72mph (111–116km/h)
Rally	90+ mph (145+ km/h)

0–60mph

Saloon & Coupé (Single Carburettor)	20–22sec
Saloon & Coupé (Sport Engine)	15–17sec
Rally	14–15sec

6 Money Makes the World Go Round

Despite money being the most vital component of production, not all who wish to read about the finished product will do more than adopt a glazed stare when confronted with a tale of more relevance to the Inland Revenue than their restored pride and joy in the garage. In the case of the Imp and its makers, so many fundamental decisions were predicated on money that it is an essential part of the narrative. Key financial events within the history of the Imp are mentioned as they occur, but more detail is offered here.

A flourishing motor industry not only assisted the country's balance of payments; it helped inculcate a terrific 'feel-good factor' within the population. Alas, the opposite led to a highly dispiriting effect on the country's morale and the belief that anything made in Britain would be unlikely to work – despite such uplifting jingoistic campaigns as 'I'm backing Britain'. By the end of the 1960s, the automobile industry would demand a reversal in the Government's attitude to it – from milch cow to lame duck.

Government tinkering with the automobile industry has always been tripartite, and the case of the Imp was exemplary. The refusal of industrial development certificates for Rootes' original plans was an example of direct Government influence that was targeted at manufacturers; secondly, the Government's use of credit restraint and both direct and indirect taxation, aimed to achieve control over supply and demand; the third, indirect, effect was caused through general social programmes, which would have a pronounced effect upon the marketplace for the motor industry's products. It would be tempting also to include the role of multinational influence on successive governments, but this is a complex relationship involving enormous levels of brinkmanship – both sides in these adversarial discussions frequently feeling bullied or impotent. In 1974, Gilbert Hunt, the chairman of Chrysler (UK), who also sat on the French board, and was the president of the Society of Motor Manufacturers and Traders, told the Secretary of State for Trade and Industry, Tony Benn, 'Detroit is nervous you are going to bully the multinationals', whereas six years earlier, when the parent company was in a more buoyant mood, he was telling Benn, 'Big industrial companies plan on an international basis and regard Governments as being mere parish councils.' That caused Benn to record in his diary:

> It was clear that on industrial matters things were decided in Detroit and not in London. It was interesting – I won't say sad because you've got to be realistic – to think that the British Parliament, the House of Commons, meant nothing. The Cabinet meant nothing. The Prime Minister was just at the other end of a phone, receiving dictation from the Chancellor of the Exchequer, who was himself being dictated to by the world monetary conference. This is the reality of life.

Tony Benn claimed to have learnt the power of the multinational company through his dealings with Henry Ford II. It is easy to forget that the unquestioned business ethos of the day was 'bigger is better', and few had heard of unknown prophets like E. F. Schumacher or his 'Small is Beautiful'.

The Imp might have received oblique assistance had the tax on petrol been raised, but the Government was reluctant to do that when imports of other manufactured goods were increasing, because so few of the economical vehicles were made in Britain. For all these reasons, future governments would no longer be able to use the old regulatory policies, whether direct or indirect, to manipulate the motor industry into acting as a social and financial instrument of control.

Money might make the world go round, but in the case of this tale, especially that of the dynastic Rootes family, it is more a case of money being made to go round the world.

There were dozens of companies under the control of the Rootes family, many without 'Rootes' as part of their name. Even today, the complexity of this web of companies causes motoring historians to differ on what to call the company that manufactured the Imp. Rootes Motors (Scotland) Limited? This was a wholly owned subsidiary of Rootes Limited, the holding company, but was any part of it attributable to Rootes Motors Limited? What about the other, probably principal, holding company, Rootes Securities Limited, often confused with Rootes Acceptances, the hire-purchase and financial arm? The correct title might be Rootes Securities, and it certainly is when talking of the aero-manufacturing business of the shadow factories, but former directors note that it never featured prominently in board discussions, and the thinking was that 'it

These three dashboards show, respectively, the difference between the original design, the post-Mk II update with round dials, and the one which was particular to the Stiletto models. The Stiletto is the only one that is furnished with a tachometer, and this example of the Mk I binnacle has the optional water-temperature gauge fitted.

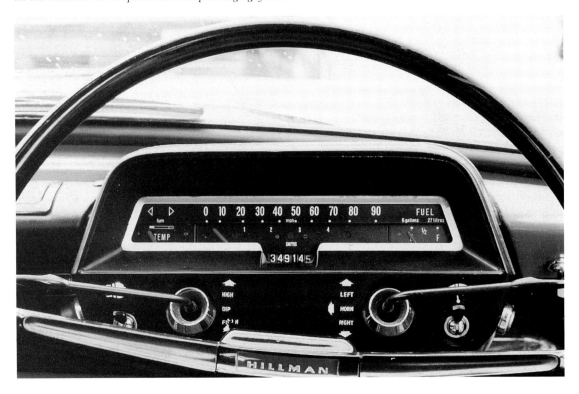

was a family concern', but then, so was the 'General Trust & Securities (Bahamas)', seemingly an obscure off-shore holding company that owned more than half of the voting shares in Rootes Limited! The company tended to be known as the Rootes Group [of companies] – which is about the only name it is, officially, safe *not* to call it with regard to the Imp, other than that the spare parts were supplied by Rootes Group (Parts). One former director commented, 'These names were only used on the "green belt".' This was the nickname given to the sumptuous green Wilton carpet leading to the offices occupied by the family – 'Rootes', 'Rootes Group' or 'Rootes Motors' tended to be the terms used by those not in the family.

As will be obvious to many readers, the tale of William and Reginald Rootes is far from being one of 'rags to riches', but during that generation of the family, it is one of from being well-heeled to enormous wealth. The Rootes brothers were exceptional businessmen, with a gift for attracting high levels of financial assistance and 'indebtedness', both by means of loans on favourable terms and through grants. The Rootes brothers were masters of negotiating loan guarantees. At this level of finance (not to mention refinance), these loan guarantees could be used as future security for borrowing or traded with other companies for profit – as was the case with the final involvement of Prudential Assurance with Chrysler/Rootes.

As many were to discover, the complex financial web that was the Rootes family empire was impenetrable to the outsider and extremely difficult to value; the term 'creative accountancy' was not invented at the end of the twentieth century! The difficulty of reading even the simplest of Rootes' balance sheets is partially because the company was so large and financially complex, while the involvement of the family trusts muddied the water even further. The archaic operations of the City of London as a financial centre had evolved along the lines of custom and practice,

so the full ramifications of apparently straightforward corporate transactions were not always clear to those outside the Square Mile. The *Investors' Chronicle* of December 1965, before attempting to establish the value of the company's declared trading profit, gross profit and net profit, prefaced its suppositions with: 'The accounts of Rootes for the last four years have posed all sorts of problems in interpretation, and analysis of the shares has been complicated by the disappointments of actual trading and the varying degrees of hope held out for the future.' Even the meaning of 'year' is not always clear cut without clarification: Rootes' financial year ended in July, and figures were in some cases an estimate as to how they related to a full calendar year.

The initial involvement of the Prudential Assurance Company (now Prudential Plc) with Rootes occurred in September 1929, when it purchased 25 per cent of the share capital of Rootes Ltd and the family's Medway Trust Limited, while also advancing a loan of £1 million – a huge sum at the time – to finance the acquisition plans described in Chapter 1.

Swinging Sixties?

The next huge step forward for Rootes Ltd was the acquisition of the Linwood site, as recounted in Chapter 3. The public purse facilitated the home of the Hillman Imp.

Following a profitable war, Rootes had enjoyed more than 10 per cent of home manufacturing output, which placed them way behind the British Motor Corporation and the American-owned Ford, but ahead of the combined Standard-Triumph Motor Company and Vauxhall. What would eventually become recognized as 'globalization' was in the air, though, and many North American manufacturers had established small levels of production in Europe in their own names. Ford was the only one that had flourished. The more common road to globalization was as a predator to identify a respected local marque and

The Man from the Pru

The initial involvement of the Prudential was at the behest of Sir George May (later Lord May), the Prudential's Secretary from 1915 to 1931. May was a theoretician, as well as a practical insurance man. He developed the strategy of smoothing markets through diversification, subsequently adopted by other insurers. May's three most lucrative investments were to include Rootes Limited, Beecham and Imperial Chemical Industries. The company minute of 19 September 1929 states:

> Rootes Limited. Authority is requested to advance to Messrs-Rootes Limited on the security of 7% 15-year Debentures up to an amount not exceeding £1,000,000. The Debentures to be secured by specific charge on the freehold and leasehold properties held or to be held by Messrs-Rootes Ltd. and on certain other companies' shares held by them, together with a floating charge over all their assets.
>
> If Messrs-Rootes Ltd. so desire £250,000 of the above mentioned £1,000,000 may take a form of guarantee by the Prudential of loans from bankers or others, the consideration receivable by the Prudential in respect of such guarantee being a premium of 1% per annum.
>
> Authority is above requested for the purchase of (A) 25% of the issued Ordinary Shares of Rootes Ltd. for the sum of £162,500, (B) 250,000 £1 Cum. Pref. shares of the Medway Trust Ltd. at par, and (C) 50,000 Defd. shares of the Medway Trust Ltd. at 2/- per share.
>
> Resolved. That this be approved, and that Sir George May be authorised to sign the necessary documents on behalf of the Prudential Board.

Other than Chrysler, the Prudential was to remain the largest non-family shareholder of Rootes Limited until the stewardship of their secretary, Angus Fraser Murray, in the late 1960s. The Prudential was consistently represented on the board of Rootes Ltd, and later, Chrysler (UK). Rootes poached Rupert Hammond from the Prudential to be Rootes' finance director, a position he occupied for forty years. It is unclear what reciprocal arrangement existed with the Prudential, but clearly the prosperous manufacturer proved to be a good investment and was frequently persuaded to place substantial insurance business with its financial guarantor and shareholder. A typical interchange is this of 1952 between the Prudential's Johannesburg office and Mr A. F. Fraser in London:

> I have received a letter from our Branch Manager at Cape Town which indicates that they have tried to persuade Rootes (Pty.) Ltd . . . to place some of their General Branch business with the mighty Prudential. They say they have tried almost every angle without making any impression . . . I have no local angle to suggest and wondered whether perhaps in view of your close relationship . . . with the U.K. Company, you might be able to put in a word in the right quarter.

Fraser confirms that a good relationship exists and he is still a director of Rootes, with whom he has raised the query, and they will 'communicate with their [Rootes] Branch in South Africa and I hope that the result will be satisfactory.'

Tantalizingly, the Prudential records from the 1930s to 1940s have not survived, but the index to these has, and it reveals a large number of entries for 'R. C. Rootes', 'Rootes Securities Ltd', 'Sir Reginald Rootes', and, in particular, 'Sir W. E. Rootes'. It would appear that a very close and mutually beneficial position existed between the business interests of both companies and their senior personnel. In 1954 we find the Prudential again confirming a new large amount of loan capital being issued to Rootes 'to finance a large programme of capital expenditure, to increase production and assembly facilities, and to provide additional working capital' – i.e. the Singer Motor Company.

Into the 1960s, various large and small dealings in Rootes' many classes of shares are recorded; one sale of nearly half a million to the Rootes family is recorded by the *Statist* and presumed to be the voting shares that preserved the family's control of the company. In January, during Chrysler's successful attempt of 1967 to obtain full control, Prudential's Finance Committee decided not to take up its entitlement to the rights issue and not to take up further share entitlements in Rootes Motors. Among all the speculative calculations, there is an instruction to sell the 'nil paid rights', initialled by AFM – this was done at a premium of 5/8d. The holding of 1.3 million 'A' ordinary shares is described as 'of negligible value'.

This might have been the end of the company's involvement with Rootes, but in 1969 the Prudential took over promissory notes to the value of £9 million that Rootes had issued when borrowing this sum from the American Manufacturers Hanover Trust Company.

The Man from the Pru *continued*

This was conditional upon a loan to the Prudential from that trust for US$21.6 million, and it is of interest to note that the Prudential was paying 6½ per cent interest on its loan, and the trust collected 8 per cent from Rootes and passed on 7¼ per cent to the Prudential. Later in the year, the chairman, Sir John Mellor, noted a telephone conversation that suggests the two companies' close relationship had come to an end:

> Lord Rootes telephoned today to me to express his thanks to the Directors for allowing Mr. Murray to remain on his Board for the time being. Lord Rootes stressed the great value of Mr. Murray's advice to his Company and

explained that his resigning at the present time would be particularly unfortunate.

> I told Lord Rootes that the Prudential Directors had considered this matter very carefully having regard to the heavy demands upon Mr. Murray in this office. I emphasised that we felt that Mr. Murray should certainly not seek re-election to the Board of Rootes when his present term expired by rotation in two years' time.

> Lord Rootes appreciated that now we no longer held any substantial interest in his company the Prudential attitude was entirely understandable and again expressed his gratitude.

---

make a take-over bid, increasing its stake until the predatory company held the necessary 51 per cent control. In reality, this was just playing out on a worldwide stage the strategies the Rootes brothers had so successfully employed on a more parochial level.

With the warning of *caveat emptor* concerning the meaning of figures, Rootes made a respectable profit of between £4 million and £5 million to the year ending July 1960, and £1 million the following year, but despite the Government's financial 'sweetener' of £10 million towards the Scottish project, the company was financially stretched by Linwood. In much the way that contemporary 'matching funding' works, the difference between this financial incentive and the estimated requirement of £22.5 million to build and equip Linwood had to be met out of the Rootes Group's funds, and the reason that Geoffrey Rootes was critical of so much of the assistance coming by way of loans, rather than grants, was that Rootes now had an 'indebtedness' for most of the assistance it received. In the year to July 1962 Rootes made a loss of between £750,000 and £1,000,000, but if we use the *Investor's Chronicle* figures, the 1962 loss would be £2.5 million gross and £1.8 million net – quite a difference.

The company, however, was in a much

worse financial state than a first reading of these figures might suggest, and it was certainly not helped by the way the industrial trouble at BLSP had been handled. The die had been cast in the decade following the war. The Rootes Group, like many British manufacturers, was extremely short of working capital: the banks were not showering them with any more loans, and the shareholders were getting fractious. The holding company started the 1960s comprising over thirty companies that were recognized as Rootes, and it would end it as two parts of Chrysler (UK). The ever-loyal author, John Bullock, might opine that, 'Although Rootes' annual profits were never high by modern standards, the future of the Group was never in any doubt while Billy Rootes was alive and the brothers' partnership remained intact', but this is not an opinion for which either the Government or the author has managed to find supporting evidence. A Government working party of 1966 concluded, 'It is clear that Rootes is a very sick company and has been so for some years.' Geoffrey Rootes' assessment of the position of the family firm in 1964 seems rather more realistic than the faith and hope of the board:

> International competition was becoming increasingly fierce, particularly from the

It is difficult to assess how serious this exterior customizing exercise was. The Sunbeam Sportsedan is left-hand-drive and to NAS (North American Specification). As the number-plate reveals, it was referred to as 'Lord Imp'. It is hard to believe that the horn mounted on the left wing would have been acceptable in any country.

Japanese, and the financial pressures involved in competing on a world basis in the manufacturing business were becoming so extreme that it made it difficult to see how a family-controlled company such as ours could survive.

Rootes, like many British firms that were still ostensibly in family hands, had its issued share capital split between classes of ordinary (voting) and 'A' ordinary (non-voting) shares, so that whatever the future might bring, there was an in-built possibility of the family retaining a significant influence that might be greater than the monetary holding it retained. In such cases, a family would be able to have the company refinanced without, at least theoretically, having it taken over.

Meanwhile, Chrysler was turning its corporate sights towards Europe. Following a good period in America, it was highly cash-rich and could afford to consider global expansion. It had been making Simca cars since 1959 and had a significant holding in the French company. By increasing its stake to a majority holding early in 1963, it effectively established Chrysler (France). Simca had become the largest French automobile manufacturer in private hands in France and Spain. At this time, Chrysler International was based in Geneva, and Simca disliked the idea of the main office eventually being transferred to London.

Chrysler Nibbling?

Chrysler had been unsuccessful in its attempts to woo Rootes' smaller competitor, Standard-Triumph, and the Rootes Group was the natural next target. Martin Adeney, in *The Motor Makers*, suggests that 'Chrysler, after sniffing round the industry for years, finally plunged in at exactly the wrong moment, and seemed to lack both the know-how and the will to improve the position of the faltering Rootes Group.' Chrysler's sniffing almost led to it becoming a neighbour of Rootes, rather than its owner. In June 1959, the American corporation had noticed similar incentives as those that were attracting Lord Rootes to Scotland. Chrysler investigated two Renfrewshire sites – Inchinnan, about six miles (10km) north of Linwood, and Barrochan Road, Johnstone, less than a mile west along the

A761 that bisected the Rootes factory. A further, more distant site, Newhouse in North Lanarkshire, was also considered, under four miles (6km) from the burgeoning Ravenscraig steelworks. Had more large firms availed themselves of the Macmillan Government's incentives, then the whole area might have become an economically viable region for lighter-industrial production. As late as the end of 1965, Ford and Vauxhall were still investigating new manufacturing sites in Scotland.

Linwood was up and running and the Imp might have been launched, but the Rootes organization was in no position to resist its suitor. With so little working capital and those repayments eating away at any small profits, Rootes was not in a propitious position to capitalize on its intended popular offering. While the establishment of the Linwood facility and the disproportionately high level of problems with the Imp might have been a disappointment to Lord Rootes, they cannot be blamed for the reduced state of the whole group nor the family's susceptibility to the advances from Chrysler International. The board of Rootes Limited concluded a protracted deal whereby the Chrysler Corporation acquired a 30 per cent stake in the ordinary (voting) shares and a larger half-share in the issued (non-voting) 'A' class of ordinary shares. The Labour Party was uneasy about this arrangement because it was rightly convinced that, despite assertions to the contrary, the concluded negotiations with Chrysler of June 1964 were only the first step to Chrysler being the outright owner – Rootes would now be beholden to what the parliamentary Opposition saw as the whims of a foreign controlling hand. The next forty years, of course, would see variations on this theme played out with greater and lesser degrees of embellishment and guarantees offered up to the prevailing governments. In reality, the Conservative Government had little option other than to agree, mysteriously finding some solace in the fact that in France and Spain, Chrysler had declared its intention

to hold 100 per cent of the equity of those firms. It was inconceivable for a Conservative Government to have turned Rootes into a nationalized state-owned concern, and without an injection of substantial sums the Rootes Group would have been heading for administration by a liquidator. It is illuminating to read Geoffrey Rootes' account of this, reproduced from his autobiography, *Carpe Diem*:

> In the spring of 1964 when we were approached by Chrysler International in Geneva, with a view to some form of amalgamation, Brian [Rootes] and I decided to recommend to my father and my uncle and our co-directors that we should enter into negotiations with them.
>
> There followed a long period of negotiation. Our advisers were Lazards as merchant bankers, Cazenoves as stockbrokers, and Linklater and Payne as lawyers. Eventually Heads of Agreement were negotiated and my father and my uncle flew to New York to conclude the necessary formal agreement. I remained in London to keep contact with the banks, stockbrokers and lawyers and with the financial press. The broad outline of the agreement was that we sold to Chrysler Corporation a considerable block of our equity shares, but not sufficient to give them control, by virtue of our retaining a sufficient number of the voting shares (the equity capital was divided into voting and non-voting shares). They would have the right to nominate certain directors to our board and would provide us with technical expertise and advice, particularly in the field of manufacturing engineering. My father was determined that we, as a family, should retain control and therefore was not willing to sell a further quantity of shares, which we could have sold at that time at a relatively advantageous price. However, all in all it was not a bad deal, assuming the working arrangements with Chrysler operated satisfactorily. This unfortunately did not prove to be the

case. Although the Chairman of Chrysler at
that time was George Love (with whom we
got on well), the Chief Executive and the
effective head of the company was Lynn
Townsend, with whom we did not have a
happy relationship. He had at that time a high
reputation in American Industry. Events
were to prove our judgement of him to be
right as the Chrysler Corporation went
through very difficult times under his chairmanship.

At this time I was still Managing Director
of Rootes Motors, of which my father was
still Chairman and my uncle was Deputy
Chairman.

The oft-used term to paper over the cracks of
'taking an interest' deals was that of 'synergy'.
With Chrysler/Rootes this would have been
difficult. Robert C. Mitchell, president and
managing director of Chrysler International,
Louis B. Warren, director of Chrysler Corporation, and Irving J. Minett, group vice-
president of Chrysler International Operations
joined the board of Rootes Motors in September 1964.

What Chrysler thought of the new
'arrangement' is not reliably reported, nor is
the point at which the American corporation
realized that, through the arcane structure of
British companies, they could own so much of
the equity of the firm without having statutory control. Lord Rootes stressed in a variety
of woolly platitudes how Rootes would
benefit from Chrysler's way of doing business,
research and marketing. The hollow tone of
Rootes' press releases and Lord Rootes' statements is hardly surprising; the family honour
and firm had been saved, but it was clear that
Chrysler would be far from being a 'sleeping
partner': whatever undertakings it had
proffered, it would be in effective control and
a take-over would only be a matter of time.
There is little doubt that Rootes struck an
optimal deal with Chrysler, but it is reliably
reported from those who inhabited the boardroom that Lord Rootes investigated the possi-

Walter P. Chrysler (and his Cars)

Walter Percy Chrysler was recognized as a brilliant
engineer and designer, and was generally thought
of in America as either a real 'car man' or the
fellow who gave his name to the eponymous art
deco building in New York that was the headquarters of the corporation he had founded in
1925 – the same year as the Paris *Exposition des
Arts Décoratifs* gave its name to this new style
where art and the automobile influenced each
other. Chrysler, who died in 1940, had been
known to, and admired by, William Rootes.

However much his name seems synonymous
with automobiles, Walter learnt his engineering
and direction skills during his first career on the
American railroads, working for both the Chicago
Great Western and the American Locomotive
Company (ALCO), among others. Having
arrived at General Motors' Buick and Willys-
Overland, Chrysler rescued the Maxwell Motor
Company and renamed it as his. Like Rootes,
Chrysler was an outstanding businessman and
acquired smaller companies while setting about
establishing their separate identities within the
corporation: Plymouth was the family car, Dodge
rather sportier, DeSoto and Chrysler further
upmarket, and Imperial maintained a definite
social distance.

By the time of the Imp, the Chrysler Corporation had established a considerable reputation for
its 5–7-litre V8 engines and its superb Torqueflite
automatic gearboxes. The European perception of
Chrysler's products was based upon their breath-
takingly powerful 'muscle cars' and the use of their
engines and transmissions to power luxury sporting cars from traditional low-volume makers like
Bristol and Jensen.

Walter's ethos had departed the company,
however, leaving behind a fairly impoverished
outlook. Having been rescued by the Government in 1979 and recovered, Chrysler then deteriorated again, and it was taken over in 1998 by
Daimler-Benz AG to make DaimlerChrysler.

bility of rescinding it after the family had committed the company, but while the final
signing had yet to take place. It is hard to
determine what alternative scheme Lord
Rootes had up his sleeve, and it is difficult to
believe that this was not the best offer the

family could have received. It is easy, however, to believe the reported tales of incredulity when various senior personnel from Chrysler inspected the Hillman Imp. If the Rootes board had been worried about the Imp being perceived as a proper motor car, this was as nothing compared to what the American Chrysler executives thought of it. As far as they were concerned, apart from its diminutive size and ridiculous engine, it failed in terms of how they saw automobile manufacturing – it was expensive and fiddly to make and it was not being produced in anything like the volume necessary to make the model or the facility profitable. It was a mass-produced vehicle that was not being produced *en masse*. The system by which Rootes had been producing all its ranges was also a complete anathema to Chrysler; in particular, the British custom of out-sourcing so much of the value of each car was quite incomprehensible, as was generating for a competitor, both plants of Pressed Steel, 40 per cent of its business.

The Pressed Steel Problem

Once BMC took over Pressed Steel in 1965, Chrysler International made its views known to the Rootes board. Little was envisaged concerning the supply of pressed panels from

Cowley to Ryton-on-Dunsmore, but within days of the announcement, the new chairman of Rootes, Sir Reginald, approached BMC about the purchase of the Linwood body-pressing facility. Whilst it was felt that the Chrysler Corporation was pulling the strings in the background, it was left to Sir Reginald and the new Lord Rootes to discuss terms with the Government and the British Motor Corporation. By now, Chrysler owned 45 per cent of the ordinary shares and 66 per cent of the 'A' ordinary equity, and the Rootes family only retained 50.1 per cent of the important voting ordinary shares through acquiring 474,500 of the Prudential Assurance's holding, along with those of smaller investors. And even then, the family had to take up 125,000 units in a rights issue. Retaining control of Rootes was getting to be an expensive pastime for the family.

In November 1965, Sir Reginald approached the Board of Trade with Rootes Motors' proposals for incorporating the Linwood Pressed Steel factory into Rootes' Scottish complex. He wanted the Government to transfer to Rootes the Pressed Steel Company's £8.5 million indebtedness to the Board of Trade (i.e. its loans), as well as amortizing the agreements in respect of Pressed Steel and introducing a moratorium on repay-

At the Paris Motor Show, September 1964. Left to right: *Robert C. Mitchell, president and MD of Chrysler International; Sir Reginald Rootes, deputy chairman, Rootes; Louis B. Warren, director of Chrysler Corporation; Lord Rootes, chairman; Irving J. Minett, Chrysler group vice-president (International Operations); and Geoffrey Rootes, chairman of Humber and MD of Rootes Motors.*

Who owns Rootes Limited?

The *Statist*, in June 1965, tried to answer this question. Even as thorough a publication as this commenced its view of Rootes with the usual caveat, with its assessment of the equity following:

> These figures are conjectural because the bulk of the Rootes family holdings are in companies and nominee names registered outside the UK presumably to avoid tax . . .
>
> What this situation really illustrates is the nonsense of non-voting shares as used by a minority holder to retain control of a company. Without that device Chrysler would have control and it is to be hoped that the Government will not allow jingoistic considerations to affect its judgement when it comes to deal with non-voting shares in the now (overdue) Companies Act.

Holder	Ordinary Shares (Voting)	'A' Ordinary (Non-voting)
Rootes Motor total equity	7,016,305	33,309,570
Chrysler	3,162,036 [45%]	21,892,701 [66%]
Rootes family and Directors	217,273	1,981,724
General Trust & Securities (Bahamas)	3,000,283	1,420,980
Hilco Ltd. (Isle of Man)	143,872	27,460
Horsford Nominees (Hong Kong)	151,852	135,000
Far Eastern Nominees (Bahamas)	2,652	522,522
Total assumed for Rootes family	3,515,932 [50.1%]	4,087,686 [12%]

ments for three or four years. The icing on the cake was the request for a further loan of £3.5–4 million. Rootes' balance sheet to July showed net assets (apart from loan stock) of about £36 million compared with £20 million before the purchase by Chrysler. The minutes of this meeting show that the Board of Trade was not cooperative, stating that loans and grants had been given to both owners with the intention of the separate facilities producing 9,700 additional jobs between them, whereas, after a peak of 6,000, the workforce had already dwindled to 4,500. No further aid would be forthcoming until the original target was met. The minute continues, 'Sir Reginald Rootes said that the Linwood project had caused his company a great deal of trouble and had cost them a great deal of money.' After claiming that Dunstable had been the family's favoured choice for the Imp factory, Sir Reginald continued that he 'was reasonably confident that employment at Linwood on the Imp project would increase substantially in the coming months, although not up to the original employment target, as a result of higher sales of the car and light van based on it which had just been introduced'. Rootes proposed the closure of BLSP in Acton, moving commercial cab production from there and the Midlands to Linwood, and commencing production of a completely new car body in Scotland. Sir Reginald suggested the cost of the Pressed Steel plant and machinery was £15–16 million, and Rootes could find £3 million from its own resources if up to £4 million was forthcoming from the Board of Trade. He reminded the government body that Pressed Steel at Linwood was repaying £1.1 million per annum, but was unprofitable and would remain in loss until Imp production

---

Sir Reginald Rootes' Dream for Linwood

Rootes' stated plans and expenditure for the Board of Trade in November, 1965.

1 Integration of manufacture between Rootes and Pressed Steel factories to improve productivity and increase capacity. .... = £550,000
2 Move Imp engine manufacture from Coventry to Linwood. .... = £200,000
3 Install assembly of new large car at 150/200 per week. .... = £175,000
4 Install equipment for work transferred from London. .... = £200,000
5 Cost of closure of London factory. .... = £300,000
6 Install additional presses and facilities for manufacture of pressings and subassemblies for new light car body. .... = £1,100,000
7 Cost of dies and special equipment for new light car body. .... = £3,000,000
8 Cost of tools for new light Commercial Vehicle. .... = £500,000

Apart from the above, we are about to spend approximately £350,000 in respect of Imp improvements and new derivative models to take effect during 1966.

---

rose to 1,800 per week from its current 1,200. Two days later, and following another discussion with Pressed Steel, Sir Reginald wrote to the Board of Trade trying to persuade it that more jobs would be created than he had previously stated, and offering slightly more detailed plans for Linwood. The Board's Advisory Committee, however, thought the plans 'sketchy' and noted that Rootes Motors (Scotland) already owed £9 million that was being repaid at £700,000 per annum, and if it were to adopt Pressed Steel's Scottish debt, then its indebtedness to the Government would be £17 million – and with the newly requested loan, over £20 million.

Even quite senior managers at Linwood puzzled over how Rootes had managed to acquire the adjacent factory, because the losses the company was enduring were fairly clear for all to see. It was incorrectly assumed that 'it must be the men from the Pru', as it was evident that Detroit was not empathetic with Linwood's aspirations. The board of Rootes eventually modified its claim for assistance from the Government through deleting its demand for an extra loan, but requesting easier terms on the Local Employment Act Section-4 loans that had been made to both themselves and Pressed Steel. As their name suggests, these loans tapped an extra funding stream and

were linked to the creation of employment at a local level. They would prove to be highly contentious for Linwood's owners through to the time of the PSA Peugeot-Citroën takeover. Many of Rootes Acceptances' customers referred to agreements for their Imp as 'on the never-never'. Here we have the company playing this same strategy: the repayment moratorium lasted until September 1968 (saving £2.75 million), with a repayment extension to 1980 (an initial reduction of £2 million for a similar sum of added cost, with only £4.7 million outstanding for the later 1970s). This, or so the Government was promised, would deliver 2.75 million square feet (255,000m^2) of covered facilities and the direct employment of 7,500 workers, with the bonus of a large area for future development and expansion.

This book is about the Imp, rather than being an analysis of the business performance of Rootes Motors, but the business health of the company greatly affected decisions about the car. Alas, having been placed on a more secure footing in 1964, over the following eleven years the company would only see profits in three or five of these, and modest ones at that. According to the company, the largest profits would be declared in 1968, with just over £3 million after three years of losses,

The styling of the complementary 'Lady Imp' is in a similar vein to the 'Lord Imp'. It is also a Sunbeam Sportsedan to NAS. This specification not only had the front under-riders, but both bumpers, or fenders, stood off the bodywork further, and this horizontal bar ran across above the rear over-riders.

and in 1973, with £3.75 million pounds. If these figures sound as if the company was not doing too badly, especially when compared with the rest of the UK manufacturers, they should be offset against some spectacular losses: in 1967 and 1970 the financial short-fall was more than £10 million, then 1974 saw the company losing almost £18 million, to be followed by a catastrophic loss of £35.5 million and not much better the year after – clearly a terminal condition for any company. In a comparative government table of the profits and losses of British manufacturers, Rootes' claimed profit for 1968 was reported as a loss of £3.7 million – it is unclear if this was simply a typographical error of inserting parentheses, making it a minus figure, or a different basis of calculation – either way, a single point does not disrupt a reading of the emerging trend represented by the graph.

It is salutary to consider the post-war state of the mass-producers of cars in the United Kingdom up to the social changes of the 1960s: few of the larger companies, whether British- or American-owned, had turned in more than the occasional loss (after taxation), and this contributed to their complacency. Had the boards of other companies chosen to ponder upon why Ford's profits were consistently superior to their own, then remedial action might have been taken before their own companies deteriorated into financial basket cases. A comparison with the British Motor Corporation/British Motor Holdings and Ford's British subsidiary reveals the enormity of the disparity – between 1960 and 1967 the pre-tax profits of both BMC/BMH and Ford UK would comfortably surpass £150 million, while the post-tax figure for Rootes amounted to a loss of approximately £10

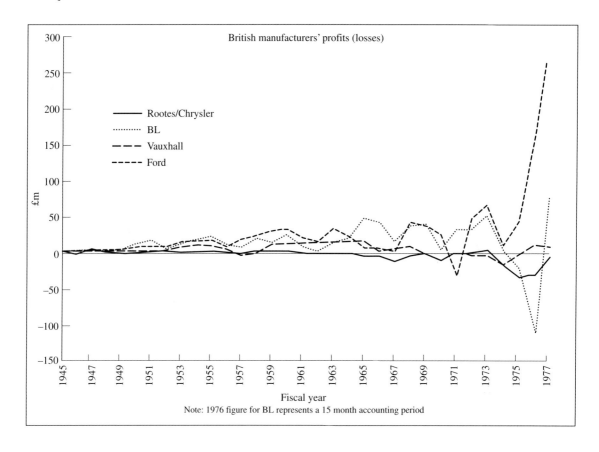

British manufacturers' profits (losses)

Rootes/Chrysler
BL
Vauxhall
Ford

£m

Fiscal year

Note: 1976 figure for BL represents a 15 month accounting period

million – even allowing for different accounting bases, the message is overwhelming.

Concomitant with the flood of new Imp variants, Lord Rootes and Uncle Reginald, at the end of 1966, were talking to the British Government again – this time about handing the family firm over to Chrysler USA, lock, stock and barrel. Opposition suspicions at the time of the original stake-building by Chrysler were proved to be justified, and those politicians had since been elected as the socialist Labour Government and so would have to sanction such a take-over. The Minister of Technology in Harold Wilson's Government was the Rt Hon. Anthony Wedgwood Benn – or under his preferred form of reference, Tony Benn, a man with leanings to the left of the party and principles above those of a mere career politician. Benn was one of the few politicians who had visited a motor-

production facility other than in a ceremonial role.

Complete Control for Chrysler?

Meanwhile, back at 10 Downing Street, while recognizing that the Government had a specific problem with regard to Rootes, Harold Wilson also realized that this was only one small part of a much larger problem concerning the country's inability to move towards freer trade. Free trade is supposedly a two-way street, but the Government knew that British light industry was in a sorry state and was possibly going to follow the once-glorious heavy industry into the oblivion of which the latter's former employees now at Linwood knew the social pain all too well. Added to these concerns were the usual political preoccupations of a deleterious national balance of payments,

A. Craig Miller, the Rootes chief engineer who had moved from Coventry to Linwood, and had done so much to cope with the problems of the Imp, is presented with a British-made portable radio on his retiral. Fortunately, he retired before the effect of Chrysler's economies came into force.

and various income and employment policies that created an adversarial labour relations climate – nowhere more so than in the automobile production industries. With the more popular press starting to focus on headline-grabbing unemployment totals, it was understandable why, for the first time in more than a generation, Government minds focused on employment policy. With reference to Rootes, there were two outstanding problems for the Cabinet.

Wilson knew that Rootes was not the only motor-industry challenge it was going to have to face: the largest British manufacturer, the former British Motor Corporation, was also a very lame, if not potentially deceased, duck and would be knocking on the Government's door. Not only would any rescue of Rootes be calling on Government funds, but its survival would intensify the competition for British-produced cars on the home market. The Government's other concern was that for years the 'Made in Scotland' slogan had been used in Imp advertising and the public had been taught to think of the Imp as specifically Scot-

tish. Nationalism was rising in the public consciousness, if not yet in terms of votes cast. After considering the weaknesses of corporate management and investment, and the lamentable state of labour relations, industrial historians suggest that Government policies and interference hindered, rather than assisted, the motor industry.

By the autumn of 1966 it was clear to those close to the industry that Rootes was in a parlous state and unlikely to continue trading. It is usually said that Rootes Motors approached the Government, but the Minister of Technology's responses were to the parent Chrysler Corporation. The resultant discussions centred on £20 million being made available to Rootes Motors Limited – £10 million through a rights issue of preference ordinary shares to existing shareholders – a transaction to be underwritten by Chrysler without commission – and a further £10 million of unsecured loan stock. If Chrysler was to take up its entitlement to buy further shares under this issue, it would obtain voting control of the British company. Tony Benn

127

Undertakings by Chrysler to the Government

i   Chrysler/Rootes to remain a UK company

ii   There should be a majority of British directors on the Rootes board

iii   Chrysler to confirm their intended expansion, development work at various factories and especially at Linwood, where the major development will take place and they are to increase employment by 'several thousands' – this is seen as essential for the company to be competitive, for exports, and return to reasonable profitability

iv   Chrysler to plan increased exports from Rootes Motors

v   Chrysler will nominate a Rootes director (British) to Simca SA & Chrysler International SA; also a nominated Simca director to the Rootes board

vi   Chrysler to leave 15 per cent of the entire equity (Ordinary, 'A' Ordinary, and Preference Ordinary) in the hands of shareholders other than Chrysler (counting the Industrial Reorganisation Corporation as part of the 15 per cent)

vii   Provided that Chrysler acquires Preference Ordinary Shares in excess of its rights entitlement of £6,263,686 nominal, it will make available to the Industrial Reorganisation Corporation, at par, up to £1,512,228 of such excess. i.e. up to 15 per cent of the total Preference Ordinary of £10,081519 on condition that the Industrial Reorganisation Corporation participates up to £10 million Unsecured Loan Stock with the right on 1 January 1972 to put these at par (and any accrued dividend) or interest. [This 'put' option was later exercised at par.]

viii Industrial Reorganisation Corporation's right to nominate one director on the Rootes board as long as it owns all the securities under vii

---

then entered into eight points of discussion with Chrysler for the Government to sanction this take-over of a British company. Benn clearly retained an eye on the implications for the future of the Linwood plant.

The Wilson Government, having failed to find either a British buyer for Rootes, or anyone prepared to merge with them, did allow Tony Benn to propose alternative solutions to that of a take-over by the Chrysler Corporation. Benn knew that to allow the third large American player into the British motor industry would not receive a warm welcome from the Labour Party's traditional supporters and would be risking the survival of the sector. With this in mind, he looked for other ways out of the problem. Benn invited Sir George Harriman, the statesmanlike chairman of British Motor Holdings, and buccaneering Sir Donald Stokes, chairman of the commercial Leyland Motors, to dinner on 15 December to discuss the Rootes/Chrysler crisis in an attempt to broker a deal to get the then-separate companies to take over Rootes Motors, as his diary reveals:

I put to them three simple questions. Do you want to see Chrysler take over Rootes? Do you think it is worth attempting a British solution – a regrouping that would include Rootes and British Motors and Leyland, in which there might be some Government participation? Would you be prepared to bring about a merger between your two companies to try to absorb Rootes if the Government were prepared to help?

Neither was interested, even with any financial inducements that went with the take-over – BMH had a model range that conflicted with Rootes and comfortably outsold it, while the commercial Leyland had only re-entered car production again through its own acquisition of Standard-Triumph and Rover (including Land-Rover), which itself had merged with Alvis. In any case, as the prime minister was later to discover when entering negotiations about the future of their own companies, this pair of captains of industry entertained an enormous level of personal antipathy for each other. Take-overs in the British motor industry had been virtually unheard of for almost half a century: the norm was that of Rootes' history – a merger through establishing a holding company. Arguably, this had been one of the fatal flaws in the Rootes structure: despite the autocratic family at the head, the constituent parts were in the hands of separate managements and practices, with the holding company unable to enforce corporate and industrial integration, let alone the concepts of cost accounting, integrated financial control or even an overall profit plan. So Benn considered nationalizing Rootes, but this was a course of action that was unacceptable to the Government as a whole. In addition to Government worries about unemployment, a high level of concern surrounded the automobile industry because it remained the country's largest manufacturing exporter and had been identified by the civil servants at the Department of Economic Affairs as being the largest problem when drawing up a national economic plan. It was known to Benn, however, that since the start of December, the Rootes family had agreed to being taken over – it had been costing them considerable sums to retain their 50.1 per cent control. A Ministry of Transport Rootes/Chrysler Working Party was established to consider the full ramifications.

A week before Christmas the Cabinet considered the possibility of a putative separate or joint take-over by British Motor Holdings and/or Leyland/Rover. It was reported that the firms could find £20 million new development money, but would be unwilling to pay more than £5 million for the equity capital of Rootes Motors. The Government, therefore, would have to find £35 million, and, while further negotiations took place, it would also have to guarantee Rootes' declared debts of £60 million. It is unsurprising that two days later the Cabinet approved the Chrysler deal in principle with general commendation. On 16 January 1967, however, the *Sunday Telegraph* ran a speculative investigative story about Chrysler not offering to buy out the British shareholders and the lack of diligence of the Government. Someone in the Cabinet Office has annotated this cutting with the reassuring information that the newspaper could not know the true extent of Rootes Motors' losses. The following day, Tony Benn made a not very informative statement to Parliament about Rootes-Chrysler, for which his own party, in ignorance of the true position, attacked him for presenting the outline of a policy they saw as more of the ethos of the opposition Conservative Party. Tony Benn describes the detailed negotiations with the

This is one of the two Rootes 1965 Farmobil flat-bed pick-up/utility vehicles that was Imp-powered. This Austro-Germanic creation came to Rootes via Chrysler Hellas (Greece), but like many other Imp ideas, including ones such as the later open-topped agricultural Gillie, it was not progressed.

Chrysler Corporation as 'very difficult and delicate throughout' – and not only with regard to Chrysler. There is a personal letter from the Chancellor of the Exchequer reminding the Prime Minister of 'substantial holdings in the hands of the Rootes family and of certain family trusts which are resident in the Bahamas'. It then goes on to suggest that the Colonial Office needed to be involved. There is a strong emphasis that the Colonial Office needed to consider the tax implications of the sale of these shares, and should the law require to accommodate the tax efficiency of this take-over, the Chancellor, of course, was the person who could effect this. If the reader is being overtaken by political cynicism at this point, this feeling might be amplified to know that, following the *Sunday Telegraph* piece on Rootes-Chrysler, the civil servants were not only working on the fine print of the negotiations and the so-called 'real' statement that would be presented concomitant with that of Rootes Motors, but they were also preparing a 'Draft Statement by Minister for release if story breaks before the main announcement can be released'!

Rootes Motors Equity

Following the take-over by the Chrysler Corporation, the share and loan capital of the company was as below. For the sake of simplicity, throughout the text shares have been referred to either as ordinary voting or 'A' non-voting classes. In reality, these types were spread over different classes.

Share Capital
5½%   Redeemable Cumulative Preference £1
7%   Cumulative Preference Shares £1
Preferred Ordinary 4/- [20p]
Ordinary 4/- [20p]
'A' Ordinary 4/- [20p]
Loan Capital
4%   Debenture Stock 1974/84
5½%   Debenture Stock 1985/89
Board of Trade Loan
8% Unsecured Loan Stock 1981
Overdraft

The deal, surrounded with miles of what would prove to be worthless fine print, progressed with Chrysler confirming its guarantee not to seek to take control of the final 15 per cent of the company without the Government's agreement, and the Government sanctioned the take-over of Rootes by the American parent company and the formation of the wholly-owned subsidiary, Chrysler UK. During this period, Tony Benn was to reveal that the figures that had been assembled for his ministry made it clear that between 1962 and 1967 Rootes Motors had returned a mere 0.3 per cent on the capital it had employed. Too late to come to the rescue of Rootes Motors, but a year later, as many readers will know, Leyland Motors did acquire British Motor Holdings to produce the British Leyland Motor Corporation (BLMC), which was to go through a number of different forms of name. Interestingly, Stokes was to discover that the figures that had been produced by British Motor Holdings during their early discussions were 'completely phoney'. It is often thought that the Government's insistence on delivering this consolidation of the remaining British-owned mass-producers was occasioned by their failure to succeed with Rootes Motors.

With the Chrysler take-over of Rootes and the formation of BLMC, the initial phase of the tripartite decline of the once-productive British Motor industry was completed. The shorter second phase could be said to be characterized by the resultant companies bumbling along, without the desired prognosis ever becoming a reality, and culminating with the actual nationalization of BLMC/BL. The final phase would be the disposal of many of the constituent parts of the corporate ventures, culminating in the foreign ownership of all, with the exception of small specialists like Bristol and Morgan, and even those that might have been protected by their multinational owners discovering that complete production of their vehicles would no longer take part within the sterling area. Lord Rootes' sanguine view of this period was:

I became Deputy Chairman of Rootes Motors Ltd. after my father's death and became Chairman in 1967 after the death of my uncle . . . The Board operated quite successfully during this period, although there was a good deal of interference from Chrysler, Detroit, with the operations. I myself was particularly vigilant in ensuring that the interests of the UK shareholders were protected, and on one occasion we had to insist that certain commitments on new model development, which had been undertaken at the insistence of Chrysler, should be debited to them rather than to the UK company.

The Pentastar Arrives

While some of the Chrysler executives who did their stint of committee-populating and finger-pointing were not entirely without their merits, their lack of inspirational leadership, their inability to communicate with the workforce, which was especially true at Linwood, and their bean-counting ways had a detrimental effect upon the whole former Rootes Group, and many leading lights of the company either left the industry completely or found themselves irresistibly drawn to positions with competitor manufacturers. Those members of the shop-floor workforce, who found that neither of these options was available to them, frequently demonstrated their dispirited morale with an invigorated irascible nature that would all too easily lead to the inevitable 'wildcat' industrial action of unofficial stoppages and strikes. The headquarters moved from the impressive Devonshire House to the more modest Bowater House in Knightsbridge, West London. It seems remarkable from this distance that at a time when the reorganized company most required the loyalty and support of both its workers and dealerships, it should disassemble the Rootes family's culture while not replacing it with anything other than vague promises of what the future might bring and an outbreak of a rash of pentastars. To show the provenance of the company, and very much in line with American corporate thinking, Chrysler's pentastar logo appeared on the cars and sales literature in 1965, extending to all dealers' signage in 1967. Or to quote from the official literature of 1970:

> In accordance with its progressive sales and marketing policy, Chrysler United Kingdom Ltd has undertaken an important programme of 'identification' to create a clear, definite and distinctive image of the Company, its products and the whole Dealer organization.
>
> An image that the public will easily recognize and remember, and which will represent the prestige of the Company and the quality and reliability of its products.

Rootes was finally removed from the company's name in 1970, the companies becoming Chrysler UK Ltd and Chrysler Linwood Ltd. The separate marques would disappear from the bonnets of the cars and trucks in 1977, to be replaced by Chrysler and Dodge respectively – an ignominy the Imp was spared. Things got quieter on the business front as the Chrysler Corporation surveyed what they now controlled, as well as owned. What this would mean for the Imp is covered in other chapters, but whereas most are convinced that it was imperative for the former Rootes company to be restructured at every level, industrial and social historians remain unconvinced that Chrysler adopted a sound rationalization of the model line-up it inherited or its production. Other than trading a few promissory notes, the life-long involvement of the Prudential Assurance was virtually at an end, but there was a small amount of background financial action as far as the Rootes family were concerned, as it chose to realize some of the minority equity it still held, and through two rights issues, the Chrysler Corporation would increase its stake in the equity capital to 83 per cent; then, following the Industrial Reorganization Corporation's exercising of its £10 million unsecured loan stock 'put' option in 1972, this rose to over 88 per cent – still short of the 100 per cent that it claimed for its French and Spanish acquisitions.

It is often quoted that Chrysler thought that the Imp was ridiculously expensive to make and lacked the essential design features that might make it suitable for volume production. Both sentiments were, of course, to some extent true. In latter years, the Rootes Motors company, along with the rest of the British automobile industry, was poor at predicting the exact reality of the former and had little experience of the latter. It is worth pondering upon the enormity of the number of units that most business advisers, especially those advocates of the 'Fordist' approach, think to be the minimum number that is possible to trigger the advantages of mass-production: certainly gigantic numbers that are only realizable with a 'global' model manufactured by a multinational company.

Tony Benn recalls that at the end of April 1970, Lord Rootes, by way of a courtesy, personally told him that Rootes would henceforth trade under the name of Chrysler and that the aforementioned increase in its capital was occurring. Benn's diary entries for May of that year contain a perceptive passage concerning his visit to Chrysler's Coventry facilities:

> I was met by Gilbert Hunt and the Rootes people for a presentation of the work of Chrysler, as it is soon to be known in Britain. They have overcome some of their problems and the Avenger is a very successful motor car. Went to Stoke [near Coventry] after lunch where the engines are built and I met the trade unions and shop stewards – a very bright and intelligent but critical lot. They said to me, 'You've been conned, you've had the wool pulled over your eyes.' I hit back and said I hadn't, but this breakdown of communication was really appalling. The company should give the shop stewards a presentation,

> exactly of the kind they have given me; there is no reason why not.
>
> This is the way forward in industry. I have no doubt about it. You have got to recognize that the shop stewards do now represent power in factories and you have to deal with them and give them higher status in your thinking than the customers or the shareholders because they are the guys that build the product.

Clearly, Chrysler was not promulgating its new corporate message to its workforce on the shop floor, but from the former employees the author has spoken to, this would seem to have been a feature of all strata of the renamed company. Many workers spoke of the undoubted savings, usually described as 'cheapening', being made to the product and the 'Profit Improvement Programme' described in a later chapter (what we would now understand as downsizing, even if its apologists would prefer the friendlier 'rightsizing'), but how this might contribute to a strategy for a glorious future seems as baffling now as it did to the workforce then. What seemed to baffle the Chrysler Corporation was how Chrysler UK could, through that earlier Paragraph vi insistence of the Government, have to leave 15 per cent of their United Kingdom equity in what they deemed 'foreign' hands, after all, this was not true in France or Spain. Also, of course, Lord Rootes might no longer be the chairman of the eponymous firm, but he was still chairman of Chrysler (UK), and the man in the street, or for that matter the Cabinet minister quoted above, still referred to the firm as 'Rootes'. The vice-president of Chrysler International wrote at the end of 1972 to Sir Anthony Part, Permanent Secretary at the Department of Industry (later to be the chairman of the Committee on North Sea Oil Taxation for Margaret Thatcher):

> In order to facilitate its operations in the United Kingdom, it is proposed that Chrysler Corporation (Chrysler) should

acquire all the minority shareholdings in Chrysler United Kingdom Limited for cash, involving a total payment of some £6,090,000. These proposals would carry the unanimous recommendation of the Directors of Chrysler United Kingdom Limited. If this is to proceed, it is necessary for Chrysler to be released from the restrictions contained in paragraph vi of its letter to the Ministry of Technology . . .

Any further Rootes money insignificant, so Chrysler proposes to reorganize its share base from four classes of Equity Shares and two classes of Preference Shares to a single class of Equity . . .

If Chrysler buys the minority interest, then total investment in the UK $139,000,000. British investors could still purchase Chrysler Common Stock on the London Stock Exchange.

The final point was to cover the prevalent attitude at the time that a 'British company', as Chrysler International still wished Chrysler (UK) to be perceived, had its shares traded in London – and for the first time, people other than specialists might understand a single class of share, rather than six different classes. The Government's Scottish Office entertained its worries about a lack of 'identifiable British participation' in the former Rootes Motors, and thought this would go down badly in Scotland. This seems to have been the Chrysler Corporation's least arduous negotiations, with the Government's and the Scottish reservations being put to one side. Having experienced a time in the United Kingdom when every bureaucrat, however minor, has been obsessed with 'performance indicators', it does seem curious to the author that successive owners of this automobile company can have promised so much for Linwood, and received so much government aid based upon these pledges, without anyone monitoring whether the company ever delivered on its promises. Lord Rootes, the retiring chairman, writes of this final scene of the Rootes family dynasty:

Although Chrysler now controlled the company, I thought it right to remain as Chairman, so long as there were substantial minority shareholdings of Equity and Preference shares. However, in 1973, Chrysler bought out these minority shareholdings by means of a Scheme of Arrangement, I remained as Chairman until this was completed and took the chair at the meetings which approved this Scheme. I then resigned from the Chairmanship and the Board, as I felt I could honourably do this, having fulfilled my obligations to the shareholders.

For all the injections of working capital, during the first half of the 1970s, along with British Leyland and Vauxhall, Chrysler (UK) was one of the least capitalized automobile manufacturers in Europe – the highest five, incidentally, were all German. None of the rescued or merged companies, such as British Leyland, ever achieved the profitability that the separate parts had, and the rescued ones were faring little better. By the 1970s, Chrysler (UK), British Leyland, Vauxhall and very nearly Ford in the United Kingdom, were close to the financial edge. This might not have been a new locus for Chrysler/ Rootes to find itself, and its shareholders were only saved from the fate that had befallen those of British Leyland by Lord Rootes' representations for the minor shareholders. It was this that really caused the Chrysler Corporation to buy out the British minority shareholding three years before it was trying to gift its European operations to anyone who would take responsibility for their liabilities.

Labour relations in the whole industry had remained exceptionally poor, but none more so than at Chrysler (UK). During the early 1970s, the British motor industry would experience its worst strike record since the 1920s, with even the still-profitable Ford experiencing an especially damaging strike. Setting the tone of Chrysler's labour relations, with the workers' evident distrust of the management, is the unofficial 'shoddy parts' dispute of 1973

– a year when the company experienced at least forty-three strikes. This acrimonious strike, which involved lay-offs across the company, took well over a month to resolve. The strike centred on whether or not the Ryton workforce should be paid for an hour and a half that the production line was stationary following the discovery, by the workers, that during a previous continuous stoppage, poorly finished parts had been fitted to vehicles on the assembly line. As was usually the case, the company paid up, and the labour relations deteriorated further – production restarted until the next issue would raise its ugly head. In addition to the particular perceptions of Tony Benn regarding Chrysler (UK), the list of reasons offered by industrial historians might be long, but it is remarkable unanimous in its analysis. The lack of investment compared to continental competitors, combined with the amateurish planning and development for new models, features prominently alongside the ineffectual management; whether one admires or deplores the actions of the autocratic owners of earlier times, they did at least know both how to manufacture and market the products that made them wealthy.

Economists will talk of the dismantling of trade and tariff barriers putting British products on an equal footing with more attractive imports, and this is certainly true later in the century, but as the comparative tests reported in later chapters reveal, the imports would still take a little time to catch up, and the Imp, despite its age, compared quite favourably with the competition. It is often suggested that Chrysler (France) fared somewhat better than Chrysler (UK); certainly the former Simca flourished in the way Rootes did not, but it did receive rather more attention from the parent company and its products were marketed freely in the United Kingdom, whilst a reciprocal arrangement seemed somewhat lacking. It was not only through managerial shortcomings in the hard business and production spheres that most levels of management were found wanting, as Benn suggests – those

of their relationship to the workforce cannot be overlooked. The archaic, one might say anarchic, industrial relations led in some estimates to a quarter of British production being lost to industrial actions in 1973 and 1974. The Chairman of Chrysler (UK), who, as it was stated above, was also on the French Chrysler board, claimed to Tony Benn that Simca had not experienced a strike for twenty-two years, as the French Ministry of the Interior surveyed the workforce for political activists – an action that Benn found an unacceptable way to treat a member of a trade union.

Although the trebling of the price of crude oil, occasioned by the Arab–Israeli conflict, did adversely affect the profits of the automobile manufacturers, two observations are necessary with this statement: this was catastrophic for the parent American corporations, but the more frugal vehicles of the European marketplace were far less seriously afflicted, with examples like the Imp actually benefiting from this. The other obvious accompanying statement has to be that, despite the small profits being made by Rootes-Chrysler during some of these years, the inexorable descent into illiquidity commenced in the later 1960s, even if it took until the mid-1970s to reach its nadir, when the British industry would see the nationalization of British Leyland and Ford making thousands of their workforce redundant. Barely half a year after the Government had, because of its importance to the national economy, committed a massive £1,400 million in support and guarantees to British Leyland over an eight-year period – effectively nationalization – Chrysler (UK) was knocking on the same door for similar support. Most readings of its balance sheet would suggest it was in an even more perilous financial state and without the obvious support of the once-guaranteed American profits.

Chrysler International might have made unpleasant financial discoveries within its overseas acquisitions, but as one of the big three North American manufacturers, the Chrysler Corporation had been viewed as financially invincible. The Chrysler Corporation's financial indomitability proved not to be so following the OPEC oil embargo of the winter of 1973/4. As suggested above, its natural home market, with its large V8-engined 'gas guzzlers', was where the catastrophe occurred. In many ways, Chrysler's production problems at home were not all that dissimilar to those it was experiencing in the United Kingdom, but writ large: little investment in product development had left much of the range rather outdated, a developing reputation for poor quality control and build, a diffuse manufacturing base that spread beyond the United States and Canada, and frequently the making of similar, but not identical, components by the different plants. To take one of the standard V-8 engines, for example, if it was produced in the Canadian plant in Windsor, then it was a 313 cid (cubic-inch-displacement) (5,130cc), but the more numerous American production was 318 cid (5,211cc), which of course should not be confused with the entirely different 'A'-series 318 cid – all of which had the same claimed power and torque output in standard form. In any case, assembly was temporarily suspended in five out of six of the Chrysler Corporation's home plants, and many in America, with typical protectionist zeal, argued that Chrysler International should be terminated forthwith.

A Migrating Lame Duck?

On the 29 October 1975, the chairman of the Chrysler Corporation, John Riccardo, held a press conference in Detroit to announce a worldwide loss of $231 million in the first nine months of the year. Britain's position as a Chrysler manufacturing base was described as 'a very grave one' and its largest single problem. Chrysler had been discussing government assistance in the region of £35 million for a new model, but this highly adversarial public discussion took the Government

by surprise. The Secretary of State for Industry, Eric Varley, firmly held the view that this time the company ought to be allowed to go bankrupt as the most propitious course of action which would not threaten the recovery of the recently rescued British Leyland; Tony Benn still favoured state administration of the British component of the company and its incorporation within the nationalized British Leyland. Varley reported that, 'The National Enterprise Board don't want it. Leyland don't want it. Vauxhall are afraid we might help Chrysler. Ford don't want it. The Industrial Development Advisory Board is split 4 to 4, not on the viability question . . . but on the question of whether we should help it, which was not within their terms of reference anyway.'

As could be expected when facing the possibility of presiding over the country's largest industrial collapse, much discussion within the Cabinet ensued. A conservative estimate of the cost of nationalizing the firm was £55 million to cover its immediate losses, with another £80 million required for working capital and development, otherwise bankruptcy was predicted within three months. As well as his infamous 'dead duck' comment, Harold Wilson felt it relevant to point out that 138,000 working days had been lost in the British motor industry in the previous ten months, concluding that he was in agreement with letting Chrysler (UK) become insolvent. Benn records, 'That was the end of that discussion and we went on to [discuss Scottish and Welsh] Devolution.' The Prime Minister later inaugurated private talks with the American owners, and an inadvisable deal that was struck extracted various nugatory promises from Chrysler, including that of moving the production of the Avenger to Linwood and to start the assembly of the Alpine model, still from French-manufactured parts, in Ryton – virtually an imported version of the knocked down kit that had traditionally been the preserve of British exports to the rest of the world. The cost to the British taxpayer was

Such was the public awareness of the Chrysler crisis that Marc Boxer could use his understated style and produce this 'lame duck' cartoon in December without a caption or explanation.

£162.5 million, spread over the next three years. The Imp was given life through secret talks between the company's owner and the Prime Minister, and it would see its cessation through more formalized talks between its American owners and a later prime minister.

Clearly the Government had, in 1975, already twice turned down Chrysler's request for aid, and the provision or guarantees for £162.5 million that occurred was predicated far more on political expediency than any hope that Chrysler (UK) would be able to recover as a sustainable British manufacturer. Eric Varley, the minister, did warn that support

for this operation could be as much as £184.5 million to see Chrysler (UK) through to the end of the decade. Not only was the Chrysler contract for Iranian assembly one of the few successful and on-going car export contracts, but wider financial considerations were involved – Britain had negotiated a loan from the Iranian Government of one billion dollars. Of secondary consideration, but one that was also of significance to the vanity of many a politician: the starting point for closures of any part of the former Rootes empire would be Linwood, and at that time it was perceived that the emergent Scottish Nationalist Party might appeal to a large sector of the traditionally socialist vote in the industrial part of Scotland – the Conservative Party then still having a representative Scottish constituency, and the Scottish Socialist Party being yet to form. For all its political expediency, support at this stage resembled a continuation of the age-old malaise of the British automobile industry and was only deferring the eventual outcome. Against its better judgement, for the above political reasons, the Cabinet changed from being sympathetic to the idea of Chrysler's insolvency to one of adopting a positive stance to temporarily preventing it. Benn thought the terms of the financial support 'was a massive further step towards industrial suicide', as the Government 'would never make sense of these issues if we insisted on confusing company viability with national viability'. This rescue was later thought to have avoided addressing the outstanding failings of Chrysler (UK) even more than the flawed support for British Leyland had done for that company. The contemporaneous perception of this bailout was that it represented the first indication of the future of the British motor industry being, albeit implicitly, placed in the controlling hands of the globalized multinational companies. By the time the Imp was nearing the end of its production run, it became clear that since the Chrysler Corporation had bought into the Rootes Group, it had lost over £400 million in the United Kingdom. The reason the Labour Government's National Enterprise Board could not support Chrysler (UK) was that, in the words of the Parliamentary Expenditure Committee, it was 'charged to be commercially viable'.

It is hardly surprising that, following the Government rescue, the distrustful workers' representatives declined to engage in worker participation at a board level, lacking all confidence in the validity of the gesture. The Government's negotiations with Chrysler had not caused the unions to feel valued, as it was only after the workers' shop stewards had protested, by way of a 'sit-in' in Parliament,

that any apparent recognition was taken of their views. The workers and their representatives, not with complete justification, assessed the position as the company decisions being made in Detroit, while the Government was not addressing the necessary reform of their company that might offer them a more secure and prosperous future. It is hardly surprising that 2,300 workers applied for the announced 1,300 voluntary redundancy positions in 1976 – between the end of Imp production and the closure of Linwood, the Scottish motor industry would once more slowly atrophy to nonexistence.

In 1978 Chrysler completed a new three-year deal with the Government, but within a month the parent was finalizing the sale of Chrysler UK and France. On 10 August 1978, the Chrysler boards would know the declared corporate intention to withdraw from its European operations with the design of selling Chrysler Europe to PSA Peugeot-Citroën. The corporation had little choice, since, following catastrophic losses in the late 1970s, mainly of the Chrysler Corporation's own making, the entire Chrysler multinational company was illiquid; despite his popularity at the time, Geoffrey Rootes' shrewd assessment of Lynn Townsend, the Chief Executive, was correct with hindsight, as he had taken the parent company to the same parlous state as its outposts. Chrysler was only saved by the Chrysler Corporation Loan Guarantee Act of 1979, by which Congress and Jimmy Carter's administration granted the corporation $1.5 billion of aid. Chrysler (UK) and Chrysler France were disposable casualties of this aid package.

Unlike the earlier part of this narrative, the documents surrounding this period are yet to reach the public domain, so the author will conclude this long and complex chapter with Tony Benn's diary entry for 20 September 1978, for where the evidence *has* been available. One finds his account to be remarkably accurate, with less interpretation than one might expect from a life-long politician:

Most people probably never realized that this utilitarian three-wheeler Pathmaster 42 Mark III was really an Imp at heart.

Eric Varley [the Minister of State] presented a paper in favour of the Peugeot take-over of Chrysler UK, which includes the old Rootes Company. There was no alternative, he said.

Bruce Millan [the Secretary of State for Scotland] thought it was the best solution, and Jim [Callaghan, Prime Minister] asked if anyone disagreed.

I said I did. 'In 1976, in what was supposed to be a planning agreement, Chrysler gave us assurances, in exchange for funds, that they would stay in Britain. Now we're supposed to just hand the company over to Peugeot. I favoured public ownership then and I favour it now because their assurances are not worth the paper they are written on.

The key phrase is on page 9 in Eric's paper: "the French Government would not allow us to take over Chrysler in France." Well, the difference between us and France is that they don't allow take-overs but we do. For years we have been told that ownership doesn't

matter, only management. This proves that ownership does matter in the end.'

Jim said, 'Perhaps we are witnessing the end of the car assembly industry in Britain, and that may be a good thing. BL has been a continuing drain on our resources and the British motor car industry has done a great deal of damage to the reputation of this country.'

That was like Samson bringing the temple down around him. Jim is violently opposed to public ownership and committed to the market economy and to Europe, and he is actually hammering an industry which earns us probably over a billion pounds a year in exports.

William Rootes' family firm, via that of Walter P. Chrysler, was now in the hands of the company started by the Peugeot family – once renowned as manufacturers of agricultural implements, corset stays and coffee grinders.

7   It's Getting Better all the Time?

Improvements All the Way

It is difficult to read the title of this chapter without the contrapuntal interjection, 'can't get no worse', drifting through the mind. The production of the Imp range in its Mark II guise from September 1965 to October 1968 does represent a golden period for the car – the automotive analogy of the musical development section: the subject's earlier teething problems were resolved, the factory had got the hang of making them and the company was solvent. These contributed to Rootes' confidence to develop the material to sporting models, a coupé, an estate and a commercial Commer van. This confidence extended to the expansion of the markets at which the vehicle would be targeted.

The Imp might have been saved by the helping hand of Chrysler, but despite the relative popularity of the Singer Chamois, things were not looking joyous for Rootes Motors (Scotland), despite a significant enthusiasm developing for the Imp – only markedly among those with an above-average level of interest in motoring. An article, 'Imp Ideas' appeared in *Car Mechanics*, the Mini-loving writer admitting that, 'A recent run of over 500 miles in a weekend endeared it [the Imp] to me so that I whip out my verbal sword and defend the honour of the little box whenever I hear it being slanged by some local peasant.' The keen observer would notice the royal 'By Appointment' crest was soon to be replaced by the Chrysler pentastar logo, with the deletion of any mention of the Imp being 'Made in Scotland'.

The 1965 sales figures reveal the commercial problem: with total Linwood output of something over forty thousand vehicles representing barely 40 per cent of the sales of the rival Mini (itself enjoying a more prosperous year than it would see again), Rootes' mass-production car was not functioning as the creator of profit for the Group. It is understandable why the Mini is the standard by which the Imp was adjudged, but one should remember that it was overshadowed by its own profitable stablemate of 1962, Issigonis's 1100/1300. The criticism that 'the car itself was badly built and very unreliable, a reputation it has never really shaken off despite conscientious development' sounds a familiar-enough one, but this 1970 group test of small cars by *Car* magazine is its description of the Mini, whereas two years earlier *Speed World International* wrote, 'The Rootes' star is clearly in the ascendant, the day of the Imp is at hand because as a nimble small car it has supplanted the Mini as the smart car to have.' The grand dreams of Rootes worked towards a manufacturing facility that would produce 150,000 vehicles per annum, but this light-industrial Scottish Utopia was not to be, and Linwood, the factory and the town, seemed non-viable without the realization of this dream.

The public's awareness of the Imp was raised through competitions, and capitalizing on the car's success in the popular fuel 'economy' trials in Britain, Scandinavia, Austria and Canada might have assisted the sales team, but like the car's growing success in motoring competition, these only reinforced an image

Once the floor panels are lifted, like the Husky estate (top), access to the van's engine (lower) is good. There is less room available to allow the owner to get at some components, while access to many others is easier – being able to remove all four spark plugs with equal ease is a pleasing feature.

A Sunbeam Stiletto engine bay with a modern alternator fitted. The generator was a popular modernization (especially on the negative-earth cars), as was the lockable engine cover. The oil-cooler can be seen above the Sunbeam script.

that the reviewers were unanimous about before the 'but' part of the review that dealt with the reliability shortcomings that predominated the public's perception. Competition successes were many and varied, but buyers knew that while this enhanced the reputation of the model, the daily life of a road-going car was very different, and Rootes' guarantee did not supply the owner with a pit crew.

Various strategies were considered in order to improve the Imp's appeal, including enormously expensive ideas like increasing the capacity of the storage space under the bonnet or the persistent intention of increasing the engine's capacity. Part of the development of the model that was taking place from 1966 might be chronologically suited to this section, but as the 'Project Intentions' of April and June concern the facelift to the next incarnation of the Imp, these will be left until the later chapter.

Someone with an eye for marketing noticed

the plethora of changes that had occurred to the Imp – understandably, Rootes had kept rather quiet about these changes as they were reactions to admitted deficiencies. Relaunching the Imp might not be feasible, but why not admit to the changes and put on them what would now be described as a positive spin? Stressing the innovatory changes, while glossing-over the reactive remedial measures, the Imp Mark II was suitably badged on the leading edge of the doors and rear. The advertisements would again concentrate on the Imp's low running costs, with statements like 'Drive the car that makes your money go further', but make a link to its known endurance successes: 'Reliability is a hackneyed word – or is it?'

Some of the Imp's most ingenious ideas had either gone or would do so in the foreseeable future. This newly codified Mark II was appreciated by those who tested it, but what of the reliability? The message had to be conveyed to the public that an Imp would be as reliable in its hands as it had proved itself to be under more arduous artificial testing.

There was a host of smaller changes for the Mark II, but some of the larger ones might also have gone unnoticed through not having to bring the previous fault to the dealer's attention under a warranty claim. The variable performance was well recognized in the company's internal appraisals of completed cars, and this was resolved through detail changes to the engine's breathing. Because of the lack of precision in matching the ports of the engine's head to the induction and exhaust manifolds, the whole gas-flowing from carburettor to exhaust was increased to accommodate the required tolerances. The carburettor returned to the original 22mm choke, feeding the enhanced ports in the head and entering

and leaving the combustion chambers via larger valves. These changes ensured that all cars would consistently behave much like a 'well-sorted' Mark I engine. Another change was to transmit the power via a larger clutch that would better withstand abuse (the increase was from 5½in to 6¼in) to a gearbox that had increased oilways to improve the lubricant distribution under all conditions and was now fitted with altered synchromesh. All this added-reliability was complemented by a new version of the ubiquitous water pump.

During Mark II production, one change would occur for dynamic reasons which would almost reinstate the æsthetic poise of the front end, but it was, and remains, a contentious alteration. The positive camber of the front wheels was reduced through resiting the pivot of the front suspension and lowering the

A left-hand-drive continental version of the new Mark II is tested in Scotland. Unlike many manufacturers, Rootes has also changed the handedness of the windscreen-wiper sweep. This one appears to be being tested under normal domestic usage.

The Hillman Super Imp had its badging on the rear and at the base of its rear quarter-panel. Like the other saloons, it has an opening rear window – something Rootes was keen to underline.

whole by half an inch. Most Imp aficionados think that the camber change did further improve the handling. From his limited experience, the author has always thought this lends a somewhat nervous feature to the Imp, so it was of interest to note Tim Fry's com-

This was the script used on the 'Imp Super' that led to the confusion of the order of words. The rectangular badges (and brochures) make it clear the order is Super Imp.

ments: 'The way Rootes did it was a bad idea as dropping the front axle lowers the centre pivot point – it reduces the front suspension roll-stiffness, made it really twitchy and it is still bad in side-winds.' Fry went on to suggest that 'the best solution for the modern owner is to modify the front damper-mountings and fit the originally planned-length springs'.

The Mark II

Gone was the basic Saloon, for the moment at least, and introduced between the Deluxe and the Singer Chamois was the new Hillman Super Imp. Encouraged by the success of the Chamois, the idea of the Super occupying a median position in the luxury stakes was irresistible. This model slotted in between the two continuing models in both specification and price. This made the all-important prices of

The Mark II version of the Hillman Imp was announced in September 1965. Not only did Rootes normally display its scale models with white-wall tyres, but these were popular with the publicity photographers – as were these floral-pattern dresses! This was titled Mark II, and the small badge on the leading edge of the door reveals this.

the new range £539, £566 and £590. With this line-up Rootes hoped there would be an Imp to address the needs of all putative customers at a price they would find tempting, whether it was as the family's first car or, as seemed to be the case of the Chamois, a daily runabout to supplement the duties of a grander family car. At this time, it was uncommon for most households to benefit from the availability of a second or third vehicle.

Fantasy, and a sense of irony, entered Rootes' advertisements for the Super. The copy-writer's banner invitation to the public was 'Go for happy go luxury!', and a short Home Counties tale followed:

All set up for a swinging safari. Four adventurers (and all their kit) off on safari in style

in their Super Imp. To set up camp is simple. They open up Super Imp's rear window and out come pots, pans and hampers. There's room up front too, for more big game equipment. Big load holding that's all part of happy go luxury motoring.

To the advertising copywriters not only was the Super declared to be 'Pretty Practical!', but its headlined seductive feature was its 'Dishy Dashboard!', and reassurance was offered to the owner with the statement, 'You're being powerfully backed.'

Along with what it considered 'minor improvements' and a change of polarity to negative earth, *Autocar* described the Super's appearance: 'Externally, the Super Imp is immediately recognized by the slim black trim strip running along the body sides and the new Super Imp motif on the flat nose of the car and by new colours. The body is now under-sealed on assembly.' As far as the improvements to the interior are concerned, the Super was furnished with door courtesy lights, larger and more compliant seats, more trim padding, liberal use of sound deadening, a pair of wind-tone horns, and, à la Chamois, new wheel trims and the stainless strips on the engine cover. *Good Motoring* was to agree with the mechanical changes when it reviewed the Super, and also mentioned the dummy grille and side flashers, but it had reservations about the seats, as it felt there was room for improve-ment to both shape and padding when com-pared to the best of some continental small cars. Other reviewers continued to mention the extremely wide-opening doors and the usefulness of the opening rear window, enhanced by the Chamois' five strips. Merito-

rious points mentioned by other reviews are the stowage of the occupants' accoutrements and the convenience for routine checks of placing the siamezed brake and clutch reser-voir at the front of the car. *Motor* and others had also liked the positioning of the fuel filler under the bonnet, as it protected the fuel tank's contents if the car was parked in an insalubri-ous location (at a time when it was more common to have petrol siphoned rather than the whole car stolen). Reviewers were befud-dled by the advice for inflating the tyres as 'few cars have so marked a differential [1:2] between the front and rear pressure recom-mendations'.

Reliability was dramatically improving, but this took a fair time for some journals to appreciate, and even longer to promulgate. Although not reported until 1971, *Autocar* published its road test of a second-hand Mark II Super Imp. It opined, 'Early on in its career,

If some of Rootes' artificial photographic publicity shots look strange today, this realistic one of the Super Imp almost defies interpretation. The strangely lit car makes it look superimposed upon the scene, whereas the reclining model on the diving board and the rear of the scruffy vernacular housing beyond is hardly aspirational.

the Imp acquired a poor reputation for durability, the state of this three year old car underlines the efforts which went into overcoming this.'

The Singer Chamois benefited from the improvements to the range, although the reviews were hardly forthcoming, or accurate, on the Mark II version. Not that Rootes' own advertisements were more informative: 'Latest refinements in the Mk. II model [Chamois] include comfort-contoured rear-seating, superior interior trim, protective under-sealing and improved engine efficiency', quoting the 'Luxury amenities: Built in heater and ventilator. Fully carpeted throughout. Three ashtrays. Courtesy light. Windscreen washers, Sun visors, Rubber faced over-riders.' The mind boggles at what is meant by 'Space-age capacity', and despite the Rootes' implication that there was now more luggage space, it remained the same, as did the 'latest refinements' – all carried over from the Mark I.

When the Consumers' Association reported on its Mark II Chamois, 'Rootes' champion in the small car walnut and chrome war', in April 1967, it was more robust. After praising the dynamic and driving qualities, *Motoring Which?*, rather atypically, offered its verdict on the handling: 'Even in the wet, it would take driving not far short of lunacy to make the back wheels slide appreciably.' This was in a comparative test with the Riley Elf and the Skoda 1000 MB. It saw the Singer as 'a Hillman Imp de luxe with more carpet, chrome and soundproofing, an oil pressure gauge, and £50 on the price', and took Rootes to task: 'The sales literature said, "The road-holding and stability are further improved by a low centre of gravity and wide, safety-ledge rim wheels with low-profile SP tyres. The advantage in *safety* cannot be over-stressed." Over-stressed or not, you now have to pay £6 14s. 5d. [£6.72] extra for the radial-ply tyres.' The only truly negative aspect of this report concerned the well-known problem about exhaust fumes.

This New Zealand-assembled completely knocked down Super Deluxe announces it is an Imp at the rear. Now repatriated to the Home Counties of England, with UK registration, it reveals its former home through small differences like the carburettor air intake built into the offside B-pillar.

We had a problem in the Chamois with exhaust fumes entering the interior of the car in some circumstances. It was fairly clear that they were being sucked in through the slots over the back window (which are supposed to draw stale air *out* of the car) if the front quarter-lights were opened. Rootes tell us that they have redesigned the exhaust tailpipe to try to overcome this.

As Rootes well knew, it was a more comprehensive problem than the shape of the exhaust pipe; it is not known if the Cosmic Car Accessories window prop to clip open the rear window avoided the problem with fumes. For the first time, *Motoring Which?* picked up one of the astonishing failings of the Imp, and one of which the author has witnessed the consequences: 'It is disappointing to see British cars falling down once again on the question of electrical safety – particularly the Chamois, which has no fuses at all.'

What of reliability? *Motoring Which?* thought that Rootes had to learn about the application of its undersealing and that the non-stainless trim items were deteriorating, but the Chamois performed well, and better than two previous Imps, although the redesigned water-pump was making threatening noises. It was the first time the Consumers' Association's members had given an Imp a 'good' for reliability.

A new Imp version was announced in October which came in two flavours: Hillman, and three weeks later, Singer – the Rally Imp. Those of Francophilic tendencies might wish to add a terminal 'e', but this suffix only appeared on the similarly entitled model from Simca – the sole emblematic identification of a Rally is a tasteful '998' on the rear, usually louvred, engine cover. Rootes declared the Rally Imp to be 'available in limited quantities', being 'primarily designed for use by experienced drivers in rallies, production car races, hill climbs and similar events'. This model is usually described as more of a 'homologation special' to allow

private and factory-sponsored entrants in competitive events to enter an Imp with the larger-capacity engine. The original dry-liner engine, which was fitted to earlier examples and previously mentioned, was not a reliable object, and most Rally models were fitted with the later version that had the integrally cast liners bored out to be replaced with 'wet' ones of a similarly increased cubic capacity.

The Rally can be comfortably cruised in excess of 90mph (145km/h) through an increase to 65bhp of the power output with a corresponding reduction of the 0–60mph time to under fifteen seconds. Inside, the Rally had a more sporting facia, with a tachometer and usually an ammeter and clock, while underneath more robust springs and dampers were utilized. The sting, of course, was in the tail: larger valves were operated by a higher-lift camshaft and fed by twin Zenith-Stromberg carburettors mounted on a water-heated manifold, aspiration being via a new four-branch exhaust manifold and cooled via a high-efficiency radiator of increased capacity and a separate oil cooler. The standard brakes received servo-assistance. Of the 'extras' offered, a close-ratio gearbox and long-range fuel tank were the two specified – the latter, curiously, being the more expensive. After conversion, the owner received 'The Hillman Imp and Singer Chamois Competition Model' or 'The Imp and Chamois Rally Conversion' supplements to their handbook. Many aspects of the Rally would eventually find their way into the sporting versions of the production cars, but *Cars Illustrated* wondered 'why the manufacturers didn't bring out a hot version earlier than they did' – one might well ask! It concluded its review, after pointing out that the Rally was not a fussy tuned car that was quicker than the ubiquitous Mini Cooper, with the thought that the Imp was 'certainly a whole lot quieter and more comfortable'.

The Rally was ordered through any dealer, but all the necessary parts and work were supplied by the Competitions Department at Humber. The extra cost on top of whichever

base car was chosen was between £250 and £300 – the silliness of the tax system meant that the 20 per cent purchase tax on the extra cost could be saved if the car was technically received, licensed by the owner, driven round the block, then taken back to Rootes for conversion into Rally specification. I doubt if many owners carried this out to the letter of the law.

And Now for Something Different

Rootes turned its attention to commercial possibilities – like most of the opposition, its Commer light van was well past its shelf life. Traders were still chauvinistic and it was thought to be unwise to drive a foreign vehicle with the firm's name emblazoned on the side.

The North Thames Gas Board in London operated a fleet of Imps, and Granada used a fleet of Huskies for its television rental business. The mainstay light van was based upon the Morris Minor, with which the new Commer Imp needed to compare favourably. Fuel economy would be easily matched, the all-important payload was achievable, general running costs were more imponderable, but there was an obvious advantage to be gained in the volume of the payload. Making a virtue out of necessity, having a flat loading deck above the rear-mounted engine meant it was a convenient height into which to manhandle bulky objects, and the cargo tended not to be loaded mechanically. The van variant of the Mini was not capacious, had a low loading deck, and was furnished with a pair of traditional side-hung rear doors – easy to better that. Classified in the 5-cwt category of light commercial vehicles, the resultant van was to go on sale in November 1965 at the highly competitive price, including the lower purchase tax, of £408. The first production models might have been sold as Commer, but the pre-production examples, though few in number, managed to occupy four different names and model numbers, including Imp Junior and Imp Senior.

Ron Wisdom (1929–2003)

Ron Wisdom was born in October 1929 in Coventry, where he also received his schooling before specializing for two years in engineering at Coventry Technical College and spending a year at the Coventry School of Art. The Second World War now being over, Ron secured a job in his local advertising agency, but after a year this was interrupted by his obligatory National Service. Having accomplished his military duties in 1950, he was employed by a Coventry advertising agency that held the Humber account – this indirectly led to him joining the Humber Motor Company's Styling Department in 1954. He worked on many detailed items over the whole Rootes Motors range of vehicles – this being done from Humber Road.

Ron's first 'Imp-related' job was to restyle the front end of the Slug in a more traditional manner in 1957. He continued his association with the development of the Imp's styling while working with Bob Saward on aspects of the evolving detail of the saloon, and contributing to the ill-fated Asp. It was in 1963 that Ron took over responsibility for the future styling of the Imp, which included his designs for the van, estate and the coupé body shapes. He continued with what he describes as the 'half-hearted bodywork updates' of the Imp range, none of which reached fruition under Chrysler's control, thus seeing the styling of the model to the end of its production. (Under Chrysler, the design studios were moved from Humber Road to Whitley, near Coventry, now part of Jaguar.)

Like others, Ron did not avail himself of a new lifestyle in France after the take-over by PSA Peugeot-Citroën, and he stayed in the Midlands. He moved to Rover in 1983 as chief stylist, initially working on the colour and trim of its ranges, then becoming the styling manager for Rover's Special Products Division.

After retiring in 1988, like others associated with the Imp's development at Rootes, Ron was engaged in diverse projects in his capacity as a freelance designer and consultant.

Alas, Ron, who had been so informative and forthcoming during the writing of this book, died during the book's later production stages.

Ron Wisdom took over the styling of the first two differently shaped Imps. When Wisdom assumed responsibility for Imp styling, there was a running prototype of an estate and he continued with the idea of separate van and estate styling. Lord Rootes, who knew the farming community well, realized that it comprised large numbers of tenant farmers who required small vans – the tale about the van requiring sufficient headroom to take the standard Milk Marketing Board's milk churn is authenticated by Ron Wisdom. The van was considered the priority, but Wisdom progressed with both the estate and the van. Because both were essentially variants of the standard Imp, he went from early sketches to cannibalizing saloon bodies and working at full size. The original estate shared the line of a saloon, so the rear metal was replaced with clay, whilst the van had the whole roof removed. A running prototype of the lower-roof estate was made.

The Commer van had involved re-engineering the body to obtain the headroom above the relatively higher floor. The roofline was raised, not in the continental manufacturers' way of having it rise behind the front seats, but by having a flat raised roof for the entire vehicle. This gave the seating area an airiness that the saloon did not enjoy. The rear door, a single item that lifted up in the manner of estate cars, revealed close on 70cu ft of space. The one-piece rear door could be furnished with a large window, and the styling exercises on the clay reveal that different depths of fenestration were tried. Vans were never supplied with rear side windows, because of the fiscal implications of higher rates of purchase tax. Ron Wisdom recalls adding transverse swaging to the roof and a horizontal crease above the drip rail to add rigidity and to prevent the roof from experiencing excessive sympathetic vibration and drumming. The eventual depressions on the upper side-panels of the bodywork became the location of the sliding rear windows once the Commer van body became the paradigm for the Husky estate.

The prototype estate adhered to the first thoughts of a saloon-based small estate car. This had the saloon's lower roof-line but the Husky's sliding windows, as well as the transverse swaging of the roof panel and the useful ability of checking the oil and coolant without disturbing the engine covers. With the sloping tailgate closed, the rear-end shape has references to the Ford styling of the time.

The Commer Imp 5cwt van was Ron Wisdom's design. One of the factory-fitted mirrors was demanded by the Construction and Use Regulations for vehicles without rear side-windows.

Items that differed from the norm of the range included the larger clutch, sturdier driveshafts, stiffer rear springs, and stronger wheels with less-compliant tyres. So as to allow the engine to use the lowest octane RON fuel on sale in Britain, an 8:1 lower-compression engine was developed – this engine was also supplied in Imps that were sold in markets where higher-octane fuel could not be guaranteed.

Attempts were made for the Commer van to become the delivery vehicle of choice of large customers, and it found favour with a few transport managers. But it was not a

Not only did the van possess sufficient headroom for the regulation milk churn, but Rootes' claim of offering space for 50cu ft of load behind the driver was credible and made the Commer a very useful little workhorse. Attention to water and oil levels is easy, as access to these is above and to the right of the number-plate, with the engine covers remaining in situ.

This Mark II left-hand-drive Sunbeam Imp De luxe has the sweep of its windscreen wipers altered to suit the position of the driver. Rootes was highly inconsistent about which models were marketed where as Sunbeams.

commercial success, although it did limp on with a few enthusiastic customers until production stopped in 1970. After 1968, most of the examples of the van appeared as the Hillman Imp Van, with the mainland European market usually receiving the identical model as the Sunbeam Imp Van. Opinion today is divided on this remodelled Imp – some find the van 'curious' or 'strange looking'; this author would tend towards those who find it and the more successful Husky estate to be pleasantly satisfying, albeit functional.

Sports' Day

The Super Imp was satisfyingly super to its new owners, but contrary to what some reviewers believed, it was not super in terms of offering enhanced performance. The Sunbeam Imp Sport offered potential owners with sporting pretensions the road-going car for them. As *Speed World International* said:

'Super if it did not go any faster, Sport if it did.' Those who admired the use of walnut could have it if they bought the identically priced 'Luxury with a sting in the tail' Singer Chamois Sport for £665 – also advertised as 'Now the most successful luxurious light car on the road becomes light fantastic'.

Extracting the potential extra power from the standard 875cc engine was the only plausible way for the company to achieve the output of approximately 55bhp gross (or 50bhp DIN) (the intention of uprating the entire range to 928cc will be dealt with in the next chapter).

The Sport would eventually replace all the Singer models, but its name has caused confusion. Up to 1969, the sales literature describes it as 'Sunbeam Imp Sport', it then is entitled merely 'Sunbeam Sport', reacquiring 'Imp' in 1973 and again reverting to Sunbeam Sport. Whichever 'Sport', the most noticeable change for the owner lifting the newly ventilated engine cover was to find the carburettor

What is a Sunbeam Imp?

This can be extremely difficult to define. There are some sporting variants that are clearly Sunbeams – the later Stiletto and the North American Imp Sportsedan being the most secure examples. Other than that, the Rootes Group engaged in badge-engineering for different markets. On the home market, not only was the Stiletto always a Sunbeam, but the sportier versions of the Saloon would either start, or eventually be graced, with this badge – even the Singer would effectively be rebadged as such.

Many left-hand-drive cars (i.e. intended for countries where vehicles are driven on the right-hand side of the carriageway) were badged as Sunbeam, but while this is so, the Rootes marketing department was far from consistent, so that *La nouvelle voiture légère dans la class de luxe* of the French brochures clearly offers a Singer Chamois to fit the bill. Taking Holland as another example, following the Hillman Imp's success in the 1965 Tulip Rally, the Sunbeam Chamois was heavily advertised, and when the Sunbeam Californian was launched in 1967, the Imp Saloon still admitted to its Hillman name, as did the Commer Imp Van. In 1968, however, *De Sunbeam Stiletto, een nieuw Chrysler-produkt* heralded the appearance of all products of the Rootes Group as Sunbeam – not only the Sunbeam Imp Van, but also the Sunbeam Minx, Rapier and so on. It is interesting to observe that Chrysler's promotion team did not pay attention to the detail that made the former Rootes team legendary – some of these Dutch brochures have the Chrysler Benelux logo on one cover, while overlooking the replacement of the Rootes symbol in other places!

Sunbeam was used for variants like the Sunbeam Imp GT which attracted attention in reviews, such as a German-registered example in *AutoMotorUndSport* in 1966. This would appear to be the equivalent of the Rally, but using an American specification Mark I body-shell, complete with front chrome under-riders and rear bumper-bar – perhaps this was mopping up some of those unsold bodies designated to the Amer-ican market. This 'GT' should not be confused with the Hartwell Imp GT or the Australian version announced as 'Chrysler Presents Hillman GT' – a completely knocked down, single-headlamps car solely for the Australian market, which did have a manufacturing code normally reserved for Sunbeams, but was most definitely badged as a Hillman. This was really somewhere between the Sunbeam Sport and the Chamois version, but virtually identical to the former. As Sunbeam was well recognized as the purveyor of sporting models, it seems curious not to have utilized the marque. It is rumoured that the unique badging was rather rapidly styled in Adelaide through combining the designs of that used by Ford for the Cortina with a common third-party accessory sold by speed shops. The later Sonic/Stilleto (*sic*) was another type unique to Australia – this time a car with a removable hard/soft top.

For a company that once took such pride in its marketing abilities as the Rootes Group did, these later mainland European brochures are pretty muddled. The cars they feature are obviously right-hand-drive models, lightly airbrushed and still complete with their British number-plates. The scenes portrayed in them are quaint to say the least – I wonder what the Dutch tradesmen thought of the English rural-village scene, with the Sunbeam Imp Van parked on a hill on the 'wrong' (left) side of the road, while the old-fashioned baker delivers a tray of his produce to the local village stores. These 'Hillman' photographs have the lettering retouched so that the seven letters become mere unreadable placeholders and could just indicate 'Sunbeam'!

The coupé versions were never assembled or sold in New Zealand, but some post-1968 Imps were badged as Sunbeam – although these had quadruple headlights, the engine was the single-carburettor type. These were the only locally assembled Sunbeams to be sold there.

After the time of the Imp, of course, the engine and name lived on in the Sunbeam 1.0LS.

replaced by a pair of Zenith-Stromberg 125CDs mounted on a coolant-heated alloy manifold and an accompanying exhaust manifold leading to a new exhaust system. The more observant might notice the adjacent compact oil cooler, a separate external oil return from the head to the sump, and the larger top of the engine block. It was possibly intended to be a Gran Turismo model, as those developing the Sport engine always referred to it as the GT – a nomenclature restricted to its Australian use. The Sport engine possessed

The Sunbeam Imp Sport is a nippy version of the saloon which was sold with rather restrained external trim and decoration that did not give away its increased performance. The 'dustbin lid' type of hubcaps fitted here proved to be rather delicate in service, and were retained by strong clips that scratched the painted wheels.

This Singer Chamois Sport combines the usual Chamois recipe of interior and exterior adornments and comfort with the improved performance offered by the twin-carburettor Sport engine. The extra stainless-steel trim strips on the roof gutter and doubled-up on the side, with painted coachline between, combined with the imitation radiator grille, makes it clear this is a Chamois. The wheel trims and over-riders are not so indicative, as they are frequently fitted to the publicity photographs of lesser Imps.

The opening rear window and its friction x stays on this right-hand-drive car are clear to see here. According to the publicity caption, this was a feature of the 'Sunbeam Imp, Imp Sport, and Chamois', and it was 'Aufklappbares Heckfenster' or 'Lunette arrière relevable'.

many modifications that owners would not see unless they delved inside. The cylinder head was given an improved gas flow to optimize its richer diet through increasing the diameter of its ports and valves, altering the geometry of the camshaft and fitting double valve springs, while sturdier pistons were deemed wise.

Because of the anticipated driving habits of the purchasers and the small comfort margin in the engine cooling department, the radiator was further uprated on this model. The temperature of the transaxle's lubricant during flat-out cruising for lengthy periods caused consternation, but it was decided to take a gamble that few would experience this. Despite Rootes' claim for a 'new suspension', it was business as usual, but with a number of modifications, including 1in, rather than 0.875in driveshafts, higher-geared steering, revised springs and dampers, and heavier suspension arms.

Rootes, in December 1966, under the heading of 'Another point of interest', notes that 'A request has been received from Home Sales and Competitions asking that a disc/drum braking layout be investigated as a track option . . . Engineering have released three schemes to Product Cost Dept.' Disc

brakes was the obvious route to go down, and they were becoming more common. *Car & Driver* had been surprised to find so many modern touches, but no disc brakes, and Rootes had experimented with disc brakes during the 1965 Alpine Rally. Subsequent to an earlier development proposal of 9in drum brakes, disc brakes were investigated on two test cars through the fitment of Girling callipers and associated brake discs – but these were thought to be too expensive, and a servo-assisted system with a larger master cylinder was incorporated that retained the status quo drum brakes. The location of this servo unit fluctuated: some cars had it fitted under the bonnet, while it migrated to the engine compartment for other production runs. With a similar eye to cost, the dashboard was not furnished with the expected tachometer, but instead the 'red line' for the engine, 7,000rpm, was a literal red line for each gear painted upon the face of the 110mph (177km/h) speedometer. The water-temperature gauge became standard and was accompanied by an ammeter. *Autocar* was drawn to comment: 'The Imp Sport is one of the finest small cars when it comes to ergonomics; all the controls are in the right places.'

Most enthusiasts claim, as *Autocar* did, that the reprofiled and fully reclining seats were the most supportive and comfortable fitted to any Imp. But the old bogey, that of unreliability, was still on the lips of every bar-room authority who 'knew about cars', and like its predecessors, the Sport did not achieve its sales potential.

More Variants

While financial chaos reigned, Rootes continued with an impersonation of the Emperor Nero and kept fiddling – and for once it was right to do so. The new model, the Imp Californian, was all about selling the idea of style. Rootes' usage of Californian had lain quiescent since the pillarless two-door version of the Minx of the early 1950s. The idea of a fastback version was not new outwith the United Kingdom, but it was an unlikely path for Rootes to take – it would not be until 1969 that Ford would introduce buyers to 'the car you always wanted' – the Cortina-based coupé, the Capri. The Californian was cheaper than the Sport, reliably outselling the better performer, saying quite a lot about image. Sentiments about image were encouraged under the banner 'Hallo Beautiful! meet the new Imp Californian', it was described as 'the rakish new car with the fastback flair', and buyers were assured that it had 'got everything going for it'. After reassuring the style-conscious of its 'stunning good looks' and its beauty being more than skin deep, the hyperbole promised that 'Envious glances are standard'.

The coupé's styling was the brainchild of Ron Wisdom – the whole idea was. It might have withered on the vine like many of the Imp's 'Project Intentions', but whereas the men from Detroit could not empathize with the true sports car, they thought the coupé was what was required. To put it in Wisdom's words, 'The Americans were beginning to get really involved by this time. I had done some sketches of a fast-back Imp derivative and when they [the men from Chrysler] saw them,

Although it would not officially be available until the start of the following year, this Hillman Imp Californian was photographed at Linwood in May 1966, and was the first production car of this variant series.

The Californian seems to be lost in this Mediterranean back-projection. The cabin's air vents can clearly be seen at the base of each side of the fixed rear window. The identification badges are on the engine cover and front wing ahead of the door. Curiously, some batches only have the wing badge on one side of the car.

they got keen on it.' It was at this point that Chrysler US made the decision to progress a coupé at the expense of a separate estate car, leaving Wisdom with another styling problem: what to do with the estate that was still required?

Ron Wisdom speaks warmly about a fellow stylist, Colin Neale, from Chrysler, Detroit. Neale, an expatriate Englishman, was the second-in-command in the styling department of Chrysler US, and it was he who was enthusiastic about expanding the range and made many suggestions during the coupé's gestation. The coupé's development went straight from drawing to full-size clay model, utilizing a decapitated Imp. Wisdom liked working with clay on the cannibalized saloon, as it gave him 'the chance to gauge all the proportions and see that they worked before going to the see-through models'. 'Everything from the waist up was new, so we tried taking the roof down [by 1½in] and putting more rake on the screen.' Wisdom remembers working on the coupé alongside work on the Sunbeam Tiger.

The rear of the coupé was influenced by the financial state of the company: whereas it was desirable to transliterate Bob Saward's idea of an opening rear window, the cash was just not there to allow for this, as it would have increased the complexity of the rear, and the extractor vents were now placed below the rear window. It was considerations of weight, cost and time that left the coupé devoid of the Imp's most advertised feature. To overcome the loading difficulty, Wisdom suggested a split rear-seat.

The Californian inherited the Super's interior appointments, including its reclining front seats. The only dynamic improvement introduced with this model would soon be incorporated into the entire range: the resiting, mentioned earlier, of the pivot of the front suspension. Some of the reviewers were convinced that this coupé actually went faster than the standard item! Thus Ron Wisdom had been successful when he says: 'We were only asked to make it *look* faster and more aerodynamic.' The coupé was not faster and was not as slippery through the air as the saloon. A few months later, the Californian was joined by the Singer Chamois Coupé, the usual recipe being concocted, with the usual Chamois imitation grille replacing the aluminium-alloy extrusion grille-like decoration of the Californian. Dunlop evidently thought the Californian was appealing enough to ally its C41 cross-ply tyre with this image.

Ron Wisdom might confirm the Californian was intended to look faster, but Rootes was taken to task by *Car* in its review. It approved of the 'fast-back version of the Imp', but also opined, 'It doesn't exactly set the road on fire. One can't help thinking that a bit of an opportunity has been lost in not installing the Sport's Imp engine which, with the car's new appearance, would make the whole thing a much more attractive proposition for chaps like you and us.' *Autocar* suggested that the Rootes attempt to establish style over content was not without its appeal: 'In the latest Californian, Rootes offer what most people will consider is a much prettier version of the Imp', and, 'Although the Californian offers less room for more money than the Imp, it does have the big advantage of individuality in an anonymous sector of the small car market.' *Autocar* did think it strange that a new model should be offered without servo-assisted braking (it was a theoretically available extra) and devoid of any face-level fresh air – how rapidly Ford had been changing the public's expectation. The observant *Autocar* reviewer mentioned one cost-saving item introduced with the coupé forms – the bonnet release was by way of a pull cable under the left-hand side of the dashboard (to the consternation of

SUNBEAM IMP CALIFORNIAN

Not having an opening rear window to assist loading, the fold-down rear seat in the coupé variants had the innovatory split seat backs.

The Hillman Husky appeared like this on 18 April 1967. The extra roof height and copious fenestration made it the lightest and airiest of all the Imps – the sliding rear passenger windows added to this feeling. The two-tone appearance is restricted to a band that lies in line with the windows, and the roof is painted the same shade as the lower colour.

many a passenger, inside the lockable glove-box on the Chamois); starting with the Californian, the release was placed behind the front badge, being operated from the outside. For the remainder of production, the rule was that all saloons with single headlights would have a cable-operated bonnet release, whereas those with twin headlights and all coupé forms would have the external release mounted behind the badge – if the badge looked reasonably flush, then the release was by interior cable; when it was the deeper, more protruding type, it swivelled to allow the bonnet to be released.

What of the intended small estate following the cancellation of the prototypes? Rootes decided that what would become the Hillman Husky estate would utilize much of the already developed van. The success of this was in the eye of the beholder; as far as the author is concerned, it was a highly practical small estate and the added headroom aided the airy feeling within, especially when all the passenger seats were occupied, and it had plenty of room for the driver's goods and chattels. Unlike the pretty-miserable and more expensive Mini estate, the Husky did not feel like the

van on which it was based. The Husky's opening sliding rear windows, a first for the rear-seat passengers in an Imp, further added to its appeal, and all-round visibility was superior.

The Husky inherited the Deluxe saloon's passenger fitments, and a more compliant rear suspension than that of the van was adopted, as were radial-ply tyres and the higher-compression engine. Throughout its four-year sales life, this little estate had a restricted, but consistent, market of customers. Rootes was correct to have addressed the estate market through maximizing its investment in the van. Chrysler/Rootes undersold this useful little workhorse when continental importers were just starting to promote their versatile small estates – ones inferior to the Husky.

In October 1967, *Motoring Which?* published a test of small estates. It compared the Husky with estate versions of BMC's 1100, the Citroën Ami 6, Morris Minor 1000 Traveller, Renault 4, and the Triumph Herald 1200. Ron Wisdom had got it right and the Husky was found to have the best headroom in its class, and once the engine cover was removed, things were easier to attend to than

The proposed Deluxe version of the estate might look less utilitarian adorned with its non-functional wood and imitation-wood panels, but it was a curious transatlantic amalgam of station wagon and English shooting brake. With its large single-pane side-windows, it predated the incorporation of the sliding rear-side windows.

on the Imp. The Consumers' Association praised the estate's dynamics: 'It seemed to corner just as well as the Hillman Imp – which is very well indeed.' The Husky had the best gear-change, and for the first time, a Linwood product was described as in good condition on delivery. A few minor points of criticism were pointed out: care was required with the load distribution so as not to make the front wheels too light; the brakes were again found to be too heavy – as in Rootes' own observation, *Motoring Which?* suggested the Husky needed disc brakes; the heater-blower being an optional extra, along with having to use the driver's foot to adjust the air distribution, was again criticized, as was having a key-lock only on the driver's door – mercifully, when the steering wheel changed sides for overseas markets, so did the solitary key-lock. Unlike the earlier Imps, this one finished the test with the underside described as new and well pro-tected, though, alas, 'above, the picture was much less happy' due to incomplete cleaning before painting. For those who were listening, the Husky was now described as 'very reli-able'; the Consumers' Association had only

experienced some minor trouble with the silencer, and the overall conclusion? 'Now that the Imp range seems to have overcome its earlier reliability problems, we think that the Hillman Husky is the better on nearly every count.'

Born to be Wild?

This remarkable fecund period for Rootes Motors was concluded when the Sunbeam Stiletto was released in October of 1967. For some this was what the Californian should have been all along, and as Rootes advertised it in those less politically correct times, 'For men whose wives think they've given up sports cars' – a curious mixed message at a time when the company was proclaiming the Imp's competitive rally achievements in the hands of Rosemary Smith! As Ron Wisdom points out, 'People talked of the success of the Imp in sporting terms; pity there wasn't a sporting version of the coupé.' After underlining the original coupé's intention merely to look faster, Wisdom continues his recollection: 'Eventually, the Engineering Development

160

A Singer Chamois Coupé, released two days after the Husky, was a popular choice for those who wanted a coupé (especially those who eschewed vinyl covering to the roof), but wished to retain the interior style and comfort of the Chamois model. The front-wing badges on this variant extend to both sides of the car.

thought it also ought to deliver the promised turn of speed and the Stiletto version of this body [coupé] resulted in the performance matching the stylist's implication.' The Stiletto used the Californian's fast-back styling, this time sensibly combining it with the Sport's engine in order to equip it with the performance its fellow coupé promised.

As the Stiletto was the most expensive Imp, launched at a price of £726, the potential buyer had to see what he was getting for his money, and no one could accuse Rootes of hiding the Stiletto's light under a bushel! As was the custom of the time, sporting cars were adorned in acres of black leathercloth or vinyl, and in this way the Stiletto cannot have disappointed. This Stiletto variation on the proverbial theme sold well, being outsold only by the Chamois variants, but after two successful

years it was no longer the desired style at the posher end of its marketplace. As with the Californian; style is a fickle quality upon which to rely.

Rootes issued a 'Point of Interest' in February 1966 that makes clear that this model was intended to have larger drum brakes:

Due to faults revealed during our development prog. we will be unable to release the 9in brakes in time for incorporation into the Sunbeam Stiletto coupe. The stiletto will therefore commence production with 8in brakes and servo situated in the engine compartment.

The 9in brakes will be introduced asap, but meanwhile, will buying dept. please suspend work on the production tooling which is in progress at Girlings.

The first of the quadruple-headlight models, the Sunbeam Stiletto, represented the top of the range for the Imp model. Rootes had been concerned at the outset of the Imp that there might not be a sufficiently perceptible gap between the Imp's performance and that of the more expensive larger cars – this was most true of the Stiletto. With its superior road-holding and handling, it and its saloon equivalent caused much comment when they were compared to the larger and newer parts of the Rootes range.

161

There were no extra-large brakes, but for the extra cash the buyer could sit in his or her new Stiletto and see that it looked very different from the Imp next door. On the way into the driving seat with its multitudinous adjustments, he or she would have noticed the emblematic effect of those four 5½-inch headlamps mounted in the car's new front panel – the traditional Rootes code, doubled-up headlights, clearly meant that this was top of the model's line – and, at the time, the owner would have thrilled at having the roof covered in black vinyl (well, even Rolls-Royce, albeit with more expensive fabrics, thought this a tasteful option to offer). The extra trim on the roof channel probably went unnoticed, as did the attention to detail of the double coachline or the car's chromed exhaust tailpipe.

So what was so different about the interior? At the instigation of Colin Neale of Chrysler US, the ergonomic binnacle was replaced by a full-width dashboard with conventional instruments, including, at long last, a tachometer – its only supernumerary item. The Stiletto's dashboard layout, which remained particular to this model, looked as if it was much more comprehensive. There was a 'more sporting' covered steering wheel, and should the going get hot, the use of the new fabric, 'Amblair', on the seat facings would be appreciated. When *Country Life*, that paragon of middle-class English taste, tested the Stiletto, it

thought the rubber washer-operation bulb to be antiquated and the single key-lock on the driver's door a frugality that did not befit the car's aspirational quality – it did, however, appreciate the fourteen-position adjustment of the front seats, even if other reviewers were to find them annoyingly fiddly.

The membership of the Consumers' Association would read in *Motoring Which?* about the next general revision to the whole series of Imps alongside a depressing report on a later Stiletto, but many of the Chrysler-inspired changes did not greatly change this model. The deterioration of the morale of the Chrysler UK workforce can be interpreted as part of the *Zeitgeist* of the British automobile industry, but it was at its most extreme in Linwood. Jim Pollard recalls how dispiriting it was to improve the build-quality of the Imp, only to have business-studies advisers descend from Detroit and tell the management that things were going to be done differently. The history of many models is surrounded by the mythical assumption that the later ones were made of thinner metal or made to a cheaper specification: in the case of the Imp both are true! Chrysler was forced to spend quite a lot on each car by way of extra sound-deadening material to rectify the results of their economies, and Tim Fry has been known to comment that the thinner-gauge metal made the body a monocoque 'jelly'. The personnel

The coupé rear of the Sunbeam Stiletto shows the cabin ventilation at the base of the rear window, as well as the copious ventilation for the engine compartment. The period Lucas reversing light and the 13in Minilite alloy wheels are an owner fitment. The identification badges on the rear wings (always two) also portray a stiletto graphic – there is still only one pentastar, though.

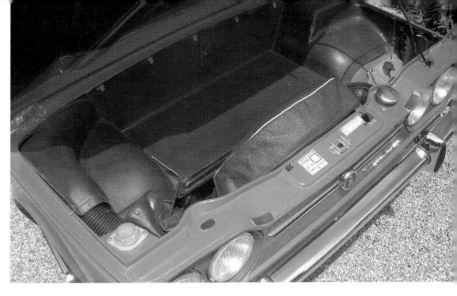

At the front of this red Sunbeam Stiletto, note that the hydraulic reservoir is moved outboard from the front panel to accommodate the twin headlights. The optional-extra spare-wheel cover is rare to find intact. The owner has added the missing fusebox.

cost-cutting exercise from Detroit, the 'Profit Improvement Programme', was much hated throughout the company and affected all levels of the staff, naturally leading to insecurity from the lowest to highest echelons of Linwood. In addition to the 'Quality Control Inspectors' being reclassified as 'Viewers', the cars' 'Lethal Tests' became downgraded to 'Safety Checks', and various other labour-intensive stages were reduced to save expenditure. Pollard, like others the author has spoken to, recalls that most of these advisers had little knowledge of the British industry and no understanding whatsoever of small cars. When Pollard was taking one of the Chrysler assessors through the Linwood paintshop, he was flabbergasted when the fellow 'said he didn't bother with small cars – and anyway, why spend so much time on a beautiful paint job?' The Imp lost its extra coat of paint and the factory lost its guardian of quality: Jim Pollard, like many other managers, left at this point 'as I felt that I couldn't guarantee quality when the [new] strategy was to reduce the cost of ensuring this'. Others, like Bob Croft, chief engineer on the body side, could drift off to another attractive position, as did Pollard. The majority of shop-floor workers did not have this opportunity within their gift, so the disaffected workforce expressed its concerns via a collective neurosis that became manifest in the atrocious industrial relations that would characterize this industrial complex in the public's mind many decades after it ceased to exist. The Linwood employees might not have been in a position to read the metaphorical *Mene, Mene, Tekel Upharsin* on the walls of the Car Assembly Building, but they knew as well as King Belshazzar's workers that Lord Rootes' kingdom was divided and their division was not likely to prosper in the new order. Jeff Torrington's fictional multinational car assembly line in *The Devil's Carousel* is only a thinly disguised account of the later culture of Linwood.

Many members of the workforce at Linwood had seen it all before, and their sensors did not have to be finely tuned to realize that the future was not propitious. Social commentators have derided the way many official 'New Towns' deteriorated, often without the full complement of supporting services being in place and without a steady and sustainable state being created within the community. Linwood fared even less well than most, for not only was the workforce at its main employer second-class members of the company, but the town had not been completed and clearly would not enjoy any further money being devoted to making it the dream of only a handful of years earlier. Whereas opinion seems divided as to whether or not Rootes was an enlightened employer, it is unanimous when it comes to Chrysler – white- and blue-collar employees alike rapidly became demoralized, and morale descended to a nadir from which it would never rise.

8 Keep Right On to the End of the Road

Not the Mark II

Nor the envisaged Mark III. It was inevitable that the new owner and controller, Chrysler, would try rationalizing the Imp range – embracing cost cutting wherever possible on this old and unappreciated design. Despite assurances and loose talk from Detroit, it seems inconceivable that anyone truly believed that there was any intention to design or build the promised direct replacement for the Imp – certainly not one based at Linwood, whatever the Government was told. Chrysler's appraisal for reducing the Imp production costs started in late 1967 – this was the oft-cited example of welding the seat panels, rather than having them stitched by an army of ladies at their industrial sewing machines, to make an intended saving of 6s (30p) on every car. There were allegedly sixty penny-pinching suggestions in total, which only made sense if the Imp was truly being mass-manufactured and the estimated life of the design still had sufficient years to run to amortize the design and manufacturing costs of such changes.

The oft-referred-to Mark III version of the Imp was the result of the suggested cost-saving changes – heralded as improvements, whereas most were cosmetic and intended to stimulate continued interest. It would be more correct to ascribe to this version the title 'Not the Mark II', as the Imp III badge was reserved for the Imp on the Australian market – technically a Mark II½, which retained the instrument binnacle. The revamped Imp was announced in October of 1968. For today's buyer, this is the crucial dividing point. In spite of the

The interior of this post-Mark II Hillman Super Imp shows the later-style dashboard complete (on this model) with a lid to the glove box and metal oddment bins on the doors. The quasi-panelled seats replace the usual fluting. The manual choke lever in front of the base of the gear-lever is particularly clear.

Today, a car can be confusing to identify if the owner has appropriated a characteristic part from another variant. This 1967 Super Imp is equipped with a characteristic Sport engine cover, which has the additional engine ventilation and number-plate illumination from above the square plate.

'Project Intentions' for this point in the Imp's life-cycle, mechanically little was changed: there was yet another change to the water-pump seal, some standardization of the syn-chromesh components incorporating Minx designs, dashboard wiring was updated with the use of rudimentary printed circuits and the Chamois models were treated to an uprated generator – still a dynamo.

The originally envisaged prolongation of the Imp series was very different. The Imp was to receive a more fundamental face-lift than the superficial. As early as April 1966, the revived idea of an automatic Imp was again proposed, with the non-sporting variants gaining the option of a semi-automatic gearbox. This time the semi-automatic trans-mission of Ferodo was to be made in the United Kingdom under licence. A known quantity to Chrysler France, it would appear as an option on a variety of Simca models. The origin for investigating its use on the Imp was that 'the instruction comes from manage-ment'. The pre-production date was to be at

the start of 1968, with full production in time for an October release. The standard gearbox, without first gear, was used in conjunction with an 8.5in hydrokinetic torque converter of similar design to the smaller one utilized by the Simca 1000 (Renault were offering a similar Ferodo Ferlec system on the Dauphine). The torque converter and hydraulically clamped friction clutch, housed in a casing that replaced the standard clutch housing, was solenoid controlled by a switch incorporated into the gear-lever knob, with the transmission having its own oil pumps and circuit. Small changes to the rear cross-member were necessitated by this unit. Changing gear, which was still accomplished by the driver, involved depressing the gear-lever knob to disengage the clutch, changing gear, then re-engaging the drive through lifting one's hand off the gear lever. An Imp Deluxe (registration FHP 551C) was pulled from endurance testing and had the standard 875cc engine mated to the Ferodo transmission (this Imp then becoming known as the

'Ferodo Imp'). It was expected that the unit would use a 928cc engine.

The performance of the Ferodo Imp was satisfyingly successful: the 0–50mph and 0–60mph times were several seconds adrift from the manual gearbox cars, but the top-gear's bottom-end time was superior and the middle-speed acceleration was only marginally slower. The top speed was the same, and the fuel consumption, the ever-sensitive point on small automatics, was virtually identical. Like many of the promising development ideas on the Imp, it is not known why it failed to reach production – the three possibilities are that: Chrysler's cost cutting killed it; the added complexity was too great a risk to take (Renault changed many back to a conventional clutch at customers' requests, although Simca seems to have produced many units without difficulties); or Chrysler failed to negotiate a manufacturing licence. The last two of these seem unlikely when one looks at the Chrysler's French usage, so one has to conclude that it was the old story of the company being cash-starved – after all, the new owner was not providing working and development capital to its United Kingdom investment at the level of support that Chrysler France enjoyed, and the Rootes Group/Chrysler (UK) was inextricably descending into bankruptcy.

The Mark III Dream

The 'Project Intention' of June 1966 betrays the dramatic intentions of Rootes to offer a prolongation of the life of the Imp, the '1968 Imp Face Lift'. This was to affect the entire range – Hillman, Singer, Sunbeam and Commer. Suggested dates had the drawings being completed by the end of the year and the Experimental Department's approval and completion of the production specification by the middle of the following year. Stage 1 of the pre-production was at the start of 1968, and Stage 2 four months later – production would commence in August in time to maximize the advantages of the autumn motor shows and to release this as the true Mark III.

Some of the specified developments were mere detail: rubber mounts were to be used on the radiator, modernized two-speed windscreen wipers (although nothing was suggested for the washing facilities), and a new (unspecified) instrument panel was envisaged. Fundamental changes were planned for the suspension: larger bushes to be fitted to front and rear, with thought being given to a cost-

This is an extant example of the proposed Ferodo semi-automatic gearbox that was fitted to the 'Ferodo Imp' for assessment purposes. The torque-converter replaces the clutch within the bell-housing, and the extra control gear fits on top of the standard gearbox.

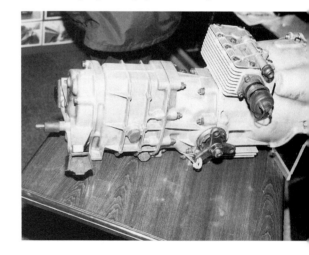

One of the many proposals to modernize the look of the Imp body mentioned by Ron Wisdom, this one progressed as far as a clay model. It incorporates fashionable rectilinear headlamps, and its raised waistline over the rear wheels produces what was known as a 'coke-bottle' shape. The designers/stylists had yet to decide where the fresh-air intake would be.

reducing redesign of the front suspension arm and a possible anti-roll bar being fitted, while the rear 'will probably consist of a new tubular rear suspension cross-member which will be mounted through rubber bushes onto the body shell'. The 9in drum brakes, under development for the Stiletto, were planned for the entire range, but without servo-assistance. The Ferodo Verto semi-automatic transmission would be offered on all single-carburettored versions.

As to the two changes that would have been climacteric for the whole Imp series, there is a paucity of evidence why they were aborted – or even how far either progressed. Under the general heading of 'Body Exterior', we know the 'following panels will be affected': redesigned front wings and panel, bonnet and its reinforcements, air intake box, spare wheel support and the front floor. Rootes intended to redesign the side assembly of the car as a single-piece item – the anticipated savings would only have been realized if Rootes Pressings had also modernized its body assembly. It was also noted that 'a new petrol tank and spare wheel storage will be required, that maximum benefit may be derived from the restyled front end'. When considering the putative considerations for the associated wind-tunnel tests for the new body, in addition to the obvious

requirement of knowing how the restyled front end would effect the Imp's drag, side-wind stability was to be investigated, as were the optimum dimensions for the rear-quarter extractor slots to ensure the new body possessed an adequate air flow – presumably through the vehicle. With these last two investigations, it would seem that at last Rootes was going to attend to the two constant criticisms of the Imp as we know it. Ron Wisdom only recalls 'half-hearted attempts' to restyle aspects of the Imp, including the 'not very serious update' of the early 1970s that was to give it the then popular 'Coke-bottle' styling and rectilinear headlamps, but none of these ideas ever progressed beyond the scale-model stage, although there were many starts made to different styling exercises. Could this again be a case of sound, logical plans becoming scuppered through the pitiful state of the company? Other updates just used the standard body, altering details like lights and grilles – there is a Sunbeam Imp, with the American date of 4/13/65, which has a front very like an amalgam of a Morris Marina with many Japanese cars of the time, through to those of the 1970s, which look curious as the basic Imp is adorned with large rear lights out of the contemporaneous parts bins. Throughout the life of the Imp it remained an under-funded

167

project, even with the not inconsiderable Government hand-outs: Rootes Limited did not have the cash and the Chrysler Corporation never spent theirs. The most gasp-making Chrysler attempt is the Simca Imp, a four-door Simca 1000 with Imp badges and the UK number-plate, APX 163!

Of the two changes for the Imp described as climacteric, the second is even more puzzling from several points of view – the company thought it important enough to work to an accelerated timescale for its development, but again there is precious little extant evidence remaining. Project 2090 of March 1966: 'Models affected – All', 'It is intended that the 930cc engine will replace the 875cc engine in all variants' – which in the company's usage meant all Imp manifestations. The drawings were executed within a fortnight, confirmation of the specification commenced in November and was intended to be finalized by the end of the year, so that pre-production could commence in May of the following year and full production by July. Although this engine was required for the hypothecated Mark III and the Ferodo semi-automatic transmission, from its development schedule there must have been the intention of introducing it for the final Mark II models. With a bore of 70mm and stroke of 60.4mm, this 928cc engine was just what the Imp, a

much lighter car than the later Sunbeam 1.0LS, needed.

Though the Way be Long, Let Your Heart be Strong

As it was, the cosmetic changes were all that would be offered in an attempt to convince the public that the Imp was revitalized. The characteristic binnacle made way for the less ergonomic but more conventional, with switchgear out of Lucas's parts bins. As previously mentioned with reference to *Motor's* review of this new model, not everyone thought this progress – some, and the author would be among their number, thought it just looked like a cheap, orthodox solution. The round dials set in a normal dashboard were utilized across the range with the exception of the Stiletto, which retained its previous different dashboard layout. An attempt was made to match the exact appearance of the dashboard to the perceived stratum of the car: therefore the Husky and Deluxe were furnished with a textured finish, the Californian, Super and Sport in black plastic, and gone was the Chamois' use of trees, to be replaced with a plastic walnut-veneer effect. The instruments were set off by imitation leather, accompanied by a padded steering wheel, and the painted heater-covering now matched the dashboard

In the post-1968 model with round instruments, the layout is simply transposed to the left-hand side of the dashboard, rather than being a mirror image, so the speedometer stays as the right of the two larger circles.

panel, with painted metal giving way to plastic. The new seats which were cheaper to produce were also adopted throughout the range – reclining on the Californian, Chamois (Sport and Coupé) and Stiletto, though not the Chamois saloon nor the ordinary Imp Sport. The seats now had catches to be released before they could be tipped forward (which many reviewers found to be too low, difficult to use, and too liable to break in a real crash). With the advancement of legislation under the banner of safety, items like the door locks were altered to qualify as burst-proof. It is only when the latter-day owner tries to cannibalize parts from a later car, he or she realizes just how many of the apparently similar components are not interchangeable. The revitalized Imp was suitably adorned with detail trim changes, different badging and front decoration, and the Chamois models adopted the four-headlamp front that had been unique to the Stiletto. The package was not to everyone's taste, and certainly deficient when compared with the intentions of the real modernization. In an attempt to stave off the criticism that the restyling also looked cheaper to some eyes, Chrysler made small, but it hoped significant, reductions to the prices of the range.

With so much having been done to improve the build quality and reliability of the breed, and to disabuse potential owners of their suspicions about the Imp, the Consumers' Association purchased a Stiletto that was already showing the signs of having been assembled by a discontented workforce – all that effort again went to dust. As part of a test published in its July 1970 supplement under the title, '3 Fast Minis', *Which?* compared the Stiletto with the more comprehensively revamped Mini 1275GT and the NSU 1200 TT. *Motoring Which?* reported on the usual excellent gearchange and 'pretty good' handling, which, for the first time, was not quite up to that of the Mini. Chrysler did not enjoy a monopoly when it came to making curious pennypinching decisions – the Mini lost the Cooper part of its designation as the new BLMC

refused to pay less than £2 per car to use the name. The Stiletto was found to be appreciably slower than the company of this test, but 'it could go as quickly as quite a lot of family saloons with engines nearly twice as large'. The whole raft of the recurrent comments were again found: the Stiletto's inability to cope with side-winds, unimpressive braking, that mean key-lock (which was easily defeated by the testers' tame burglar), fumes entering the car, too noisy for the price, difficulty in using the jack, with a new coupé-based criticism of the drivers hitting their heads on the underside of the roof.

The abysmal state of this Stiletto on delivery and during service caused *Motoring Which?* to report:

> holes in floor under back seat; engine compartment cover had half-inch gap along front edge, and its gutter was bent; oil cooler brackets corroded by battery acid; felt under back seats sodden and mouldy; body seams poorly fitted; windscreen and front quarterlights leaked; gear change stiff; 26 other faults . . . Our Stiletto arrived in appalling condition – with poorly fitting bodywork, dents, water leaks, and an off-tune engine. Its condition was the worst we have seen for some years.

And, 'Our members were not very happy with either the mechanical condition or the bodywork of their cars. By the end of testing, our car was in poor condition.' In its conclusion, *Motoring Which?* did offer a crumb of comfort for the prospective Imp owner: having suggested the Stiletto might have the edge over the faster Mini through being more comfortable to drive and less noisy, it reminded its members that the Imp Sport was cheaper, with much the same performance, and might be a better buy. Reliability had now been established, but with the factory's deteriorating build quality and productivity, the path to the future looked irreversible for the Imp and Linwood. Jeff Torrington's fictional factory

A later Singer Chamois Saloon shows the quadruple headlights and the slimmed-down imitation radiator grille that is similar to an inverted Super or Husky.

The quadruple-headlight Stiletto has simpler badging than some of the later four-headlamp models, and of course is adorned with Sunbeam badge and script.

undoubtedly produced this Stiletto, and its finish is reminiscent of Torrington's portrayal of the underseal and paint divisions. 'Underneath, under-body sealing was still working well . . . but there were several places which it had not covered', and the standard of finish was best summed up by the observation that, 'The Stiletto's doors were not well painted, and large areas of rust had got a grip (fed, in one door, by a puddle at the bottom).'

The Sunbeam Stiletto, like the remainder of the range, would reflect its corporate ownership. If not emblazoned on the bonnet, then the appearance of the Chrysler pentastar logo, which had been a feature of all advertising,

now spread to the dealers' forecourts and signage, as it had to Simca in France. Chrysler UK did not benefit from Britain entering the European Economic Community, as little attempt was made to market its British products in mainland Europe – this role fell to the much more flourishing Chrysler France SA. As far as Scotland was concerned, Chrysler gave to the British Government and Scottish workers repeated assurances about its continuance of Linwood and its intention to develop an Imp replacement. The sheer size of the Linwood facility, which was rarely achieving above a third of its output, counted against it and it had to be productive for its survival.

Although this is a left-hand-drive version of the Sunbeam Imp Sport, in this press photograph it appears that the sweep of the windscreen wiper has not been altered to suit.

Extra lines had to be established to make the facility more productive – but as to how to realize this, certainly producing more Imps was not a feasible proposition.

A precedence that would remain until its demise started in 1969 when the Arrow-range production (mainly the Hillman Hunter, but also including the Sunbeam Vogue and fast-back Rapier) was transferred from Ryton-on-Dunsmore to absorb Linwood's spare capacity while liberating production space for the rather dull, but new, Hillman Avenger – the highly conventional and inexpensive front-engined, rear-wheel-drive vehicle. The Avenger's claim to British motoring fame at the time was that it represented the first British use of an all-plastic radiator grille! The Avenger would be the last Rootes and Hillman new car, and the final bearer of the latter's name. The British-designed, but Spanish-built, Chrysler 160/180/2-litre of 1970 was intended to be a Humber, but it was never made in Britain. Linwood would also produce some of the Avenger's components. Chrysler was committed to Ryton, and the inconvenient Scottish outpost was a place where the last ounce of potential profit was wrung out of any ageing model – the Imp became such a model.

Though You're Tired and Weary, Still Journey On

With the 1969-model update, the Imp might be revitalized, but alas, the sales figures were not. Chrysler did little more to the Imp other than drop some variant models, while keeping the others going until the company thought of a more productive use for part of the Linwood plant. Commencing with all the Chamois models in 1970, the up- and down-market Imps started to be pensioned off. Within four months, the Imp Sport, Californian, Husky and the Hillman/Sunbeam van would all be consigned to history, with the Stiletto backing up the procession in the following year.

The virtually full-width front badge on this Super Imp is characteristic of the post-1969 models. Inside, these models have the later round-instrument dashboard.

Production of the base-model Imp was recommenced, still aimed at paring the all-important handful of pounds off its advertised list price. Lots of remaindered parts from the Chamois were used alongside the Sport engine to produce the Sunbeam Sport. By April of 1971, Chrysler was advertising the range, with a hint of what was known as 'knocking copy' against the Mini, VW 1300, and even Ford's Mustang, proclaiming 'The Imps. Built by the car craftsmen', and giving the current prices as Hillman Imp £672, Deluxe £725, Super £769, Sunbeam Sport £871, Stiletto £942.

The reviews of this unornamented statement of the original theme were good. Not as ecstatic as the original press coverage perhaps, but motoring was moving on and the expectations of the testers were becoming both more demanding and more catholic. It is instructive to look at group or comparative tests of the 1970s that included the Imp, now with the inclusion of the continental European and Japanese models reflecting the changing motoring tastes of the south-east of England – if not yet the whole country. In his book *The Motor Makers*, Martin Adeney starts with the interrogative assumption, 'Why should it be that my street is full of foreign-made cars when the British, as I was brought up to believe, are one of the greatest manufacturing nations on earth?' Upon the answer to this is predicated the demise of the Imp, Rootes, and the British motor industry as it was known – by the end of the Imp's production run, imported cars started to approach half those sold in the United Kingdom.

The assumption throughout much of this book is comparing what was occurring in the industry, and how Rootes, and subsequently Chrysler, was reacting to it with reference to the Imp, with an implied sub-plot of 'if only . . .'. Perhaps this is a fallacious dialogue and one should just accept that the Imp was an extremely interesting small car that one might choose to enjoy today, but it was made at a time when the whole industry – an industry that was poorly understood by successive interfering governments – could not easily embrace the changing world.

For these contemporaneous comparative tests, the Imp would have to match up to either the ubiquitous Mini or its more successful stablemate, the 1100/1300, and now the Datsun Cherry, Fiat 127, Citroën Dyane and Ami, Renault 5, Simca 1000 and the like would be considered comparative fodder rather than strange and exotic breeds. By this point in Britain, the ageing Imp and Mini were competing against at least thirteen imported models for sales in their market sector. The utilization of space in the newer cars, especially where the genuine hatchback concept was realized, was far superior to that of the Imp's generation. What is astonishing is that after a decade, the Parkes and Fry ideas were still winning out against the newer designs – the Imp's engine might not have benefited from the desired update, but it was usually considered as far superior – the roadholding, handling, and gear-change were also deemed superior to the opposition. *Car's* giant test of the Super Imp, after finding minor items like the new seat catches awkward to use, offers an apologia for the original design and styling:

> At Chrysler the styling department has so far resisted the temptation to meddle more than superficially with the Imp's appearance, which is a good thing for it is an attractive, light-looking car with the ageless quality of basically correct and complementary lines . . . The real difference [with the Mini] lies in the fact that the Imp is by far the nicer car to drive . . . In fact the Imp remains one of the most satisfying of all small cars to drive. It is actually enjoyable, where the worthy Mini is now only practical.

Every Road Thro' Life is a Long, Long Road

Even the basic Imp, without much of its sound-absorption padding, metal door pockets and trim, much of the external bright-work and with rubber floor covering, was considered by *Good Motoring* to be 'Outstand-ing value for money'. The sixth and final sup-plement about an Imp that the Consumers' Association produced for its members in January 1972 was entitled 'Four Cheap Saloons', and tested the basic saloon. The thinking behind this test was that of the fifty or so vehicles *Motoring Which?* had tested in the previous two years, only three remained under £900 – the inflationary pressures of the 1970s were under way. The four vehicles were the Mini (£655), Imp (£667), Citroën Dyane 6 (£688), and Renault 4 (£739). (*Which?* was not playing the manufacturers' pricing games, and quoted the price of the British cars inclu-sive of their virtually compulsory heaters.) The Imp was the sprightliest performer with precise and positive steering, but was not thought to respond well to bumps and irregu-larities in the road surface. Carrying out a more precise assessment of the problem of fumes entering the car, *Motoring Which?* described the carbon monoxide levels as not toxic, but certainly unpleasant. Other than water leaks through the rear window and pas-senger door, the multitude of other delivery faults centred on the Linwood assembly line's inability to tighten nuts and bolts – nearly all the trim screws and bumper bolts were loose (the Mini was delivered in an even worse state and the Renault had potentially dangerous deficiencies; only the Citroën was in a reason-able state of preparedness). As in all the later *Motoring Which?* tests of the Imp, the brittle paint was not surviving well, allowing rust to spread, especially in the seams, the underseal was imperfectly applied and there was a problem with battery acid spilling onto the surrounding body.

As far as reliability was concerned, 'Our Hillman needed a lot of attention, often for faults which could have been avoided by better assembly.' There were lots of faults, none that serious, but several forming a refrain and couplet structure: to have the windscreen wipers inoperative four times seems more than misfortune. Of the Consumers' Association membership, half had reported failed radiators, exhausts, paintwork and rust problems and sticking windows. By the end of the test, apart from an engine oil and grease leakage, 'it was running fairly well' – not that any of the others, except the outstandingly reliable Renault, fared any better. The verdict on each car is interesting: Imp, 'Not happy on the open road, but some virtues as a town car'; Citroën, 'Had very little to recommend it'; Mini, 'Like the Imp, better as a town car. But we think the Imp – and especially the Renault 4 – better value'; Renault, 'Good value for money as a small "work-horse".'

The Middle East would trigger the most significant oil crises for quarter of a century, and Chrysler shelved its plans to delete its most economical model and tried to respond through an advertising campaign across the media as, for the first time since the earlier 1960s, the Imp was just the car that was easy to sell within a context when the fuel costs of running any car rocketed. Like many aspects in the tale of both this car and Rootes Limited in general, it was too little and too late, following a period of stagnation. For too long, Chrysler, like Rootes before it, had been ignoring the old Ford dictum that 'without product, you don't survive!' Although the Imp might have represented a moribund model in the public's consciousness, the motoring press were redis-covering it – if only to represent the known 'old guard' when assembling their newer gen-eration of economical small cars. The millen-nium may have ended with protracted high fuel taxation by the British Government, but it should be remembered that during most of the time of the Imp, British petrol had been cheaper than that available on mainland Europe – one of the reasons why most of the economical small engines emanated from France or Italy. Relative to the overall domes-tic cost of living in the United Kingdom, fuel had never been cheaper than just before the oil price crises that were triggered by the belligerent Middle-Eastern political situation and the market control by the Organization of Petroleum Exporting Countries (OPEC); expensive fuel came as an unpleasant shock to a nation that had yet to exploit the riches of its own oil and gas production. It is also worth casting one's mind back to the government decisions of the late 1950s and early 1960s about the Development Areas: Linwood was in a more extreme position than the other automotive ventures, but all these more-distant projects now found that their transport costs were becoming a highly significant feature of their running costs.

Fill'd With Joys and Sorrows Too

Even if the parent company was fast approaching its own financial nemesis and could not be relied upon to fund the redevelopment of Chrysler UK's outdated product line-up, it is a testament to the advanced nature of the Imp that it was not hopelessly anachronistic a decade after its launch and without the benefit of its later envisaged improvements. In *Motor's* 1973 group test of the Sunbeam Sport in the company of the type of much more modern opposition mentioned above, the Sport not only had the best gear-change, but 'In nearly every aspect of handling and roadholding the Imp was, once again, the highest scorer.' It did think the minor controls had been ruined. In its retrospective appraisal of the preceding decade, *Motor* elevated the Imp to the position of the most under-rated car, a theme embraced by *What Car?* magazine when it produced its buying guide for the Imp in 1974. Under the title 'Living down a poor reputation', *What Car?* proceeded by advancing the notion 'Time and time again the Hillman Imp has been called the most under-rated small car on the market, yet it has never shown any sign of matching the phenomenal sales of the Mini.'

Motor, joining in the general air of the motoring austerity of the time, treated the basic Imp to one of the model's final contem-poraneously published tests: like so many that preceded it, if not those from *Motor* itself, it was against the Mini. 'With the cost of petrol soaring and the production of both cars being stepped up to meet demand, this seemed a good time to return to basics and revisit both cars with this comparative test.' Like the author, *Motor* considered this Imp not so much as a Mark III, but 'Mark II discontinued as a designation'. Like most non-Australian purchasers, *Motor* paid for the 'optional' heater, making this basic Imp's ex-works price £748.87, comprising net price £613, special car tax of £51.08 and Value Added Tax of £66.40 in addition to the £18.39 for the heater. In the manner of many reviewers of the post-1968 cars, one of the things *Motor* felt incumbent upon itself to chronicle was how enlightened the styling of the original interior had been: 'Sadly, the two-stalk system we praised so highly back in 1963 has been replaced: there's now just one, mounted on the right, which operates the horn, the indicators and headlamp dip and flash. The wash/wipe button and main light switch are grouped together on the facia to the right of the steering wheel.' Of the newer layout, *Motor* opined 'Chrysler fill the redundant instrument pods of this basic model with blanks or large warning lights. This gives the facia a rather cluttered appearance', as well as giving the owner the unbridled impression that he or she had bought one of the cheapest cars available, or, in the reviewer's words, 'Though spartan inside, neither car is unattractively finished . . . Large expanses of bare paintwork and cheap-looking cardboard door-trims endow the car [Imp] with an unnecessarily cut-price appearance. For some reason even the vinyl-covered facia and seats lack the quality of the Mini ones.' The untrimmed door panels, lack of door bins, unopening quarter-lights, single sun visor and the instruments being 'small, poorly defined and unattractive' contributed to the ascetic feel that *Motor* had forgotten such base versions conjured up, although the reviewers thoroughly enjoyed driving both cars. It was felt that there was little to choose between the pair, but as the Mini was now 11 per cent more expensive, this became 'a decisive margin in favour of the Chrysler'.

As the 1970s progressed, Linwood would continue to produce the Imp, as it was by now an under-utilized facility and the development costs on this car had long since been amortized (if not those of the factory itself). No further significant updates would be considered, nor for that matter would much Chrysler cash be forthcoming for the advertising budget, which is reputed to have descended to a mere £1,000 for an entire year. Ron Wisdom remembers the 'half-hearted enquiries' from managers, passing on questions allegedly emanating from some corner of a multinational board-room, about the superficial updates to the Imp, but like all previous attempts, these never progressed beyond scale models or sketches. It seems highly unlikely that there was ever a serious intention beyond that of the cancelled update of the later 1960s to do more than keep the Imp ticking along until a more profitable use could be made of the Linwood facility – not that there ever seems to have been much commitment to that either, not since the halcyon days of the Macmillan/Rootes dream for central Scotland: vacuous words of comfort when the corporate hand was out for supporting funding perhaps, the level of commitment to, and strategy for, the region, nugatory.

In the midst of this unpredictable period for the future of private motoring, Chrysler UK was making the final changes to the remaining models in the range – some refer to the Imp that was announced in October of 1974 as the unofficial Mark IV, while others prefer to call it Mark IIIb in an attempt, no doubt, to stress that it was not a redeveloped car. Chrysler, of course, did not entitle it anything, having given up counting at two. Alongside Chrysler's production strategy was the company's behind-the-scenes negotiations with the Government. Two problems remained unresolved for the moment – how to continue manufacturing any of the former Rootes cars, and what to do

about the disastrous labour relations, especially in the dispirited Linwood factory – there are a truly staggering number of Government files on both of these topics. Chrysler benefited from rescheduled repayment terms that the Rootes family had renegotiated during the mid-1960s, but the financial metaphorical chickens, in the form of the premier's 'lame ducks', were coming home to roost.

The American Chrysler management was singularly inept at dealing with the British labour relations, and the tough-talking stance of a dispirited Glaswegian shop steward was beyond its ken. The Chrysler approach was not so much that of a 'good-guy/bad-guy', but both attitudes from the same people: Chrysler UK's strikes in the 1970s were characterized by a well-publicized resolute stance being adopted by the management, only to be followed by it losing all credibility through complete capitulation. Strikes in 1972 cost Chrysler UK 14 per cent of its production, a figure that rose to 22 and 17 in the following two years. By 1974 it is reputed that Chrysler UK was losing the equivalent of more than a week's production per annum from each member in its employ through what is described as 'lost time'.

The revamped Imps were to embrace a number of small changes to the engine, interior and exterior, and further modernization of the electrics. The engine would now benefit from the improved gasflow of the Sport engine, including its sportier camshaft. This engine, however, was detuned somewhat through the retention of the standard smaller valves and ports, still fed by a single Solex carburettor, something that had been tried some years previous on the Australian GT production. Both to save on materials and speed assembly, separate individual circuit-wiring was replaced by a limited use of simple printed-circuit boards. The other updated electrical features, in addition to installing the long-overdue fuse-box, would be the replacement of the direct current dynamo with an alternating current alternator via a larger negative-

---

Outwith the Company

The lack of 'vertical integration' in Rootes/Chrysler – the degree to which a firm's own production handles the supply chain from raw materials to final customer – meant that, like most British producers, it bought components from outwith the company – some 1,600 for the Imp. A Parliamentary report suggests:

Bought-out (sometimes called bought-in) components in 1973

Vauxhall	85%
Chrysler/Rootes	71%
Ford (UK)	70%
BLMC	65%
US Ford	61%
Toyota	59%
US General Motors	46%

The alleged advantages of using so many outside suppliers were that it released the need for the manufacturer to pay for plant and machinery that might be under-utilized; cost-pressure could be brought to bear when writing contracts with a third party; flexibility of ordering was possible – more in good times, cutting-back when vehicles were not selling. As with all things in life, these advantages were a two-edged sword. The company's capital might be saved, but at the price of direct control over the manufacturing and, sometimes, the exact specification – the ingenious pneumatic throttle of the Imp comes to mind. The largest drawback was a result of the appalling labour relations within the industry and its suppliers. Not only did a manufacturer still have to honour its orders if it went on strike, but it would have to contend with the multitude of stoppages and 'go-slows' that its suppliers were enduring. Because of the location of Linwood, supply difficulties would also extend to transporting so many outside components to Scotland.

Statistical caution again! It is claimed the 1973 local content of Chrysler UK for the home market was 97 per cent by value (a questionable figure); by 1983, this as Peugeot-Citroën-Talbot, had fallen to 30 per cent – admittedly not as dramatic as General Motors' Vauxhall outpost, which fell from 98 per cent to 22 per cent.

---

earth battery, which enabled the fitting of an electrically heated rear screen and more powerful heater fan. All cars were now blessed with better storage; the over-riders, however, were reserved for the Super and Sport models.

The aforementioned fuel crisis would have devastating implications for all industries, none more so than the automobile manufacturers. As previously suggested, the Chrysler Corporation was not a bottomless pit, and the board back in Detroit was forced to reassess its worldwide operations. A critical appraisal of its European operations would reveal that Chrysler UK was in reality, like Rootes before it, bankrupt – and in terms of the parental larder, the cupboard was bare. The weakest of the European parts of Chrysler was Chrysler UK, whereas the former Simca and Barreiros companies were considerably more secure, albeit suffering. The British Government no

longer had any illusions about any of the British-owned car industry, but for political credibility it still wished to see continued employment of the various workers in the main companies and their satellite suppliers, which were much more significant employers than in most other countries.

Tartan Imp?

With no conscious reference to the Scottish motoring heritage of a turn-of-the-century automobile concern in Union Street, Aberdeen, or the Granton, Edinburgh, taxi producer of a decade later, the Caledonian was launched in October 1975. This was to be the final statement of the Imp theme played out in a glorious cherry-red loud tutti. It was more a case of making sure that Linwood would not be left with huge amounts of spare parts than

Here we see a close-up of the Deluxe's rear Hillman badge in the final year of production. The pair of number-plate lamps affixed to the bumper have been adopted from the Stiletto. Even on this late car, the hole for the starting handle remains.

a truly new Imp, and the Caledonian combined the characteristic 'extras' from across the range and added a few of its own. The seats were trimmed with a chequered cloth fabric – a quasi tartan effect for this highland fling – and were the fully reclining type. At long last, a radio and reversing lights were fitted by the factory. The exterior incorporated the well-tried side adornments, including the later Stiletto's stuck-on coachline, wheel embellishers, and the over-riders of other models, and added exterior mirrors.

The usual promises of continued Imp production were heralded in 1976, but few can have thought their resonance was that of authenticity, despite the circulation of photographs such as the new moulded one-piece Imp dashboard and, yet again, loose talk of redesign. Mutual trust had irreparably broken down between the dispirited workforce and the increasingly remote management. With the potential to transfer the no-longer-new Hillman, about to be Chrysler, Avenger assembly to Linwood from Ryton-on-Dunsmore, the remaining completed Imps would be distributed and sold, but Imp production would not see another Scottish spring, never mind a winter. The Linwood workforce was asked to endorse the Government's rescue plan for the company on 5 January, and after the social pain was mitigated through the number of anticipated redundancies being reduced, the workforce dutifully acceded to the desired democratic outcome. As was the case with the Government, most workers knew this was likely to be a temporary reprieve for their employment in the form of this 'mortified duck', and it certainly sealed the fate of the Imp. The announcement for most of the former Rootes employees was carried by the internal telexes and the *Coventry Evening Telegraph* of Wednesday, 7 January 1976: the paper's front-page headline read 'END OF THE IMP AS CHRYSLER AXE FALLS'.

The Linwood production log for 9 February 1976 reads: Arrow 101 cars, Apex 32, and 80 minutes 'lost time', with 0 appearing against the Imp for the following and subsequent days – the first time the log seems to have used the 'Imp' name. The Linwood production day, which was partitioned into eight segments, tells the tale of the last production Imp (vehicle numbers are expressed as Arrow/Apex): 8.45: 10/7, with a note that labour shortages lost 8 minutes from the production (it was a Monday morning). The day continues: 9.45: (Arrow/Apex) 9/5 with 6 minutes lost production (one for a jammed cradle on the line and five for an over-run rest break); 10.45: 15/3 (two minutes rest-break over-run and a seven-minute safety dispute); 11.45: 12/3 (two minutes lost, including a faulty sling); 1.25: 14/7 (one minute lost);

Representative Test Data

Model	Source	Date	mph (best) top speed	Economy (test mpg)	Touring mpg (Imperial)	0–60 Time, Secs	Engine (if not 875cc)
de luxe Mk I	*Autocar*	1963	83	38.1	35–50	23.7	
de luxe Mk I	*Motoring Which?*	1963	85	39	–	–	
de luxe Mk l	*Motor*	1963	81	35.1	43.7	22.9	
de luxe Mk I	*Cars Illustrated*	1963	76.7	–	35–40	23.5	
de luxe Mk I	*Motor Rally*	1963	>75	43	–	18.4	
de luxe Mk I	*Sporting Motorist*	1964	77	37	>40	21.8	
de luxe Mk I	*Car & Driver*	1964	80	–	34–47	23	
de luxe Mk l	*Good Motoring*	1964	81	36	41	23.2	
de luxe Mk l	*Practical Motorist*	1964	78	–	–	23.4	
Singer Chamois	*Autocar*	1964	84	35.4	33–43	22.9	
Nathan–tuned	*Autocar*	1965	107	30.7	36.9	12	998
Hartwell Stage 3	*Autocar*	1965	100	29.2	40.1	14	
de luxe Mk I	*Motoring Which?*	1966	78	36	–	–	
Sunbeam Imp Sport	*Autocar*	1966	90	33.1	40	16.3	
Californian	*Good Motoring*	1966	81	–	35–41	22	
Californian	*Autocar*	1967	81	34.6	35–39	21.9	
Californian	*Car*	1967	76	–	–	19.7	
Hartwell Californian	*Car*	1967	93	–	–	13.8	
Fraser Racing	*Sporting Motorist*	1967	118	*c*.12	–	7	998
Rally Imp	*Cars Illustrated*	1967	93	30	–	15.2	998
Rally Imp	*Sporting Motorist*	1967	90	–	33–34	15.5	998
Singer Chamois Mk II	*Motoring Which?*	1967	80	37	–	–	
Husky	*Motoring Which?*	1967	75	39	–	–	
Super Imp Mk ll	*Good Motoring*	1967	80	33	40	23.7	
de luxe Mk II	*Motor (Group Test)*	1968	*c*.76	38.5	35–40	–	
Emery Stage 1	*Cars & C Convrsns*	1968	90	–	–	18.6	
Hartwell Stage 3	*Cars & C Convrsns*	1968	100	–	*c*.40	13.5	
Sunbeam Stiletto	*Country Life*	1968	*c*.90	–	36	16	
Hartwell Stiletto	*Motor*	1969	100	27.2	30.4	12.7	998
Singer Chamois III	*Autocar*	1969	78	35.7	38	26.2	
Sunbeam Stiletto	*Motoring Which?*	1970	88	35	–	–	
Super Imp III	*Car*	1970	78	35	44	21.4	
(Standard) Imp III	*Good Motoring*	1971	81	–	38–42	–	
(Standard) Imp III	*Motoring Which?*	1972	74	37	–	–	
Sunbeam Sport	*Motor*	1973	88.3	34	37.8	16.1	
Standard Imp	*Motor*	1974	76.4	31.2	43.8	20.3	

(This comprises a representative, rather than exhaustive, table of published test results.)

2.25: 18/4; 3.25: 11/0 (eight minutes lost through extended rest break); 4.30: 23/0 (one minute lost for material shortages). The final four Imps had rolled off the production line in the sixth period, and with a bitter irony, its literally final hour was a trouble-free one.

But Onwards We Must Go

The Imp was dead. It is tempting to add 'Long live the Imp', as outside its strong following in competition circles, the car had been an acquired taste by those who savoured the ingenuity and success of its stronger features over the obvious trials with which in life the model presented its owner. It is the much appreciated successes of so many aspects of the vehicle that have engendered the enthusiastic following the model quickly acquired. Whereas the proverbial bar-room motoring expert pontificated on the Imp's shortcomings, with its fire-pump engine, his son or daughter tends his or her lovingly restored version and appreciates the racing pedigree of the engine, along with the original philosophy of Parkes and Fry, through finding the Imp such fun to drive, while finding that Saward and Wisdom gave it one of the few 'three-box' rectilinear formats that has an enduring, as well as an endearing, shape. Some authorities claim that only sixteen or so of the final two hundred Imps were sold, and if this was true, the author suspects the others are likely to have been used for a Chrysler scheme to lease cars to employees: the Imp was £7 per month.

Since the narrative of the Imp as a manifestation of social change (or Rootes' response to such change) is so inextricably entwined with the economic and social manipulation of the Linwood factories and their communities, to stop with the Imp's demise would leave the tale incomplete. In any case, parts of the Imp were to live on a little longer in the guise of one of the replacement cars. Multitudes of Her Majesty's civil servants had been compiling a welter of files since 1972 for their respective ministries with subject lines conveying the true position of Linwood: 'Chrysler (UK) Ltd: financial position', mutates into 'its potential collapse', followed by 'Government support'; the end of Imp production was barely three months after the British Prime Minister, Harold Wilson, had announced to his Cabinet that the motor industry 'was not a lame duck, it was a dead duck' – but an extremely costly one. Michael Andrews, the assistant to Tim Rootes, recalls he was in Bowater House, the overseas exports centre of Chrysler International, the day when the early evening television news ran the story that Chrysler was on the point of collapse without a massive Government hand-out for its United Kingdom operations. A telegram was delivered that read: '6.00 news says you have gun to government's head. Please pull trigger and oblige! Signed: John Bull.' This was not a cultural reference to the eponymous English Renaissance composer, but John Arbuthnot's eighteenth-century character who, following the cartoons of the satirical magazine, *Punch*, personified the spirit of the British nation with its portrayal of a solid, land-owning figure who wore a Union Flag waistcoat and was accompanied by his trusty bulldog. It was suspected that the anonymous telegraphic John Bull was a prominent financial trader in the City of London.

The Imp might have loved the snow and ice of Canada and the far north of Scotland, but it was no longer pining for the fjords – it had passed on. In terms of Harold Wilson's metaphorical duck, this one was no more, it had ceased to be, it was bereft of life – the Imp was now an ex-duck! As far as the wider British car industry was concerned, although it might not have seemed like it at the time, there was always a price to be paid for improvident Government short-term assistance. Along with the other terms the Chrysler Corporation had agreed with the Government was the undertaking to design a new car to replace the Imp which would be built at Linwood – how could Chrysler not acquiesce? It was the Government that was paying for it. The project, often referred to as 424, had to be executed with remarkable speed, taking a mere two years to come to fruition: financial prudence also had to be the order of the day. Despite being an entirely new model, the resultant Chrysler Sunbeam (the former Rootes marque now being relegated to a model name) achieved both of these through its reliance on its Rootes predecessors. The highly conventional format was largely dictated by its utilization of the Hillman Avenger's floorpan combined with either its 1,300cc/1,600cc engine, or, as in the favourably named 1.0LS, the 928cc modified version of the Imp's engine – the size that the Project Intention had specified for the Mark III Imp. The Sunbeam was described as a hatchback, but the other feature it shared with its Linwood predecessor was that it is more accurately described as having an opening rear window. The Sunbeam, launched in 1977, was not a bad car at all, but hardly a model that was going to be the saviour of Linwood.

The Hillman Avenger, or Plymouth Cricket, was the ultimate episode of the dynasty that was the erstwhile Rootes empire. It sold well on the home market, but by the time of the demise of the Imp, it was approaching the end of its shelf-life. In the manner of the move, mentioned earlier, of the Arrow range to Linwood, when the production facilities of Ryton-on-Dunsmore were being devoted to the latest model, now it was the turn of the Avenger. Something was required to occupy the liberated Linwood capacity, as the Sunbeam was not going to have the whole facility devoted to it, so the Avenger moved to Scotland in 1978 and the new Chrysler Alpine was manufactured in Ryton. Despite being designed and developed at the Chrysler/Rootes design department at Whitley, near Coventry, the Alpine was imported from the former Simca plant in France. (The Horizon forms no part of this story, as it was never made in the United Kingdom until after the time of Linwood.) The completely knocked down kits were still

produced for some overseas markets; for example, the Todd assembly plant in Porirua, Wellington, New Zealand, took the Avenger for local assembly until Linwood closed. Coincidental with its move over the border, the Avenger became the Chrysler Avenger, and the last of the Rootes marques died. This would not remain so for long, since, as previously mentioned, the Chrysler Corporation required rescuing by the American Government. President Jimmy Carter proved to be a more confrontational businessman than various Europeans who had been bankrolling the former Chrysler International outposts, and as part of the American rescue package these had to be sold. Chrysler UK, almost overnight, but technically from the start of 1979, became the debt-ridden liability of the French holding company, PSA Peugeot-Citroën, with the former Rootes Ltd part being designated to its subsidiary, Peugeot Ltd (then Peugeot-Talbot Ltd). From the few records that are in the public domain at the time of writing, like many of the 'surprise' announcements in the history of Rootes Limited, the proposed deal, then referred to as 'Chrysler (UK) Ltd, Chrysler France SA, and PSA Peugeot-Citroën proposed merger', was worked out in essence by the start of August 1978, with the visit of Eugene Cafeiro, president of the Chrysler Corporation, to the United Kingdom. It would take until the end of the year to flesh out the detail – or until October 1980 before the British civil servants would make the final comment. As long ago as 1975, Eric Varley, the Industry Secretary who believed that the whole former Rootes concern should have been allowed to become bankrupt, did entertain the hope that Volvo, as the foremost former customer of Linwood, might have been interested in its purchase. As Varley's plan was not adopted, no one ever found out whether Volvo *was* interested, but considering that Volvo had only acquired the DAF company in the preceding autumn and was in the process of converting the Dutch Born factory for the production of the small

Proof that the dream is irrevocably over, six months before the new millennium – the Car Assembly Building is no more. Some readers will think it ironic that the dream's final demise is at the hands of a machine made by Hyundai.

Volvos, it is hard to credit that this government hope was any more informed than others related to industry.

With fortuitous coincidence (although 'Talbot' had not been a live French marque since the Talbot-Lago of the 1950s or the Rootes Sunbeam-Talbot that had been moribund since 1954), in the wake of the demise and break-up of the Sunbeam-Talbot-Darracq (STD) company in 1935, the name had had separate Anglo-French (or for that matter, Franco-English) meanings – Darracq using it in France until it was bought by Simca in 1959, only to become slowly absorbed into Chrysler from 1963. All the extant Chrysler models were rapidly rebadged as Talbot, not that this situation would endure for long, either. There seemed a strange irony that the once prestigious Sunbeam-Talbot marque was now reversed as the final Linwood model, the Talbot Sunbeam.

The End of the Road

Linwood would not emulate the lyrics of Harry Lauder's most famous song – the dreaming was over, and even if Rootes had had a stout heart, the hill was too long and steep. It was felt at the time that the main attraction to PSA Peugeot-Citroën (the holding company) of purchasing Chrysler UK was to obtain the comprehensive former Rootes dealer network, which, although smaller by 1979, in 1965 had been claimed to offer 'access to 1,100 outlets'. Of the three main assembly areas, for all the reasons that have formed one of the sub-plots to the story of the Hillman Imp, the Coventry centre appealed to the new owner immeasurably more than the Scottish or Dunstable ones. Despite all the assertions of PSA Peugeot-Citroën as to its commitment to Linwood – hollow sentiments that the workforce and Government alike had witnessed from its previous owners – on 11 February Peugeot-Talbot announced its impending closure.

The official closure took place on 22 May 1981, with nigh on 5,000 Scottish workers finding themselves redundant (a long way short of the fictitious 9,700 jobs that the company had always claimed to be producing to enable it to attract its regional aid) and following in the footsteps of the 2,000 who had left two years earlier. Some workers relocated within the industry in the West Midlands – a handful even staying within the company – but most were not in a position to do so. The newly automated West Works at Longbridge (CAB1 extension) for the Austin Metro of 1980 was designed by the same architects as Linwood – Weedon also worked on associated amenity housing projects to accommodate the enlarged workforce, ironically, many recruited from the Linwood factory. Whereas the Conservative Government of the patrician Harold Macmillan had gone to some lengths in its attempts to expand the economy of the region, the later Conservative administration of Margaret Thatcher was preparing the Scots, and for that matter most areas of England and Wales, for the brave new monetarist world where its advice to the unemployed was to 'get on your bikes' and find employment where it was available – with a dwindling United Kingdom manufacturing base, however, the bicycle ride would become an increasingly long and arduous one. The Dunstable commercial facility was eventually sold to, and used by, Renault, before closing in 1993. Ryton-on-Dunsmore survived, even if it did not fare that much better. It would be many years before it could safely be described as profitable, and during the latter days of Chrysler and those of PSA Peugeot-Citroën, car assembly was virtually an imported version of the knocked down

kit of French-manufactured parts, something that had traditionally been the preserve of British exports to the rest of the world.

The completely knocked down version of the Hillman Hunter, the remaining part of the Arrow range, which had started life at the Stoke plant, near Coventry, before moving to Scotland, had been transferred to other production sites, with the entire manufacturing equipment being sold to the Iranian state-owned Khodro Company in 1989 so that it might continue with its production as the Paykan. The Paykan had been in production since 1967, and this contributed to making Rootes' Arrow series the country's most financially successful model. Some industrial economists see this original Iranian deal as the single reason why the Chrysler Corporation persisted with its Chrysler UK operations for as long as it did. At the time of Chrysler's rescue by the Government in 1975, it was reported by the Chancellor of the Exchequer, Denis Healey, that the Finance Minister of Iran had told the British Ambassador in Tehran that if the Government allowed Chrysler (UK) to become illiquid, it would destroy British credibility in Iran, which would therefore have a profound impact on Britain's weapon sales to all Organization of Petroleum Exporting Countries. With Linwood's closure, the Sunbeam model and marque ceased, as did the British production of the Avenger, although this latter vehicle, which was still selling well, had a life after Scotland, continuing to be made for another decade by the Volkswagen Group in Brazil.

Not only was Linwood immediately prepared for resale, with its development potential being stressed, within a decade the other bright beacons of regeneration, Gartcosh, the huge Ravenscraig steelworks and many more would be advertised as offering new development opportunities. The Linwood aluminium–alloy die-cast factory and the main office block survive, but are dwarfed by recent warehouse and storage constructions for the distribution of goods made outwith the

Linwood–Washington: New Car Factory

For those interested in such socio-industrial comparisons, although beyond the scope of this book, it would be fruitful to compare the establishment of the Linwood complex with that of Nissan's facility in Washington, Tyne and Wear. Nissan also trained and employed a hitherto heavy-industry workforce that included redundant ship-workers. But the similarities, other than a brand-new factory, rapidly cease: Nissan stipulated a single-union agreement with its workers, and both white- and blue-collar employees were salaried.

country; and the site of Pressed Steel houses a shopping complex with fast-food outlets. The redevelopment of Ravenscraig is frequently the subject of meetings of local government strategic planners and the promissory statements of politicians from the Scottish Executive to redevelop the site with shopping and leisure facilities with accompanying private housing – apparently recycling scripts of outworn platitudes from England. Looking north of this, mentions of Gartcosh in guide-books will stress the leisure facilities and the golf course, certainly a more green and pleasant land, but it is difficult to maintain a sense of pride in a 'call-centre' or a manifestation of the amorphous concept of 'tourism'. It is understandable to appreciate why the Imp and its time now represents for some a Scottish golden age of opportunity. So to apply a colloquial American invitation to the product of this latter-day Scottish industrial golden age that is the Imp, Enjoy!

The façade of Linwood's main office block, boardroom, and showroom survives at the time of writing, but it is unlikely to do so for very much longer; neither will the other surviving part, the former die-casting plant.

9 Sporting

Going Faster?

Because of the many strengths of the standard production Imp, especially that of its handling and the potential of its engine, Parkes and Fry's originally fun quotient was, and still is, being extended. This chapter is not intended either as a tuning guide or a comprehensive review of the Imp's contribution to motor sport. It reviews some of the contemporaneous offerings that were available, and then considers some of the more celebrated events in the Imp's competitive legacy.

Being a modestly priced vehicle, the Imp was a popular choice of those whose entertainment was competing in events at a local or club level – rallying, racing, hill-climbing, and rallycross. Most tuning firms were involved with the cars at all levels of competition, and naturally it was the higher-profile outings that were of most value to them; the intelligence gained through this was made available in a less extreme and more affordable form to the owner of what was essentially a road-going car.

Many tuning firms, some of which were involved at a more competitive level, offered the usual fare for improving the performance or handling of one's production Imp – most categorized their preparation into a series of 'staged' levels of tuning, which only had comparative meaning within that firm's other stages, starting with stage one as the mildest. Roger Nathan, Paul Emery, and Motortune of London, Janspeed Engineering, Leonard Reece, Arden Conversions, Mangoletsi, V. W. Derrington, Ruddspeed and Jack Knight

(Developments) all contributed to the sporting equipment available to the Imp owner, while some of them undertook a full conversion and preparation that would include both engine performance and revised suspension and brakes. Many other firms offered the usual accessories of wheel-spacers, wider wheels, wooden steering wheels, suspension-lowering kits and the usual panoply of goodies to make one's car faster, either in theory or in practice. It was the dealership of George Hartwell of Bournemouth, however, himself a competitive race and rally driver, that gained the most respected reputation, mainly through Hartwell's close relationship with Rootes Limited, as well as some of the later racing and rallying teams. George Hartwell also ran the Thomas Harrington Company, wholly owned by Rootes Motors, which was involved with the Sunbeam Alpine. Hartwell's independent dealership is one of the few British dealerships to survive more than seventy years.

Hartwell's stages of tune commenced with better gas-flowing of the cylinder head and careful matching of the manifolding in a way that Linwood did not. The next discrete step, entitled Group rather than Stage 2, would involve a more efficient four-branch exhaust manifold and silencer, while the Group 3 also incorporated twin Zenith-Stromberg carburettors, higher-lift camshaft with larger valves and double valve-springs and optional improved suspension and braking, including servo-assistance – the obligatory tachometer remained an extra, as did the other ancillary gauges, but few can have specified their

Hartwell cars without them. Unlike some of the commercial competition, George Hartwell retained the standard-capacity engine for some years, whereas most others, like the factory itself, opted for a version of the 998cc unit.

Roger Nathan offered four stages of tune, also ranging from simple bolt-on improvements through to race preparation with an enlarged engine. Nathan was to produce his Impudence II racing car which was modified to the extent of rotating the engine through 90 degrees and displaying a top speed of approximately 120mph (195km/h) with a 0–60mph time of seven seconds. As early as 1965, Nathan offered the 998cc engine, with a re-ported and gas-flowed cylinder head fitted with larger valves, high-lift and large-overlap camshaft, with uprated springs, camshaft carrier blocks, and fitted with twin carburettors (either SU or 2 × 38DCOE Weber) with four-branch manifolding. As the engine was 'red-lined' at 8,000rpm, it was carefully balanced and crack-tested. A full range of suspension and braking options were available, including a conversion to disc brakes. Paul Emery was to produce one of the greatest increases in engine capacity, extending it to 1,150cc. Whichever engine conversion or suspension modification was employed, the alternative gearbox of choice for competition was from Jack Knight in Woking, Surrey. The simplest type would substitute third and top gears of different ratios which were straight cut rather than being helically toothed. A more advanced gearbox was furnished with a constant-mesh, straight-cut gear set with its gears running in needle-roller bearings. This competition version was offered with twenty possible ratios to embrace most demands. There was also a similar five-speed gearbox equipped with a limited-slip differential.

Hartwell did go on to produce its 998cc-engined version, named of course, Group 4, but in many reviews, Hartwell's popular Group 3, with its 875cc engine, acquitted itself with honour against those from the other tuning firms with larger engines – it was

reputedly also a somewhat more reliable object for wider road use. A substantial proportion of *Cars & Car Conversions* in September 1966 was devoted to reviewing prepared Imps and the tuning accessories that were available. *Cars & Car Conversions* might have thought the Group 3 Hartwell Imp was the fastest road-going version they had tested, but when the more reliable wet-liner 998cc engines became the norm, the Bournemouth Mecca produced the Imp GT, a more reasonably priced version being directly based upon the Sport – a comfortable road-going car with a top speed well over 100mph (160km/h). Hartwell's final Clubman model was fairly and squarely focused on competitive events, and its fractionally slower top speed than the GT was because of the Clubman's Jack Knight close-ratio gearbox. The engine was 'red-lined' at 8,000rpm and the acceleration was far superior. When *Motor* tested a Hartwell Stiletto in a comparative assessment with other tuned cars, it had the joint top speed, with *Motor* concluding that 'it is just an incomparable and very desirable little car'. The competition for this test was a LuMo (Ford) Piranha (with a Cortina GT engine), Downton BMC 1300, Master (Hillman) Hunter, SAH (Triumph) 1300 and a Blydenstein Viva.

Competitions

Rootes' competition department was based at its Stoke facility, near Coventry. Rootes enjoyed some success through rallying Sunbeam-Talbots and Alpines, and had offered support to a number of private entrants as well as its official team. The Imp had not been thought of as a potentially competitive car, but it was during its testing that its performance capabilities became evident and infamous with those who lived near the chosen test routes – after all, the engine had been detuned before its launch. Rootes' rallying success became the thrust of its election for the Imp – an arena which was not as much of a spectator sport as it was to become in the future. The competitions department required revitalizing, and Marcus Chambers was appointed as the competition manager. Chambers, who would later write an account of his efforts, *Works Wonders*, had worked for BMC, being associated with what would become 'the enemy' – the Mini-Cooper 'S' rally car. Des O'Dell, whose pedigree was Aston Martin and Ford's 'Advanced Vehicles' (which included the GT40), joined him. Other than in private hands, the Imp did not receive much attention in 1963, as Rootes was still preoccupied with the problems it started to encounter with the production cars. From 1964 until 1970, when the programme received the familiar cost-cutting attentions from Chrysler, the official works rally team was to flourish, initially using largely unmodified Imps, with some bought-out parts from the tuning firms mentioned earlier.

The usual 'classes' the entrants competed in were the 'Grand Touring' class, which in terms of the Imp was the category up to 1 litre – being prepared in accordance with a strict book of rules. The other main classifications of relevance to the Imp were the 850cc–1,150cc category for modified Production Touring cars (in some events, referred to as 'Group 2') and, if just as on the dealers' forecourt, 'Group 1'. Rallies also had a Coupe des Dames, or Ladies' Prize, and as the Rootes team would include the highly gifted Rosemary Smith, this bonus prize would frequently find its way home to Coventry; like Pat Moss before, Rosemary Smith had been chosen because of her skills rather than because of her gender. Smith's name would become synonymous with Imp rallying. (The author fails to see why the much-hyped description at the time of Smith being an Irish dress designer should be of any more significance than Cowan being a Scottish farmer.) I. D. L. 'Tiny' Lewis became the other regular works driver, Andrew Cowan and Nick Rowe being offered works support (including works-prepared cars), with Colin Malkin, David Pollard and Patrick Lier featuring as technically private entrants.

Because of its media coverage, the 1964 Monte Carlo Rally was to be the initial outing of the official works team. The Imps were pretty-well carefully prepared standard Linwood issue. It was not a barnstorming arrival of the team, but a confidence-building exercise: of eight entrants, seven arrived safely in Monte Carlo. It was the privateers who picked up minor trophies: Hunt and MacCrew for the best performance from a British private entrant and from the Glasgow start (which was then one of the originating points). A locally entered Imp driven by Truillet would also win the under 1,150cc class in the Belgian 12-Hours Rally, with Lewis achieving a first-in-class in the Welsh Rally. It would be the RAC Rally, the 'International Rally of Great Britain', that was to offer the Imp its greatest publicity in its first year. Pollard won the 1-litre GT class, Cowan the Group 2 class for cars under 1,150cc, and Smith mopped up the Coupe des Dames with her overall fourteenth position.

By the start of 1965, the 998cc engine was available to the works cars, and its first outing would be during a testing Monte Carlo Rally, when only thirty-five of the 238 who started would find their way to the Mediterranean. Private entrant Pollard and Rosemary Smith were placed in their class. The Imp's rallying successes moved up a notch from here: the international Circuit of Ireland saw Smith and another Irish lady, Sheila O'Clery, a privateer, joining Lewis and Malkin as recipients of class trophies. Also in Ireland, the '2,250km Rally' saw six finish out of a small field of fourteen, two-thirds being Imps.

It was the 'Tulip' Rally that attracted the most immediate publicity. Despite it being held in April, the drivers experienced truly atrocious weather, including substantial snowfalls that contributed to the elimination of more than two-thirds of the 157 starters. Straight one–two positions went to Rosemary Smith and 'Tiny' Lewis, both for their overall performance and in their class; adding Smith's Coupe des Dames meant that this rally harnessed seven awards for the Imps. *Autosport* was to conjecture: 'Undoubtedly it was the superb road-holding and handling of the Imps which was the main contribution to the success.'

Private entrants were having a lot of success at a local club level, but also on terrain as varied as the Tanzania, Tanganyika, International London Gulf and Polish rallies. The works-entered and -supported cars were also flourishing: the Canadian Shell 4000 produced a class win for Smith; the Scottish returned an overall second and class win for Lewis, with Smith being the class runner-up, fifth overall and, now almost taken for granted, the Ladies' Trophy. Rosemary Smith's popularity was increased further, along with the publicity for the Imp, with a class win in the

Austrian International Alpine Rally. Rootes made a promotional film, *Miss Smith and her Imp, 1965* – the highly articulate Smith also being entrusted with the commentary. The year closed with Lewis, Smith and Cowan taking the Manufacturers' Team Prize in the RAC Rally – another event held under really testing climatic conditions, with only sixty-two of the 162 cars finishing.

This year and the next were undoubtedly the most successful for Rootes from a publicity standpoint, partially because of the successes it was enjoying, but also because rallying was considered popular enough to benefit from a lot of popular media coverage. The Monte Carlo Rally kicked off 1966, but this was the year of the fiasco concerning the newly introduced rules, and Rosemary Smith

Despite the 'Rootes Sunbeam' stickers with their accompanying pentastar, the press release reads: 'Dress-designer Rosemary Smith has emerged as one of the toughest as well as most glamorous drivers in international motor sport by winning the Coupe des Dames in the world's longest rally – the coast-to-coast across Canada Shell 4000 event . . . driving her Hillman Imp.' In 1966, this six-day event was unusual, as it made the drivers and co-drivers do all their own servicing.

Andrew Cowan and Brian Coyle are seen on a Scottish special stage in the 1966 RAC International Rally of Great Britain. At the two-thirds stage, Tiny Lewis, Rosemary Smith, Colin Malkin, Rodney Badham and Paul Burch in Imps, and Gerry Birrell in a Chamois, were still going strong, but a spate of failed transaxles would ensue before the end.

was disqualified through a technicality, as was the whole BMC winning team. Patrick Lier won the production touring class in his privately entered Rally Imp, and Lewis and Phillippe Simonetta took the top two places in the modified production touring group. This busy year would include differing levels of celebration in the East African Goodyear Rally, the Nairobi event and both Irish events; and Lewis, Rowe and Heijndijk took positions 1–3 in their class for the Tulip Rally. Imps continued a successful year by taking three out of four places in the Austrian Arboe and Veralpen rallies, with Smith securing her first-in-class and Coupe des Dames for the Canadian Shell 4000 Rally, a third place with the Coupe des Dames award for the Greek 'Acropolis' event and, along with four other Imps, similar glory in the Scottish. With Lier managing a second place in Geneva, Rootes' competitions

and publicity departments were as busy as the drivers. Smith, Cowan and Pollard achieved the team and the first three places in their class for the International Gulf Rally, adding even more to the feeling that notice had to be taken of the Imps. The RAC finished the year with a lower key, as the Imp transaxles of Lewis and Cowan would submit to its rigours.

Despite the concomitant free publicity, the works and works-supported events started to be scaled back. The 1967 Monte Carlo drive would see Lier in his privately entered Rally Imp leading Peter Harper in their class, and Cowan taking the Group 1 prize, but things were getting quieter. Cowan would achieve a respectable ninth position in the Alpine Rally, with the Circuit of Ireland offering Smith a class win and, for the seventh successive year, the Ladies' Prize, and she also led a trio of Imps home for the top three class positions in the

Scottish Rally. The year did not end with the traditional RAC Rally, as it was cancelled because of a severe outbreak of foot and mouth disease affecting many parts of Britain. This did benefit the Imp, however, as it led to the immediate invention of Rallycross, in which the Imp excelled and the television cameras seemed not to be able to resist it.

Andrew Cowan took his modified Sunbeam Sport 875cc to the class win in the

1968 'Monte', and Rosemary Smith achieved her usual level of success in the Canadian event. Malkin won the Cambrian Rally, with Malkin and Smith being placed in, for the Imp, the all-important Scottish Rally, Smith winning the Ladies' Trophy for the fourth consecutive occasion. Malkin was having a good year, too, as he won the 1968 *Motoring News* Rally Championship, the BTRDA Gold Star Championship and, with his Rally Imp,

Perhaps better known as Triumph works' drivers, even winning the 1966 RAC Rally Championship and the BTRDA Gold Star Championship for them: Roy Fidler and Alan Taylor are seen here driving their Imp in the 1967 Alpine Rally.

190

the RAC Championship – the icing on the cake was to win, with Andrew Cowan as co-driver, the London–Sydney Marathon, this time in a works Hillman Hunter. Malkin continued in 1969 by winning the Manx Rally, and in this quiet year, Cowan secured the second place in the Scottish Rally. Luckily this was local, as it is reputed that after suffering transaxle problems his rally unit was swapped for the one from his normal road car. This would be the final international outing for the works Imps, as Chrysler withdrew from official rallying at the end of the year.

On Tarmac

It could be said that the Imp spotlight shifted in 1970 to its antics on the track, with the appearance of Bill McGovern's Sunbeam Imp, prepared by George Bevan, winning forty-eight out of fifty-one of the races and the RAC Saloon Car Championship. The story of the racing Imps starts much earlier, and in different hands. As a car that was relatively inexpensive and one that handled so well that it was also fitted with an engine from which so much extra power might be extracted, the Imp quickly became the popular choice of amateurs who wanted to race in local events but whose financial support did not extend to the budget of the factory teams. There never was a factory team of Imps; the closest the company came was to supply a small level of support to third-party teams – the competition budget was devoted to supporting the ral-

lying side. Prior to the Bevan Imp, two friends established their separate teams – the afore-mentioned George Hartwell and the Anglo-Scot Alan Fraser.

George Hartwell had been involved with the sporting side for years, and his engineer Ray Payne, who prepared a lot of Hartwell's cars, is attributed with the inspiration of adding the Imp not long after its announcement. As previously described, the main thrust of Rootes, Hartwell and others was extending the engine's capacity to 998cc (and later, beyond) to extract the maximum horsepower from the little Coventry Climax unit. Several would follow, but Payne also seems to have been the originator of the idea of reducing the engine's capacity to result in the 850cc version – still bedecked with all the tuning paraphernalia. Within the club racing rubric, this car could be entered in the under 850cc class, but would benefit from its 65bhp (with twin-choke Weber 38 DCOE carburation, front-mounted radiator and many more detailed modifications). With Payne as driver and development engineer, Team Hartwell would meet with success in the British Automobile Racing Club saloon car championships, and Hartwell-prepared cars would become a popular choice of many private entrants. Like most of the other tuning firms involved with making the Imp go faster, the company would devote most of their efforts to developing the 998cc version.

The only officially supported Imp racing team was that of Alan Fraser with its charac-

Two years after the invention of the televisual Rallycross with its combination of track and rough ground, the Imp was excelling in these short rally-races. Peter Harper, successful Imp racer and rallyist, excelled in his Alan Fraser Racing Sunbeam that, like the Emery car, extended the engine's capacity to 1142cc – necessitating surgery to the engine bay/rear seat space and using a Hewland transaxle. Here at Lydden Hill, Kent in December 1969.

teristic livery: resplendent in blue over white, with a saltire, the cross of St Andrew, emblazoned on the roof. Fraser was also a competitive driver, driving Bristol-engined Coopers for the Fraser-Hartwell Syndicate in the early 1950s and devoting six years of his life to 'things Imp'. Fraser recalls that he was minding his own business while driving a Sunbeam Rapier in the early 1960s when a Mini-Cooper overtook him – and driven by a female at that! As Mini-Coopers and Lotus-Cortinas were starting to beat him in races, he realized that the world was changing. Like Hartwell, Fraser investigated the possibilities offered by the Imp. In 1964 Fraser experimented with a rally car whose sole outing was in the Scottish Rally, 'purely for evaluation purposes', and 'tested a virtually standard vehicle at a few meetings'; other than improving the Imp's suspension, Fraser chooses to be unspecific about these outings. Under the development eye of Norman Winn, Alan Fraser Racing persisted with the Imp and achieved thirty-one awards in 1965, including nine first places in twenty-seven events. Rootes designated the Fraser team as factory sponsored; thus commenced the unsatisfactory relationship between the two. Fraser, a friend of the Rootes family, claimed that it would take him three years to deliver the prize of the international saloon-car championship; the company could benefit from publicity and access to his development work, and in return the team received a modest amount of sponsorship and details of Rootes' research.

Things got off to a fine start in 1966 which complemented the successes the rally team were also enjoying, and the press proclaimed that 'the Alan Fraser team were cleaning up everything'. This started at Goodwood in March, with the team winning four races: the usual drivers at the time, Nick Battan, Ray Calcutt, and Bernard Unett excelling in the different classes – Tony Lanfranchi, Jaqui Smith and Peter Harper among others would also have team roles to play. The talk of the Easter Monday at Brands Hatch was Unett

setting a new lap record for the under-one-litre class of less than a minute (59.8 seconds), and also winning the trophy race, with Batten taking the honours at Oulton Park and another visit to Brands Hatch. Things were getting really hectic for the team. Managed by Leslie Shirley-Price, it comprised two teams – one international and one that raced at a club level. Fraser entered at least sixty races that year, having to distribute cars over three simultaneous meetings.

In 1967, a year that Calcutt was not racing, Unett scored three class wins and a similar number of second places, with one third and a fourth place, while Lanfranchi amassed four seconds, and a third and fourth place. This placed them second and third in the BRSCC championship with 'Group 5' cars. To accommodate the regulations for this class, these cars benefited from extensive mechanical modification, but standard bodywork. The engines were usually 998cc with a compression ratio raised to 11:1, delivering their maximum power of c.115bhp at 9,000rpm. Either twin carburettors or Tecalemit-Jackson fuel injection fed these engines, which were normally kept in a band of 7,000–9,300rpm, as they delivered little useful torque below 5,000rpm. Fraser still believes that his real secret weapon was the copious refinements he carried out to the suspension, that combined with the careful selection of gears for the five-speed gearbox to optimize the cars to each circuit. These cars were fitted with front disc brakes and $13 \times 5.5J$ wheels (up to 7J for club events). Unlike club racing, where front-mounted oil coolers and coolant radiators were allowable, these cars retained the rear radiator, supplementing it with another in place of the heater. Fraser made his own, more reliable, distributor drives, extra-deep pulleys and special jockey wheels for the fan belt. The club cars, some of which reputedly used the 'deep' cylinder heads with which Rootes had experimented, retained the proprietary 'bottom end', although the pistons were of Fraser's specification. By the end of his involvement with Imps, Fraser had increased the engine's capacity to 1,142cc, alongside those of 850cc and the regular 998cc.

Just when it looked as if Fraser would be able to deliver his promised championship for the forthcoming third season, 'Chrysler pulled the plug ten days before the first race . . . we did the first two races and the last – winning all of them – we then went to Formula 3.' Having previously visited Tenerife, the somewhat dispirited Fraser returned there, initially to investigate the production of what he considered his baby – the Imp-based CUB that he had been developing in Hildenborough, Kent – as a Maltese kit car. The Maltese Government pledged many things under advantageous terms if Fraser established his kit-car company there. Through restrictions that the Government wanted to place upon the length of stay in Malta of Fraser's engineers (originally one year, later extended to three), the project failed to reach fruition. At this point, Fraser experienced a change of career to that of animal rescue, which he now does from his Mountains Animal Sanctuary in Angus, Scotland. To paraphrase Fraser about the 140+ inmates of his equine rescue: he started his concerns with single multi-horsepower, and now he worries over multi-single-horse-power!

The final phase of the track Imps was the partnership of George Bevan, contributing his skills of tuning to Bill McGovern's skills as driver. This was not a factory-supported team, but a private entrant, although Rootes dealers did contribute to the sponsorship of the 'Bevan Imp'. During the 1970 season, out of eleven race-entries, McGovern, a former Emery Team driver, won seven and came runner-up twice more – this was more than sufficient to achieve the RAC British Touring Car Championship. McGovern, again assisted by Bevan, was to have similar successes with his Sunbeam Imp in the following two years, giving them a hat-trick with these consecutive wins. Incidentally, Bernard Unett would go on to win this same title three non-consecutive times at the wheel of a Hillman/Chrysler Avenger.

Ray Calcutt in his George Bevan-prepared Imp at Brands Hatch in 1972.

10 Buying One

Do I want one? Presuming that you have begged, borrowed, or stolen this volume (you might even be fortunate enough to live in an area where local council 'efficiencies' allow your local library, or 'Ideas Store', to be furnished with books as part of its 'core activity'), and having read thus far, you must either already possess a fleet of Imps, from basketcase to immaculate, and just wanted some respite from skinned knuckles and oilencrusted fingernails, or you are envisaging becoming the next owner of this highly practical 'classic' car.

Older cars are entertaining to own and are a pleasing hobby. Before you ask yourself which Imp model you most covet, give some thought as to how it will find a place in your life. How will you use it? Everyone appreciates economical cars, as the Imp is, but if your mileage is low, then this will not be as significant as if you undertake many and lengthy journeys. Can you accommodate all your customary paraphernalia within what is a small car? The question of whether your garage will accommodate an Imp is not likely to feature other than during restorations – it is comforting to have a covered work area, as a partially dismantled car takes up an astonishing volume of space. This author is among the ranks of those who believe that older vehicles should be used as day-to-day transport in order for the owner to gain full satisfaction from his or her interest. Others, however, are content to restrict their outings to driving to prearranged alfresco picnics in the muddy field of a stately home, where they meet up with fellow enthu-

siasts of the marque. Both categories of owner gain pleasure from their pastime, but it is useful to know which type you are, as it will affect the way you hope to relate to your Imp.

The financial aspects of older cars are highly dependent on what you are comparing them with. If you are hoping that your chosen car will reward your investment beyond the financial dreams of avarice, then might I suggest a book on trading financial derivatives? Should your motoring experiences have been mainly purchasing 'new previously owned' vehicles, then an Imp compares highly favourably from a financial standpoint. You will occasionally find yourself looking at a large bill, but it will usually involve the rectification of a fault of which the vehicle has been attempting to inform you for years, but you will not experience depreciation. Even if you are unlikely to experience a large appreciation in its value, your Imp will not depreciate, something worth comparing with a modern car. A word of financial caution, though: very few cars in need of a full restoration will allow the restorer to recoup anything approaching the full cost of such an undertaking, and the Imp is no exception. At various times in the United Kingdom, there has been a fiscal advantage in owning a car built before a certain date as the road fund licence might qualify for the vehicle being classified as an 'historic vehicle'. Governments are capricious, however, and it would be foolish to base one's buying strategy upon such fiscal advantages.

Cars of the age of the Imp are not intrinsically less reliable than a newer model – there is the assumption that your chosen Imp will be correctly serviced and kept up to date in terms of replacement parts. Herein lies one enormous advantage of most cars from this period – simplicity: they are relatively straightforward to understand and work on. This is a benefit to your patience if you personally attend to their every need, and to your wallet if you divest this to someone else. As has been made clear, the Imp earned for itself a fearsome reputation for unreliability. Most of these shortcomings were attended to during its production run (and recognized to be the case by all but the bar-room 'expert'). Early cars that the owner is likely to encounter today will have benefited from the necessary corrective treatment.

Conventional wisdom suggests that if you are acquiring any older car, then you should buy the best you can afford. With the peculiarities of the English language, a 'dog' might be man's best friend, but it is also his worst conceivable car. The problem is that the latter use of the colloquial canine is relatively easy to portray as the product of the proverbial 'lengthy restoration', with an unrealistically high expectation of gain from a vendor. For this sage-like proposition to have some validity, you have to ensure that the car you envisage buying has truly enjoyed knowledgeable and thorough attention – a grubby cardboard box of receipts is no substitute for a properly recorded log of mechanical and body care over a reasonable period. If any major dismantling and restoration has taken place, then a comprehensive photographic record might reassure one that it was worthy of a higher price. Paying such a price for a vehicle that has had a lot of attention is galling if the work has not been correctly executed and the new owner just has to repeat many of the jobs. With the sweet innocence of the newly converted, some prospective owners of older vehicles hope to find the proverbial one-previous-owner (hopefully a local member of the cloth or the ennobled female aristocracy), low-mileage, unrestored example. The author was fortunate

enough to achieve the latter himself; but the chances of this occurring are becoming vanishingly small.

My feeling about the type of car would concur with the accepted wisdom of buying the best you can afford, but with the enormously important *caveat emptor* that this presupposes you are assured that its condition is worthy of its price. Before addressing the alternatives, the author should provoke the reader into a mood of truthful introspection without wishing to invoke a state of inactive navel-gazing! To what extent do you wish your relationship to flourish through the input of your own effort? This question, of course, contains the thinly disguised subsidiary question about your own skill and ability. Some grander vehicles might attract an ownership that would best be described as 'bonnet polishers' or 'cheque-book owners', but thus far, the Imp has largely avoided this type of owner. Should your forte be more mechanical, then concentrate on finding an Imp that is bodily in good condition, whereas those who find metalwork pleasing will not be put off a car that is suffering from the effects of corrosion, but might find the prospect of rebuilding an engine truly horrifying.

Knowing yourself is a useful adjunct to purchasing an older car, as the number of abandoned restoration projects in advertisements confirms. Taking one of these over can be an excellent way of achieving a useable car that is restored according to your preferences, but do not overlook the testing of your personal mettle that this will involve. The safer strategy, especially if this is one's initial venture, is that of 'rolling restoration'. For this to be a reality, you will be looking for a useable vehicle, or one that can quickly become so following an initial onslaught, and then one's spirits can be sustained by the pleasure of owning and driving the vehicle, while one plots future improvements, whether cosmetic or mechanical. Alas, achieving an equilibrium between usage and restorative attention might require much deft spanner-work and diagnosis, but in the author's experience, if achieved, it can greatly enhance the spirits, not to mention the synchronous pleasures of owning, driving and restoring one's pride and joy.

Getting to Know You?

The one-make (or model, as in the case of cars like the Imp) owners' club should play an important part in your auditioning process. Other than being an unconscionably lucky person by nature, your painstaking research is likely to be rewarded by way of your satisfaction with your purchase. My advice would be to acquire a feel for the object of your desires through purchasing many books, reprinted contemporaneous road tests, and back numbers of older-car magazines that had features on your targeted machine – such expenditure is small compared with making a costly mistake. At this point, it is worth joining the appropriate one-make/model club and accessing its Internet site with its undoubted links to other enthusiasts scattered round the globe. Prospective Imp owners are again fortunate in these respects, as the Imp Club is run by realistic and knowledgeable enthusiasts, its club magazine, *Impressions*, contains many helpful pointers to Imp ownership, and the Internet sites and closed-user groups are more comprehensive than those enjoyed by other models. Your research will mean that when you attend an Imp event, not only will you have some idea of which model is which, but you can enter into meaningful conversation with present owners. Their opinions may not accord with yours, but this can be educative: find out why an opinion is held. Is it personal or held by the entire fraternity? Is it based upon technical observation or aesthetic preference? Examples would include choice of engine for the former and dashboard layout – earlier or later type – for the latter. There is no 'right' answer in its abstracted form, but you should establish what constitutes a correct answer for you.

I should point out that this author has made the decision not to give any contact details for either the Imp Club or the many specialist firms that concentrate upon this marque. The current details of both are easily obtainable, either from the specialist publications or through a few moments spent entering the relevant details into an Internet search engine. At this juncture, it is worth saying that some of these specialist suppliers of Imp parts and services are of extremely long standing, and their accrued knowledge of the model's strengths and weaknesses is substantial.

From time to time, magazines publish estimates of the difficulties of owning the objects of their attention; usually by way of bar-charts headed with spanners, to represent the availability of parts, and the other with one or more £ signs, representing the obvious. The good news for the Imp owner is that such a chart portrays the model with an abundance of spanners and not many £s. Not every part is available all the time, but all normal 'running spares' are available at modest cost. The various specialists, often in conjunction with the club, remanufacture scarce or unavailable parts, and here again the Imp Club can come to the rescue of its members through locating elusive parts or suggesting a modern substitution.

Your Choice From the Imp Fare

You will wish to decide to which of the different models you are drawn. Naturally, I possess my own preferences, but not knowing yours, I can only put forward a few considerations that are often contradictory. If you have made up your mind that you must be the next proud owner of one of the rarer manifestations of the theme, then you will have to take what is on offer, as an example might only come on to the market very infrequently – I was about to write 'once-a-flood', but areas of Britain seem to experience these with far greater regularity than a Zagato-bodied Zimp appears on the market! Whereas it is fairly well attested that only three of these were ever produced, there are not that many more extant examples of the once more-profuse genuine Rally models or those performance-enhanced cars prepared by the likes of Fraser, Nathan and Emery, or even the authentic Hartwell ones. Those of known competition provenance, whether as part of a racing or rally team, comprise another specialist market.

The two obvious divisions in the Imp line-up are by year, or by body style – whether saloon, coupé, or van/estate. Obviously, the last of these variants is dependent upon your usage, but if you want a small carrier, then these might fit your requirements rather well. Some dislike the higher roof line, but I find this an attractive feature and it does make the interior feel very spacious. Neither Husky estates nor Commer vans are as numerous as the other forms of Imp, but their relative rarity is not usually reflected in a higher price. I entertain a soft spot for the look and practicality of the Husky, so I am surprised by how many enthusiasts overlook its advantages.

Saloon or coupé? This is mainly a matter of taste, as both are available with the Sport's engine. The only obvious practical observation is the lack of a opening rear window in the coupé manifestation. This orifice is useful for loading lighter items into the luggage accommodation behind the rear seat – to my mind, more advantageous than the coupé's divided folding rear seat. Aficionados of the coupé's styling like its lower roofline and the rake of the front screen, as these contribute to its more business-like appearance. In the Stiletto form, either the vinyl exterior roof covering is something you could live with as a period feature, or it is the determinant of your choice for another variant.

As far as the division-by-year is concerned, more than any other consideration is the dashboard and the more modern, but less characterful, instruments – should you be considering the Chamois version, then it is

This otherwise-sound Imp, subsequently restored, displays typical corrosion points (marked) along the leading edge and rear corners of the bonnet, complete cills, and lower-rear of the front wings. When inspecting a vehicle, care needs to be taken to ensure that, if rectified, such perforated panels have been thoroughly replaced with sound metal.

Sometimes the owner gets a pleasant surprise; the corrosion of this 1965 Chamois is relatively light, being restricted to the rear wings surrounding the wheel-arches and the cills (not shown). When the paint was removed, the only filler found was rectifying minor motoring mishaps of old. The liberal use of wax-based corrosion inhibitors has greatly assisted the preservation of this Imp. The advantages of owning a car for several decades is that one knows exactly the extent and quality of past refurbishment.

This Stiletto reveals the typical Imp wheel-arch corrosion (not too severe in this instance) and the penetration of the lower rear wing corner (highlighted).

unlikely that you would prefer the later use of cheap, sticky-backed plastic as imitation wood. Again a matter of taste and personal preference, the decision is the simple trade-off between some fitments that are more modern and small detail improvements to the ride against the obvious later cost-cutting feel.

A Hole in Your Car and Pocket

The popular mythology of any model is founded on an element of truth, although it may now be insignificant. Corrosion is one such subject. One belief suggests that the pre-Chrysler-control Imps are more resistant to the ravages that eventually befall all cars. This thought is because they are made of sterner stuff – well, thicker pressed sheet-steel (the earlier models used sheet-steel of 0.031in thickness, with 0.035in being used for the roof panel). Whilst this line of persuasion is undoubtedly true, a contrary argument is that they are even older, and that, anyway, it was not until during the Mark II stage that the factory really got the hang of applying the more effective bituminous protection to the underside (early treatment relied purely on a phosphating dip under the paint). A believer in the earlier-is-better theory will retort that unless the undersealing products have been resuscitated regularly, then the treatment has

Despite looking not-too-bad superficially, this 1969 Chamois coupé is beyond any economically viable refurbishment and was recycled for spare parts. The corrosion of the rear wheel arch is visible, but the deterioration of the car's structure was comprehensive. This could act as a warning about trying to assess the condition of a potential purchase from a photograph.

This 1968 Californian offers an example of a typically rotten near-side rear wheel-arch. On closer inspection, a previous owner's inexpert 'bodging' of a cill repair with sheet aluminium alloy is obvious – and dangerous!

The off-side rear wheel arch of the same Californian showing (marked) the corrosion of the join between the wheel-arch and the outer rear wing, the rear of the cill, and the worrisome penetration of the inner wing near the suspension cone. This car has since been restored.

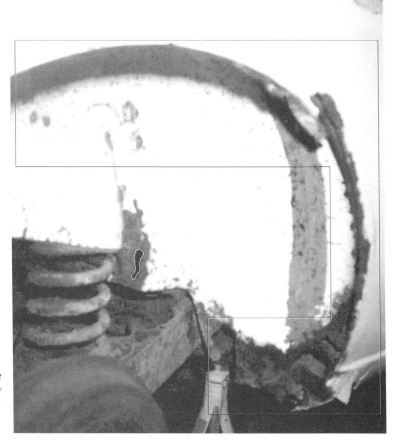

Looking forward along the off-side cill of this Husky from the rear wheel-arch shows the extensive penetration of the metalwork (highlighted). An unpleasant discovery, but despite this, the remainder of this vehicle is in reasonable condition and awaits restoration, which will be a practical proposition.

probably been more detrimental than the protection it initially afforded. He or she will then seamlessly return to the refrain of the thickness of the metal, while a proponent of the other side of the argument will resort to the obvious – newer is less old! Intellectual fascination apart, the undoubted truth is that the newest example you can encounter is over a quarter of a century old, and despite the Imp being rather more resistant than the lamentable British average of its peers, it would be surprising if some corrective action was not now required. It is also worth remembering that although Rootes and Chrysler trumpeted about their use of sophisticated seam-sealers, this was a long time ago. As far as corrosion is concerned, it will be more a question of how much? How structurally serious? And where? For its period and size, the Imp was a well-finished motor car that used modern materials. For today's owner, materials like the seam sealers and protective coatings are now well past the end of their useful lives, and it is worth checking that any replacement work has been carried out to at least the original standard. Most modern materials, however, will be even more effective at protecting the car for decades to come. For the record, Linwood's Jim Pollard favours the early-1967 vintage as the best-assembled Imps.

Thanks to its almost over-cautious designers, Imps are remarkably rugged little things. So, if remedial work has been done on areas like the cills, ensure that it has been done properly and that the replacement panels retain the integrity that gave the original its superb strength. Many useful clues whether this is likely to be so can be gained through the photographic record I mentioned. It is beyond the intention of this chapter to catalogue each vulnerable place where corrosion occurs – most are the same as on any unitary-construction car of the period. It is worth recalling that Imps have inner as well as shiny outer wings and wheel-arches, and that any corroded cill structure has to be replaced with new metal that is firmly attached to the floor-

pan, etc. Some consolation can be gained from the realization that it is likely that someone somewhere (it might be continental Europe, India, the Far-East, or the Antipodes) will be offering a high-quality reproduction of just the panel, or part thereof, that has rusted on your example. Not every seller is happy to let you lift the edges of the carpet, and some seem insulted if one applies a small magnet to the outer-cills of their 'guaranteed pristine' car: but these precautions are essential.

Briefly, areas that are worthy of your suspicion would be the cills, both outer and inner, and especially the adjacent couple of inches of the floorpan – this is likely to be the most costly and difficult area for the owner to rectify – front suspension mounting points (best viewed from inside the boot with the cardboard lining dislodged) and the seating for the rear springs (which, of course have two ends!); the rear cross-member is worthy of inspection, as are the front wishbones and the rear trailing arms. It is essential to inspect all of these thoroughly: the rear trailing arms will have led a tough life and are vital to the Imp's safe handling – it is worth remembering that, like the front, they are fabricated from pressed steel box-section units. The other areas are, perhaps, more obvious, but when welding do remember the heater-piping and wiring runs close to the corrosion-prone rear wheel-arches – neither does this piping benefit from being bathed in some types of anti-corrosion cavity wax. Although purely cosmetic, the typical corrosion bubbles of the leading and trailing edges of the bonnet can be troublesome to rectify, as can the deterioration caused in the vicinity of the battery.

Getting Down to Nuts and Bolts

Before embarking upon any maintenance, it is advised that any owner equip himself or herself with the appropriate Imp manual. Different owners will express a preference for different publications, but the two essentials would be the original factory manual combined with T. C. Millington's *Hillman Imps: Tuning, Overhaul and Servicing*, which is available in reprinted form from the Imp Club. As the title suggests, Millington embraces both the normal points of servicing and overhaul, and his idea of tuning extends to improvement from both a competitive and a road-going standpoint. These two publications can be further supplemented, as auto-jumbles allow, with the usual fare of do-it-yourself manuals like those produced by Haynes and Newnes (Pearson's Illustrated) with the less-technical owner being catered for by the Haynes *Owner's Handbook/Servicing Guide* series.

Turning to the engine, after its launch, the Imp's mysterious metallurgy, and the ramifications of this, might have puzzled many, but we and our garages have become accustomed to these materials. We no longer require the dire warnings of articles about the necessity of using a torque wrench or reminding us that it is easier to over-tighten a bolt when working on an Imp engine than an iron lump. I would recommend, however, that the purchase of an accurate torque wrench is essential.

Reviews highlighted the turbine-smooth operation of this engine, something that should be none-the-less true today. Engine design has moved on, but this unit was at the leading edge of design and it is comfortable in today's traffic. While an owner might have fitted the 998cc version or the 928cc incarnation of the engine, it is more likely to be the different forms of the 875cc that the reader will encounter. The engine might have been considered mysterious, but it is not magical and it wears with use over large mileages. Performance improvements aside – and there are a multitude of these that can be made to liberate further the engine's inherent sporty characteristics – the most obvious to concern many owners is the ability to run the vehicle on 'lead-free' petrol. The aluminium-alloy cylinder head was fitted with valve-seat inserts. Whenever a head requires lifting, this is an opportunity to replace these with specially hardened ones matched with new higher-specification valves that do not rely upon the lubricity that the lead additives in petrol used to supply. If the head has been skimmed a number of times to return it to a flat state, it could be that the compression is above the original 10:1. Should this be so, when preparing the head for lead-free fuel it might be worth having the compression slightly lowered. Combined with some attention to its gas-flowing, then any slight loss of performance will be compensated for through the engine's better breathing. Unless the reader lives somewhere with fuel of a very low octane rating, then it is pointless to use the van's concave-topped pistons. One reason for the huge differences in the performance of the reported test cars appears to have been poor matching of the engine's ports to the inlet and exhaust manifolds – whichever type of manifolding has been fitted to your engine, this is the time to adjust any sloppy alignment. At this stage, owners of Mark I cars might also like to consider swapping the engine head for a Mark II or Sport type to benefit from larger valves.

The original carburettor fitment was either the single-choke semi-downdraught Solex B30 PIHT series or the twin-carburettor installation of a pair of constant-vacuum Zenith-Stromberg 125 CDS carburettors as fitted as original equipment to the Sports versions. Earlier owners exchanged the Solex unit for either the once-popular Fish (both Reece- and Minnow-types) or twin-choke Weber or Nikki carburettors. You might still encounter one of the earlier automatic-choke Solex carburettors – if it has survived till now, then it is likely that it can still be correctly adjusted. Those readers contemplating the jetting of carburettors, matching these to manifolds, heads, camshafts, exhaust systems and the like, are best referred to one of the many books on tuning this engine. It is best to follow any work with a visit to a rolling-road dynamometer to ensure the necessary fine tuning. If you envisage tuning your Imp engine then it is better to start with a Mark II block, which is rather more robust, and a Sport Imp head – the Mark II block is essential for anyone wishing to bore out the old liners and increase the capacity to 998cc. It is unlikely you will find a car with an operational Dunlop pneumatic throttle.

Whilst perhaps not being as oil-tight as some modern oriental units, the engine should not leak much oil. After checking the obvious gaskets during servicing (a smear of modern sealant on new ones is usually beneficial to the cause), it is worth checking the engine crankcase breather tube to the air filter-housing, or its flame trap, for blockage – either congealed sludge or kinking. On the earlier type that vents to the outside world, it is unlikely to have had its 10,000-mile (16,000km) filter change, or even been cleaned in living memory. When the engine is warm, after checking the oil pressure (on cars with this helpful gauge) or the extinguishing of the warning light at tickover, try raising the engine speed and letting it fall back while you listen for noises from the camshaft drive. Rattling noises can indicate that the tensioning system is not functioning, rather than a stretched chain itself – not expensive *per se*, but a fiddly job to replace. The engine, by the way, can be removed either with or separately from the transaxle; however, the combined unit has to be removed from the Husky and van.

The coolant system was marginal, and a close eye needs to be kept on it by today's owner. Rootes recommended that the fan belt should not be over-tightened so as to preserve the remote water pump's bearings. This advice is essential knowledge, but these bearings are more likely to fail through sitting in coolant that has seeped past the pump seals. The later-model pumps (there were three different models in all) are more durable due to drain holes and deeper grooves to assist the bearings' environment, but the water pump remains an Achilles heel that is not inexpensive to replace. Two other areas worth taking care over are the radiator and air in the cooling system. Assuming the former is in good condition, not always

a wise assumption, then check that the area between the fan and the radiator is free of debris. A problem with an 'oily' engine is that the oil particles are drawn forward by the fan and can easily restrict the radiator matrix. The other side, nearest the road surface, might also reward cleaning, along with the stone guard. All bar the earliest models have a bypass junction with a wing-nutted tap so that the coolant can be bled into the header tank. This should be done when the engine and coolant are still cold.

The gearbox/transaxle can and does wear, but if it is reasonably quiet in operation and the synchromesh works, then it should last a goodly time. There are reprinted detailed instructions on rebuilding the transaxle, but assume this will not be a task you will have to undertake. The gear-change should be very light and positive, but a heavy or stiff gear-change usually involves no more that a thorough cleansing of the nylon bush and shaft at the rear of the gear-change shaft, followed by a copious application of grease. A common place for oil leaks from the transmission is the oil seal for the output shafts located on each side. Remedying this is not a particularly difficult task, but an essential one to prevent oil building up on the Rotoflex couplings. These endure a long and hard life, but their life expectancy is severely compromised if they remain bathed in oil.

There are no special precautions as far as the diaphragm clutch is concerned, other than that many owners of the earlier 5.5in ones might like to fit the later 6.25in when the time comes for renewal: this will require acquiring the later engine flywheel.

Concerning suspension and steering, the Metalastic bushes used in the various locations throughout the suspension display no Imp-based foibles. The steering, however, is worthy of comment. The appearance of the front wheels on the earlier cars has been unkindly described as 'knock-kneed', and that is correct. The steering should be exceptionally light to turn. If this is not so, the usual two suspects are the steering rack and the kingpins – the former is pretty durable, the latter less so. Access to the steering rack is straightforward, but it is difficult, but not impossible, to keep it topped up with its lubricant without removing it from the car, and naturally, the rack will fail in short order if one of the bellows ruptures and the oil escapes.

Should you encounter an early car that still has functioning PTFE 'sealed-for-life' bushes surrounding the kingpins, then if the steering feels light leave well alone other than treating the outside of the joints with grease to prevent the ingress of water. Failure of these and their replacements (which require lubrication) is caused through interloping water causing light corrosion of the kingpin, which then makes short work of any bush. Even if proper lubrication of the later pins is followed, stiff kingpins are usually the result of inactivity. Rootes suspected that the fault of many of these pins was caused through the centreless-grinding process it used not leaving the hard-chrome coating uniformly distributed over its surface as the pin's centre was off-centre of the original, unmachined, blank – thus corrosion ensued (as the seals did not keep all the moisture out), and this abraded the PTFE bushes, a fate that can also befall the later design during long periods of inactivity. From time to time, Imp specialists have stainless kingpins remanufactured – an option that was thought too costly to implement by the factory. If your car might face periods of inactivity, then this type might prove to be an economic choice.

The other system that hates inactivity is the brake system. The Imp was only ever fitted with drum brakes – twin-leading shoes at the front and leading and trailing at the rear – with servo-assistance only on some later models. (Remember, such assistance only reduces the effort applied to the pedal, it does not improve the quantity of retardation available.) In addition to rust on the inside of the drums, inactivity can lead to problems caused by the wheel-cylinders sticking or seizing, those of the rear being designed to slide on the brake backplate – failure to do so will result in poor braking efficiency. The usual reviewer's term for the Imp's braking system as measured by a Tapley meter was 'adequate', and being a light car, an overhauled system should give the impression of being very effective at stopping the vehicle. Some owners have uprated the system through fitting servo-assistance and dual master-cylinders, and some have gone as far as converting to disc brakes. Parts for the original equipment system are likely to remain freely available as they are all common implementations used for another decade. My feelings about updating the braking system is that the original can, and should, be made to work well, with the temptation of servo-assistance being appealing when driving an Imp over mountainous terrain. Dual-circuit brakes and a disc-brake conversion could be introducing a multitude of problems. Incidentally, access to the brake and clutch master-cylinders requires the removal of the fuel tank.

The electrical system employed by these cars is straightforward – because of the lack of fused circuits, somewhat too much so. Many an Imp has been saved from a premature end through connecting the main battery lead via an isolating switch that permits immediate disconnection without the owner fumbling for the correct spanner.

Despite its age, the Imp is a thoroughly practical alternative to a small modern car. Most owners I have met use their cars as their main mode of car-based transport and find the Imp to be quite at home in today's traffic conditions. It is just as happy cruising for very long distances under modern conditions as it is squeezing into small urban parking places that others have had to eschew.

Bibliography

Specifically Imp

Allan, R. J. *Geoffrey Rootes' Dream for Linwood*, Bookmarque (1991)

Griffiths, W. *Tuning Imps*, Bookmarque (1996)

Henshaw, P. and D. *Apex: The Inside Story*, Bookmarque (1988)

Millington, T. C. *Hillman Imps: Tuning, Overhaul and Servicing*, Bookmarque (2001)

Motoring Which? 'Hillman Imp', Consumers' Association (October 1963)

— 'Imp v. Vauxhall Viva', Consumers' Association (January 1966)

— 'Three Small Saloon Cars', Consumers' Association (April 1967)

— 'Small Estate Cars', Consumers' Association (October 1967)

— 'Three Fast Minis', Consumers' Association (July 1970)

— 'Four Cheap Saloons', Consumers' Association (January 1972)

General Motoring

Bullock, J. *The Rootes Brothers: Story of a Motoring Empire*, Haynes (1993)

Collins, P. and Stratton, M. *British Car Factories from 1896*, Veloce (1993)

Rootes, G. *Carpe Diem: The Memoirs of Geoffrey Rootes*, (Private, 1991)

Setright, L. J. K. *Drive On!: a Social History of the Motor Car*, Palawan (2002)

Worthington-Williams, M. *The Scottish Motor Industry*, Shire (1989)

Industrial and Political

Adeney, M. *The Motor Makers*, Collins (1988)

Benn, A. W. *Out of the Wilderness: Diaries 1963–67*, Hutchinson (1987)

— *Office without Power: Diaries 1968–72*, Hutchinson (1988)

— *Against the Tide: Diaries 1973–76*, Hutchinson (1989)

— *Conflicts of Interest: Diaries 1977–80*, Hutchinson (1990)

Church, R. *The Rise and Decline of the British Motor Industry*, CUP (1995)

Dunnett, P. J. S. *The Decline of the British Motor Industry*, Croom Helm (1980)

Fiction

Torrington, J. *The Devil's Carousel*, Minerva (1996) Alpine 181

Also various Imp brochures, documents, service and parts manuals, and the journals, magazines and records referred to in the text.

Index

206